HIGHBURY

AUTHOR INFORMATION

Bruce Smith attended his first Arsenal game in 1969 when Bobby Tambling ruined his day by scoring the only goal of the game to send Chelsea home 1–0 winners. Thankfully things were to change for the better and it was '1–0 to Arsenal' that became a way of life as he found himself a committed Gooner. The following year he attended all of the club's European Fairs Cup games at home and clearly made all the difference as the club went on to lift its first trophy in umpteen years.

Fully bitten by the Arsenal bug, he did not miss a game in the 1970–71 season and the club, equally inspired, performed an incredible Double. Life, children, work and travel commitments meant that his lean attendance years caused the club to suffer. But a return to full-time homage in the middle of the '90s propelled the club to new heights and has seen him celebrate at Manchester and in Milan, and witness the birth of the Untouchables and their 49 games undefeated.

An award-winning writer, he has an unhealthy love for stadiums and events and has worked in this field for well over ten years. He likes to think his original reports to Arsenal on stadium naming rights had some influence on their ultimate £100 million deal with Emirates, whilst in his capacity of consultant he provided advice on the design of the waste infrastructure incorporated into the new stadium.

A member of the Football Writers' Association, he is an Arsenal bond and season-ticket holder. He currently lives in Sydney, Australia, but travels regularly to see matches and watches all the others live on TV.

BRUCE SMITH

HIGHBURY

THE STORY OF ARSENAL STADIUM

MAINSTREAM
PUBLISHING
EDINBURGH AND LONDON

This edition, 2006

First published in Great Britain in 2005 by
MAINSTREAM PUBLISHING COMPANY (EDINBURGH) LTD
7 Albany Street
Edinburgh EH1 3UG

ISBN 1 84596 104 8

A catalogue record for this book
is available from the British Library

Typeset in Caslon and Gill Sans

Printed and bound in Great Britain
by William Clowes Ltd, Beccles, Suffolk

Acknowledgements

Special thanks go to several people not least Dave Old for the FA Cup chapter and the Old family (George, Pat, Sam, Dave and Pippa) for hospitality and Arsenal memories down the years, and to my wife, Melanie, for her understanding and support.

Thanks to Jeff Baker, senior project planner (Arsenal) at Islington Council, for access to files and records, and an amazing insight into the scope of the new Arsenal development, although it is a shame that records prior to the rebuilding of the South Stand have long since been lost to history – what fascinating reading they might have made. Thanks to Mark Webb (editor of *Stadium & Arena Management* magazine) for his reading and work on the original manuscript, and to Chris Williamson for details of the Rangers games played at Highbury, along with others who have supplied their own memories of Highbury. Thanks to the staff at the Islington History Centre for access to the many copies of local papers from 1913 and to dedicated Gooner Samir Singh. Also thanks to the many people who wrote or emailed me with suggestions and corrections for inclusion in this paperback edition, in particular Nigel Phillips. Thank you also to Mandy Mead for the photographs from the Final Day. I am indebted to Deborah Warner, my editor at Mainstream Publishing, whose comments and suggestions have proved invaluable.

The substance of the text dealing with managers at Highbury is taken, in an updated and revised form, from my book *Arsenal Fact File*, published by Virgin in 2000.

* * *

I hope that all readers will find *Highbury* of interest and informative, as well as providing a memory resource in the years ahead. I welcome constructive comments and any pertinent information which might be of use for future editions of the publication. These can be sent by post to the publishers or directly to me via email – go to www.brucesmith.info and click on the Highbury link.

FOOTBALL TRUST

With the changing ownership structure of several clubs in the FA Premier League, the Arsenal Supporters' Trust was formed in 2003 to represent and unite the minority shareholders of Arsenal and supporters in general. Whilst the directors and ITV own about 75 per cent of the club, about 1,500 shareholders own another 15 per cent of the shares, many of them descendants of the original shareholders, dating back to when the new Arsenal Company came out of liquidation in 1910.

One key objective of the trust is to broaden supporter ownership of Arsenal, as the share price – at the time of publication this was £5,000 per share (there are 62,217 in issue) – is prohibitive to most. The trust has plans to launch a sharesave scheme that allows supporters to make monthly contributions towards shares that are mutually owned by the trust on behalf of the contributing supporters.

For more information on the trust, visit www.arsenaltrust.org.

Bruce Smith

Contents

A DIFFERENT ERA

Although a bitterly cold east wind kept many indoors there was still a large crowd in Highbury Hill awaiting the Prince's arrival. One small schoolboy stood on the kerb in front of the crowd which had gathered. He had waited hours to secure a good position. Then a mounted Policeman came riding down the hill on a great white horse, clearing the road.

The crowd moved back obediently – all but the small boy. He stepped forward and hid himself from the policeman by walking under the head of the horse. The horse seemed nervous and pawed violently at the ground. The crowd held its breath. But the boy just looked up into the horse's mouth with a smile. Then the horse dropped its head and nestled gently into the boy's cheek. The crowd roared its approval.

A memory from the official opening of the West Stand,
Islington Daily Gazette, Tuesday, 13 December 1932

Preface

In the end, it was a fairy tale. Arsenal won their final fixture at the grand old stately home that will be forever football. Thierry Henry scored the final goal on the hallowed turf – it completed his hat-trick and he sank to his knees to kiss the lips of the luscious green in front of his adoring North Bank. Dennis Bergkamp – the greatest-ever Arsenal player – made his final competitive appearance as he entered the fray ten minutes from time; the roar that greeted him shifting decibels higher as news flooded through that Arsenal had secured a Champions League qualifying place at the very least, Tottenham having fallen behind in the dying moments of their final game of the season and thus losing out on fourth place to Arsenal. And so Arsenal left Highbury as they had arrived: to the angst of their near neighbours. The irony would not have been lost on any north London football fan that afternoon.

It was fitting to that, having been for so long derided as the 'Highbury Library' for its alleged lack of noise, the stadium boomed louder than ever for its final bow. Decked in human stripes of red and white, the four stands were picture perfect, while the final game culminated into another feast of Wenger football. It was a Henry who scored the first Highbury hat-trick; another Henry scored the last. The first was by Henry King, the last King Henry – perfect symmetry.

HIGHBURY

The holy grail of the Champions League came so close, but it was not to be. Highbury would not see the European Cup and another chapter would close in its life. When the famous trophy finally arrives – as it surely will – it will be into a new home: the Emirates Stadium. When that day arrives, the journey that brings it back to N5 will surely take the shortest of detours, swinging down Avenell Road to receive the acclaim of a certain ghost waiting patiently within the Marble Halls.

Farewell, Highbury

Introduction

I am standing on a small circle of whitewash. Around me it is pandemonium. People are pulling others one by one over the low-railing arches. Arsenal supporters in their hundreds are cascading down the North Bank terracing and flooding onto the pitch. The netting on the goal is tearing as feet get tangled and bodies tumble in good humour within its constraints. The white light beaming down illuminates a misty haze of heat rising from sodden turf and overheating bodies. The noise is uncoordinated: chants begin and fade in hoarse-throated confusion; men and women (mainly men) are screaming at the top of their voices. No one is really listening, everyone is screaming at each other and at themselves. Tears of joy threaten to flood the pitch. The clock shows it's a little after 9.30 p.m. A silvery glint catches the eye. The number '5' surfaces above heads, riding on a sea of shoulders. McLintock! We've won the Cup!

It's 28 April 1970 and Highbury has never ever seen a night like it. Arsenal have just secured their first trophy in 17 years beating Anderlecht 3–0 on the night, 4–3 on aggregate, to win the European Fairs Cup. We all have memories about football and about the theatres they are played out in, but this is the one that will be forever imprinted on my mind. Many others will have theirs, but, for me, this was Highbury's greatest night.

HIGHBURY

For countless thousands of people down the years Highbury has been a second home – for many probably even a first home – standing on terraces and sitting on seats for hour after hour. It has been home not least to the whole range of emotions, from both ends of the spectrum, that have been shared with friends and colleagues, and often with total strangers with the same obsession, who come together as brothers and sisters to share 90 minutes or more at a time. Joy, heartbreak, elation, hope, desperation, anticipation and more; for so many the journey to Highbury has been a pilgrimage; one that is sought with nothing but complete anticipation from the moment the final whistle has sounded and the next match looms on the horizon. There have been weddings and ashes scattered or buried: Highbury *has* been a matter of life and death and not just figuratively. It really is *that* important.

The final game at Highbury was an emotional affair. It was a spectacle both on and off the field. It was a thrilling encounter that Arsenal had to win and duly did in the swashbuckling style that had become their hallmark after a decade under manager Arsène Wenger. It was a visual feast as every fan donned the red or white T-shirt left on their seat that, together, painted the stadium with red and white stripes. It was a poignant event as fans savoured memories and watched past heroes in a spectacular parade before the large digital stopwatches that had adorned Highbury on the scoreboards for that final season slipped to zero and initiated a firework display that delivered the final curtain.

Highbury as a football stadium has passed on. Thankfully, its shape and being – if not the entire physical structure – will remain, and people will be able to continue to visit something tangible.

Every football ground is special, but in true Orwellian style some are more special than others – Highbury certainly comes into this category. And how ironic that after examining the possibilities of relocation from King's Cross to London Colney, a new home should be found almost within a booted clearance of Highbury itself. That in itself means the old stadium will be at the centre of a massive regeneration programme within the Wards' bounds and beyond, which will change the face of north London forever. In doing so it will catapult the club into a superleague of sporting wealth that it could never have imagined – not even when initial planning permission was being sought. Whilst the media was full of the cost of the relocation and the effect it could have on the club, what was actually happening behind the scenes was the creation of a money monster as the club turned into a property developer. The project will see the creation of some 2,700 new homes within Islington, combined with a massive boost to the local council coffers.

Highbury is the story of Arsenal Stadium. It is also the story of Arsenal at Highbury. It tells of the club's relocation from a south London suburb to N5 and reveals how in just 60 days simple playing fields were transformed into a usable stadium thanks to an army of willing workers. An instant fan base simply queued in an orderly fashion outside wide open doors until they were told to come forward and take their places for the first game. The subsequent developments were largely down to its patron at that time – a man who would end his life banned from football – and a succession of secretary– managers who had the vision to create a masterpiece of design that would stand the test of time. In those pre-war days each brought innovations that would go on to shape football, not just Arsenal football.

Having survived two world wars not quite unscathed, Highbury saw pioneering developments in the use of floodlights, under-soil heating, turnstile counters and video screens to name but some, and lived through the arrival of the all-seater age and the Premiership, until the realisation dawned that ultimately home was simply too small to encompass a new future.

Then there are the eras and players that have captivated the crowds down the years, from the Team of the '30s through to the Untouchables and three Double-winning sides. Highbury has also played host to a variety of events, from England internationals to FA Cup semi-finals, not to mention European Cup encounters even before Arsenal themselves entered the UEFA arena. Highbury has also seen World Championship boxing and been transformed into a movie set.

The post-war managers wielded little influence on Highbury itself as stadium development stagnated, simply amounting to patch-up jobs before the arrival of David Dein. The club then went into another gear, both on and off the field, with the very significant arrival of Arsène

Wenger and the transformation of a team of hopefuls into a side with potential and delivery. With this came the need for a stage far bigger than Highbury could provide.

The future of Highbury is assured, with the Marble Halls to be preserved and the East and West stands metamorphosed into contemporary dwellings. The actual playing surface will be lost, but the space will be retained in green as a series of gardens and water features.

Long may the memories live and long may we cherish them.

ONE

Prelude to N5

Highbury was a gamble. It was a gamble by a desperate man who was a visionary but who was going to take a football club from liquidation to the verge of extinction. His dream was to own the best club in the land and for them to play in the best stadium in the land. It was a dream that was realised, but along the way some of his methods weren't quite legitimate and, ultimately, as Highbury evolved and Arsenal succeeded, he could only witness it from afar, banned from football. A sad end for Sir Henry Norris, but he could never have imagined that the footballing icons he helped create in both team and stadium would become known around the globe.

Arsenal played their first game at Highbury in September 1913, but the journey there from across the river, then north along Upper Street, started many years earlier in another part of London. From the club's formation in 1886 to manoeuvres north in 1913, Arsenal were a modest side looking to become great achievers but continually failing to do so. Those very early years saw 'the Reds', as they were known locally then, become *the* glamour club: they were the first club in the south of England to be elected to the Football League and so attracted crowds and players from all over London. However, it was gaining professional status that first worked against them; then it was the local economic environment. Both made it necessary that they relocate, so it was as much a move for survival as through ambition.

* * *

The Royal Arsenal was a huge government munitions factory to the south-east of London. Woolwich was essentially a military town dominated by this massive works, but it also housed many army units, including the Royal Military Academy, the Royal Artillery Regiment and several military hospitals. War was big business and was extremely labour intensive, both in its fighting and preparation. The Royal Arsenal was a huge employer, attracting workmen from all over the British Isles.

In 1886 a group of men working in the Dial Square workshops within the Royal Arsenal discovered they had a common interest in football. Woolwich was set in an area where the predominant sports were rugby and cricket, but they decided to try to form a football team if sufficient men were interested. The inaugural game was almost certainly played on wasteland in what is now Tiller Road in Wapping on the Isle of Dogs (which, curiously enough, now houses a sports and leisure centre). Indeed that first 'ground' was wasteland in every sense of the word, and by the time the opposition, the Eastern Wanderers, were soundly beaten 6–0, it was almost unplayable. The result, as opposed to the initial set-up, led to an enthusiastic response and word of the team spread quickly through the Royal Arsenal factory. Within a very short time Royal Arsenal Football Club was born.

Their home ground for that first year was Plumstead Common and, as the name implies, this was an open public playing area. This proved totally unsatisfactory since it was constantly in use by either other local teams or horse-drawn artillery practising military manoeuvres, which left the field deeply rutted. They urgently needed a ground of their own, and in September 1887 the club opted to move to an old pig farm next to Plumstead Marshes. Teams in those early days used the local Sportsman's pub to get changed. Royal Arsenal only played friendlies at that time and did not have a 'competitive' match until they entered the London Cup. Newspaper reports at the time noted some 500 spectators turned up for the encounter to witness the 3–0 defeat of Grove House in October 1887.

(Some reports suggest that Grove House actually conceded the tie prior to the game because they did not have their full team available and that this encounter was just a friendly.)

Being so close to the marshes, the area and pitch were frequently waterlogged and on 30 March 1888 overnight rain made the pitch totally unplayable for a game against local rivals Millwall Rovers. It was Easter Friday and a large crowd was expected. Anxious to play the game, the club's committee members elected to hire the better-drained Manor Field adjacent to the marshes, and after some frantic work by club members a pitch, including fixed goalposts, was laid out.

Arsenal continued to hire the field and played their home games there for the next two years. Club officials drew military wagons from the armaments factory for each game and used them for attaching ropes to block off the club ground. The pitch itself was also cordoned off in an endeavour to keep over-enthusiastic spectators from spilling onto it. The wagons were also used as a form of terrace to give better vantage points since the crowds were by now several people deep. At the start there were no on-site changing-rooms and so the backrooms of pubs, such as the Green Man and Railway Tavern on the local Plumstead High Street, were used, players from both sides making the short jog to the 'ground'. Spectators were now being charged for entry and it was often down to a couple of the home players to help collect the admission fees.

By now the Manor Field had been renamed the Manor Ground (although it barely resembled what we would call a ground today) and crowds of up to 1,000 people were not uncommon. Indeed an attendance of over 1,500 is recorded for a friendly match with Tottenham Hotspur in September 1889 in which the Royals won 10–1! The biggest reported crowd at the Manor Ground around that time came on 7 December that year with an estimated 6,000 turning up despite an earlier snowstorm to see the visiting Swifts win 5–1. With bigger crowds making it difficult for players to get to the pitch, the local pubs were abandoned and a disused railway hut was commandeered and used as makeshift changing-rooms.

The 1889–90 season was a momentous one for the club, it being both accepted into the FA Cup and playing four rounds of the qualifying competition. In addition, Royal Arsenal won their first-ever trophy, the

Kent Senior Cup, beating Thanet Wanderers 3–0 at Chatham, as well as reaching the London Senior Cup final, losing 1–0 to Old Westminsters at The Oval (where FA Cup finals were played at the time). The London Charity Cup final saw them gain revenge over Old Westminsters at the Spotted Dog ground in Leyton, winning 3–1 to claim their second trophy. Royal Arsenal were starting to become a formidable side.

Apart from those paying an admission fee to witness proceedings, there were also plenty of non-paying spectators who could get a raised view of the game for free from a vantage point on top of the Southern Outfill Sewer, a massive pipe which still exists today. Its name clearly indicates the type of atmosphere games were played out in. That these people could gain 'free admission' irked the club, whose members were also feeling cramped, and so they started looking for a more secure setting where they could also attract bigger crowds for their games, which were by now averaging around 5,000 per fixture.

INVICTA GROUND

In September 1890, after some investigation, the move was made to the Invicta Recreation Grounds in Plumstead. They were accessed directly from the High Street and boasted concrete terracing with a grandstand and dressing-rooms. The ground was a multi-purpose facility and had been used primarily for the cycle track that ran around its perimeter, with Sunday cycle meetings often attracting five-figure attendances.

The ground was the property of a George Weaver, a mineral water manufacturer with a company of the same name, who charged Royal Arsenal £200 per year in rent for the ground – a grossly inflated price since Football League clubs were at most paying only half this at the time. Still, the club was ambitious and the Invicta Ground had been described as the 'finest in the South', boasting, as it did, a grandstand that could accommodate around 1,500 people.

Crowds of 8,000 were regular occurrences now, with admission just 3d (1p!). They were also treated to a pre-match band, the 2nd Kent Artillery Volunteers playing a selection of music at half-time, something that would become commonplace at Highbury many years later. It proved so popular the band would often surface at the end of the game and play the fans out of the ground, which often took an hour or so as they remained to listen to the music!

In 1891 the club were accepted into the first round proper of the FA Cup, losing to Football League professionals Derby County 2–1 at the Invicta in front of 8,000 fans. Looking to make the most of their pulling power, the Arsenal committee staged an Easter Tournament for the first time, which culminated in a contest against then Scottish champions Heart of Midlothian, which attracted 15,000 paying customers.

Fed up that their better players were being poached by clubs in the professional league, it was decided that Arsenal would likewise join it. They opted at this stage not to form a limited liability company but simply to elect to change their name to Woolwich Arsenal Football Club (a curious decision as the club had never played in Woolwich at any point). The London FA, which at the time was vehemently opposed to clubs becoming professional, immediately expelled them. This meant that Southern teams were effectively barred from playing Woolwich Arsenal, so the club set about arranging fixtures with professional sides from the Midlands and the North: no fewer than 57 matches filled their initial professional fixture list, some 48 being played at the Invicta, shrewd marketing attracting locals for the chance to see the big teams from 'up North'. It worked to perfection. Woolwich Arsenal's first professional game took place at the Invicta on 5 September 1891 – there is no recorded attendance, although a full house can be assumed – and their opponents that afternoon, Sheffield United, won 2–0.

Another season of friendlies in 1892–93 (a further 56 games with 41 of the encounters at the Invicta Ground) ended with Woolwich Arsenal applying for Football League membership. With the League anxious to expand and attract clubs from the South, Woolwich Arsenal were readily accepted. The joy was short-lived as the club was handed another bombshell as a direct result of that election success: Weaver, their landlord at the Invicta, on hearing of the club's successful application, decided to increase the rent for the season ahead. With less than three months before the new campaign got under way and probably believing he had the club over the proverbial barrel, he informed the club they could hire the ground on a fresh one-year lease for £400 with an additional £100 payable for rates and taxes. After some discussion the lease element was reduced to £350 per year with the proviso that Weaver would be elected on to the Arsenal's club committee. For that final season of friendlies the club had paid £200, including rates and taxes, for an eight-month lease, but were also spending £60 a year in repair bills. As a comparison, Sunderland and Wolverhampton Wanderers at that time were paying £45 and £76 a year respectively for their leases; the norm was certainly no more than £100 per annum.

The club made their own offer to Weaver, reported as being £300 per annum inclusive, but this was rejected. So with just three months to go before the 1893–94 Football League season was due to kick off, the club had no ground. Some decisive action was required. The obvious immediate solution was to move back to the Manor Ground. The club had continued to use the Manor Fields for training and practice so the area was familiar to them and the supporters. After lengthy debate amongst the club officials it was decided to purchase the ground if at all possible and if not, take a short lease and continue to look out for a facility over which they would have total control; one which wouldn't put them at the beck and call of unscrupulous landlords.

SHARING ARSENAL

After some negotiating, the club came to a deal with the owner of the Manor Fields, Mr J. Morris, which allowed them to purchase the ground immediately. The cost of acquiring the 13.5 acre site was £4,000 and this money was to be raised by the issue of 4,000 shares at £1 each and the club's formation into a limited liability company, Woolwich Arsenal Football & Athletic Company Ltd. Reports on the take-up of shares are mixed, but it would seem from newspaper reports of the time that around 2,500 were issued to around 1,500 people. This left the club well short, but the sale of season tickets at 10s 6d certainly boosted funds. (NB: *The Official Illustrated History of Arsenal* by Phil Soar and Martin Tyler differs from these local accounts, reporting that 860 people bought 1,552 shares.)

But it was not enough to simply purchase the ground: massive improvements were needed as well. The club could not hope to contain supporters using wagons and rope especially after the relative splendour of the Invicta Ground. So the summer of 1893 saw a huge effort mainly by volunteer supporters who converted the Manor Field into a football ground that could clearly be called the Manor Ground.

First the designated playing area had to be levelled to remove a substantial slope – this was done by using a base of hardcore which would also aid drainage in the marshy area. Truckloads of loam and earth were imported and spread to create an even surface onto which the best quality turf was laid. The playing area was roped off and low-level fencing would be applied around the perimeter of the pitch when the rest of the work was completed.

Next, the spectating area had to be addressed. On the north side of the ground a five-tiered terrace was constructed along the length of the pitch (this was ultimately extended right around the ground with the initial terracing being covered with an iron stand which could enclose some 2,000 spectators). Fencing, mainly of galvanised iron, was added to enclose the area. Iron was also used to erect buildings on the south side of the ground, comprising changing-rooms for the home and away teams and a committee room for meetings. A small press-box for 12 reporters was also constructed, although this wouldn't be used to its full potential.

The Manor Ground's main access was from the Griffen Manorway, which had three gates, whilst two exits led onto a private road, which required the London County Council's permission to be used. Over 10,000 turned up on 2 September 1893 to see Woolwich Arsenal play their inaugural Football League match in the Second Division. The opponents were another newly elected club, Newcastle United, and the game ended a 2–2 draw. Attendances settled in at around the 6,000 mark, making Woolwich Arsenal the best-supported club in the Second Division. A reported 12,000 squeezed onto the terraces in November 1893 for the FA Cup third-qualifying-round encounter with Millwall Athletic (formerly Millwall Rovers).

Off the field, the outbreak of the Boer War in 1899 deprived the club of many of its key officials as the introduction of shift work to increase output at the Royal Arsenal factory played havoc with people's lives. Likewise attendances at games declined and cash started to get tight. Equally the number of non-paying 'viewers' started to increase as fans, strapped for cash or unwilling to pay to see part of a match because of work commitments, sought out vantage points on areas such as the popular Southern Outfall Sewer pipe, just as they had done during the club's first stint at the site.

PROMOTION INTEREST

By 1904 the club had finished runners-up in the Second Division and were promoted to the First Division. Interest was now immense as they were the first Southern club to play in the top flight. Attendances were set to rocket so the capacity of the Manor Ground had to be increased to accommodate the extra spectators. This was done by building a huge terraced area in front of the Southern Outfall Sewer pipe which also rendered its use as a spy point useless – the club therefore solving two problems in one go. The ground's capacity swelled to over 25,000. Because the new terrace reminded the many soldiers who supported the Reds and who had recently served in the Boer War of Spion Kop, an infamous hill in Natal which claimed many lives in a horrific battle, they opted to make the embankment its namesake. Spion Kop ultimately became known to locals as simply 'the Kop', and the concept then spread around the rest of the teams in the Football League, where, for most, the biggest area of terracing became known as the Kop.

As predicted, First Division status brought with it the big teams and the big crowds as attendances swelled to a regular 20,000, occasionally reaching 30,000 for specific matches. However, despite all this, the club's finances were not in a very good way. The club's fortunes were just about to experience a downward spiral.

In a *Kentish Mercury* account of that FA Cup encounter with Millwall Athletic it was reported that fans had swarmed to the ground using a variety of methods. It said special trains, trams, buses, traps and even steamboats had taken what it reported was a 20,000-strong crowd to the Manor Ground. There was no easy, direct way to get to the venue even though the train station itself was directly opposite. The services that did exist were sporadic and unreliable and only when games were high profile were special services run.

Chelsea and Clapton Orient were admitted to the Football League in 1905 and were soon followed by Fulham and Tottenham Hotspur, so there were other opportunities in London to watch Football League, invariably at grounds that were much more accessible. Indeed George Allison, a local reporter covering Arsenal games at the time (and who would later become a manager at Highbury), noted that even journalists couldn't be bothered to travel south from Fleet Street to cover games at the Manor Ground. Allison would often be a loner in the 12-seat 'Press Stand' and simply syndicated his reports to the other journalists to use in their newspapers.

Locally the workforce was in decline with the government reducing staffing levels at the Royal Arsenal munitions factory by over half. Locals were either moving out to seek new employment or remained with no spare cash to spend on attending football matches. These factors combined meant that attendances at the Manor Ground sank back to the levels they'd been before the club had moved to the Invicta Recreation Grounds. In 1911 Woolwich Arsenal could only attract 3,000 for a First Division fixture with Sunderland.

The club had appointed George Morrell as secretary-manager in 1908. Morrell was regarded as a financial whizz-kid in football circles after having achieved a complete turnaround with the fortunes of Glasgow Rangers. He had then taken the debt-ridden Greenock Morton into solvency and on to election to the Scottish First Division. Initially, his appointment saw a lift in results, but ultimately players had the same travel problems as the fans – the ground was difficult to reach by public transport and so many supporters simply stopped bothering. With the subsequent reduction in gate takings, cash became increasingly tight. The club couldn't meet its wage bill and was ultimately forced into selling its better players to reduce the wage bill and provide injections of cash. A vicious circle. In 1910 Arsenal were averaging 11,000 through their gates. Chelsea, with better access to their ground, drew close on three times that, despite finishing second bottom. When Woolwich Arsenal had played a fixture at Stamford Bridge the year before Morrell arrived at the club, a crowd of 65,000 had been witnessed. None of this was lost on him.

In March 1910 Woolwich Arsenal went into voluntary administration with debts of £12,500. It was the job of the administrator, Mr Brannan, to sell off the club's assets, such as they were, and to use whatever was raised to pay off the club's creditors. The only real asset the club owned was the Manor Ground. In fact, Brannan sold everything as it was to a consortium of small businessmen headed by one George Leavey. Leavey had been part of the club for a number of years and, although not an official, had often helped out by putting his hand in his own pocket.

Wishing to ensure the club survived, the consortium offered shares for general sale in May 1910. The large majority of these were subscribed to by Henry Norris and William Wall, who purchased 240 each, giving them over a third of the total shares on offer, and so started an association with the club that would ultimately lead to Highbury. Other notable shareholders included Leavey himself, who took 100 shares. Tottenham Hotspur FC also reportedly purchased 100 shares which they subsequently sold before the new football season started. None of the original founders of the club bought shares and so links with the early days and Dial Square were fully severed.

HENRY NORRIS ESQUIRE

Henry Norris was born in 1865 and became one of the most influential figures in football at the turn of the twentieth century. Socially he was the ultimate Edwardian bounder of his time: he was football's first dictator and hard man, and in modern-day terms might be described as Robert Maxwell, Ken Bates and Doug Ellis all rolled into one – although, in truth, he wasn't as soft as that! His influence on the evolution of a number of London clubs should not be overlooked. Without him it is doubtful whether Arsenal or Chelsea would exist today, certainly in their present forms, and Fulham owe much of their early growth impetus to him.

Born into a working-class family, he aspired to the upper echelons of late nineteenth-century society. His first job, aged just 14, was at a little local solicitors firm where he read articles for just a year. From there he looked to the building trade, and within a few years had developed the hard exterior and no-nonsense attitude that set him apart from others and gave him an air of superiority that few challenged – and when they did, they always wished they hadn't. He ruled not so much with an iron hand as with an iron fist!

Norris, just like the aforementioned moguls, was a self-made man. Based in south-west London he made his fortune in the property market with his company Allen & Norris. Moving between the building and banking professions, he was able to establish a useful network of contacts and use a mixture of brawn and finance in the process of converting rural Fulham into a sprawling south-west London suburb.

Having seen the growth of the building industry and, in particular, the need to house an exploding population, Norris turned his attentions to the real estate market. During this process he extended his networking contacts deep into the local council and areas of government. He had already established his reputation as a bully and someone to be avoided at all costs. Although there is no record of any gangster-style persuasion methods being used, his underworld connections probably stood him in good stead. These contacts – 'his boys' – were invariably used to the full, not least when planning permission was slow in coming forward or looked as if it might be refused.

Norris loved football with a passion and it was a source of great angst to him that the Northern sides dominated the professional game. His dream was to see a London club at the top of the tree. At this stage Norris was involved with Fulham Football Club. In 1903 Fulham were admitted to the Southern League and as part of that process converted into a limited liability company. The resulting board of directors included Norris.

Norris was totally ambitious and although Fulham were elected to the Second Division in 1907, the club's constant failure to earn promotion to the First Division rankled with him. The ultimate reasons for the purchase of a majority share in Woolwich Arsenal at that time can only be guessed at: Norris was ambitious; Fulham were a Second Division club,

Woolwich Arsenal were in the First Division. Perhaps Norris saw Arsenal as an immediate meal ticket to the First Division? This theory would seem to hold water since Norris did apply to the Football League for a merger of the two clubs. The assumption was that the new club would play at Fulham's Craven Cottage stadium, one of the finest in the country at the time, with crowds to match. By taking over Woolwich Arsenal's First Division status, crowds would swell even more and there would be the mouth-watering prospect of west London League encounters with the well-supported Chelsea.

Norris's merger proposal was rebuffed. He then looked to move Woolwich Arsenal from Plumstead to share the Craven Cottage facility, but this too was firmly rejected by the League. So, Norris remained as a director at Fulham – a Second Division club with excellent facilities but with little prospect of gaining promotion in the short term, and with nearby Chelsea drawing away the crowds – and the chairman of Woolwich Arsenal – a First Division club struggling in the lower reaches of the League whilst its geography made it difficult to attract the players and attendances required to remain solvent. It was a quandary, to say the least.

Given these factors, and Norris's drive for success, it would seem he simply took the decision to relocate Woolwich Arsenal. This in itself seems curious given that he had not been allowed to move the club to Craven Cottage: perhaps the League's thinking was that three clubs (Woolwich Arsenal, Fulham and Chelsea) in such close proximity to one another would have been detrimental. Why ultimately, then, they allowed Woolwich Arsenal to move to an area in which Tottenham Hotspur and Clapton Orient were also based remains a mystery. It's likely that Norris needed time to set relationships in place and lobby the parties whose votes he would need to get his way – something that would also help Arsenal's 1915 promotion to the First Division again.

Norris, as ever, argued his points well, noting that cities such as Birmingham and Sheffield, whose populations equalled a small percentage of London's, were already supporting two top-flight teams each, so why couldn't north London with a population double that of Birmingham and Sheffield combined support one more? His arguments, and no doubt his iron fist, carried weight within the Football League.

Central to the weight of these arguments and the lobbying was his sidekick William Hall. A metal merchant from nearby Putney, he played second fiddle to Norris and was always on hand to help carry out his mentor's wishes. He served on the boards of Fulham and Arsenal and at the start of 1913 he sought and gained election to the Football League Management Committee (LMC). Political manoeuvring of the highest order indeed!

In February 1913 Norris announced that Woolwich Arsenal would be leaving their Manor Ground home in Plumstead and relocating to Highbury, N5 for the 1913–14 football season; the move had been ratified by the LMC.

TWO

Highbury Dawn

Leicester Fosse were Woolwich Arsenal's opponents for the opening game of the 1913–14 season: the first game to be played at Highbury. The crowd of around 20,000 witnessed the home side win 2–1. The Highbury facilities on that day were well short of completion: there were not even dressing-rooms for the two teams. However, it had been a Herculean effort to get things to standard for the opening day of the season on 6 September.

* * *

By the time the club had announced it was moving from the Manor Ground to Highbury results had deteriorated. Woolwich Arsenal had finished bottom of the First Division and so would be starting their next league campaign in the Second Division. Norris now found himself involved with two second-tier clubs. He remained a Fulham director until the outbreak of the First World War, whilst William Hall, a director at Arsenal, remained the Fulham chairman until that point: the conflict of interests must have been intriguing, although there is no record of anything untoward.

As we know, the move to Highbury had been set in motion some three years before the opening encounter with Leicester Fosse when the amalgamation with Fulham was vetoed by the LMC. Struggling in Plumstead and with decreasing crowds, the club at this point had barely £19 in its bank account.

Given the huge accessibility problems the club had encountered at the Manor Ground, it was clear that easy access for public and media was of paramount importance and a defining factor in location. Norris and Wall set about looking for locations with the right amount of space onto which a 'world class' facility could be built. They also wanted to be able to pick a location which was not too close to any of the other London clubs, so as to attract a new fan base and to help ease an application for a move which would become prickly if it was too near any of the other grounds. A number of sites were investigated but all proved unsuitable. It soon became obvious that it was going to be impossible to locate somewhere meeting the criteria which wasn't in close proximity to other major clubs.

GOING UNDERGROUND

Norris hit upon looking at the route of the growing underground network of trains as a focus for his location search. How Norris hit upon the Highbury Hill area is lost in time: maybe he or one of his underlings visited stations in turn and had a general scout of the area, or perhaps he used his mayoral contacts to find potential sites for sale by word of mouth. We'll never know. What is known was that he found a site literally on the doorstep of the Gillespie Road Underground station. The location was perfect. At that time the Piccadilly Line, which had opened just prior to Christmas 1906, ran from Finsbury Park to Barons Court. Finsbury Park itself was just a brisk walk away and even nearer was the then Metropolitan Line-based Drayton Park station. Three stations: one on the doorstep and the other two just a few minutes' walk away. Perfect.

The site in question was St John's College of Divinity. Although large, the site was mostly laid to field. The open area was Aubert Park and this was marked out with a couple of football pitches, two cricket pitches and a number of tennis courts. These facilities were being used by the college's students as it was and were accessed via the building or through two huge wooden gates on Avenell Road. Negotiations took several months to complete and were resolved when Norris agreed to terms for a 21-year lease. These involved a payment of £20,000 and a reassurance that games would not be staged on Good Friday and Christmas Day, nor would alcohol be served in the grounds. The lease deed was signed by none other than the Archbishop of Canterbury. However, there was to be further divine intervention as the locals – residents and clubs – vented their full anger.

Quick to object were the two local clubs: Tottenham Hotspur and Clapton Orient. Both clubs were livid at relocation into their patch – Tottenham, perhaps rueing the sale of the club's shares they had owned just a couple of years beforehand, placed an advertisement in one of the local newspapers requesting locals not to go and support Norris's Arsenal. Both clubs objected to the League Management Committee in the strongest terms, but after an emergency meeting the move was sanctioned. Remember that Wall was on the committee, and the then LMC president, John McKenna, was a close friend of Norris – not such a surprise then. The ruling by the LMC was that never having objected to other clubs moving before they could hardly do so now (the fact they would not allow Woolwich Arsenal to move to Fulham seemed to have been forgotten . . .). Tottenham were a First Division club and Orient would be competing against Arsenal in the Second Division during that first Highbury season. Tottenham had, of course, previously objected to Clapton's election to the Southern League and then the Football League.

Interestingly Chelsea also joined in the LMC objection process, perhaps fuelled by the disagreements that had gone on between Chelsea chairman Gus Mears and Norris, and Norris's refusal to move Fulham and become a tenant at Mears's Stamford Bridge facility a few years earlier. This refusal had resulted in Mears forming his own football club: Chelsea.

Islington Council would also initially object to the proposal to build the stadium in its borough (and this would create permissions problems in due course), whilst the local residents were outraged at the prospect of Christian fields being replaced with the hell of football crowds. Indeed an action group was formed and petitioned vehemently in every way possible.

Eventually the action died down, no doubt aided by Norris's contacts, and works on the stadium commenced.

ARCHIBALD LEITCH

With the land found and a lease purchased and any legal or competition-based objections to the move going ahead dismissed, Norris required a plan for the ground. As chairman of Fulham he had already associated with an architect by the name of Archibald Leitch.

Born in Glasgow in 1865, Leitch became the leading light in stadium design in the early part of the twentieth century. He initially trained as a marine engineer and after sailing the world for a number of years turned his mind to more stable structures. After six years working for one of the more pre-eminent engineering firms in his home town, he broke out on his own as a 'consulting and inspecting engineer'. Success wasn't immediate, as he spent his evenings lecturing; but then, at the turn of the century, he got his big break, securing a contract with his first love, Rangers FC. The result was the biggest stadium in the British Isles, with a capacity of 80,000, but one that was constructed totally from wood – terraces and all.

Sixteen months after its opening, disaster struck when a section of the terracing gave way during a Scotland v. England Home International clash and football had experienced its very first stadium disaster. How many people were killed or injured that day in the capacity crowd is not known, and despite being cleared of blame, its impact on Leitch was immense. He began to set about looking at new techniques and methods to make stadiums safer. In this respect he pioneered terrace standing, using raised banks of earth and stepping them with rakes and risers. He also patented his own crush barriers, which were still being installed as late as the 1960s. His gabled grandstands also became a feature of his work.

His innovative and forward-thinking approach catapulted him to the forefront of every club board, and by the time he turned his sights south to London he had completed or was working on new stadiums for numerous clubs, such as Bramall Lane, home to Sheffield United, and Middlesbrough's Ayresome Park. He was also working on a replacement facility at Ibrox and would go on to have a major influence at just about every major facility in the country, including Anfield, Goddison Park, White Hart Lane, Stamford Bridge, St James' Park, The Dell, The Den, Roker Park and Valley Parade, to name just a selection.

Norris had been hugely impressed with Leitch's work at Craven Cottage in 1905, including the pavilion, which would later become known as 'The Cottage', so it was no surprise that, needing a quick solution, he turned to the stadium designer from north of the border.

Swamped with work, Leitch turned to his right-hand man for support – his chief assistant and designer, A.G. Kearney, who only found out about the project's nature when he arrived on site! This was pretty much the way the whole project was managed. Forget about city offices with rows of drawing boards and draughtsmen working through the night; forget about engineers with slide-rules calculating loads and stresses. Instead imagine scraps of paper with hand-drawn sketches and notes. This is how the initial concepts behind Arsenal Stadium came about.

Kearney's personal account of his role in the project makes interesting reading: he describes arriving at the St John's College site in a two-cylinder Renault taxi with 'rod, poles and perches' in hand after having been made 'head cook and bottle washer' on the project by Leitch. With his engineer's eye he did not see the fields for what they were but was taken by the obstacles surrounding the site that would prove barriers to his work. St John's College occupied the southern end of the site: to the west was a long unbroken row of tall Victorian houses, to the north a laundry, and to the east on the Avenell Road side houses with a high brick wall. Prior to travelling to London from his Manchester office, Kearney enquired of Leitch as to plans and specifications. His reply was that he was to do them on site as the ground was to be ready to open that coming September – less than six months away.

Kearney's first contact at the site was with two representatives from Messrs Humphreys Ltd, Civil Engineers of Knightsbridge, who had arrived on site to install the builders' huts. Having found accommodation in nearby Sotheby Road, Kearney felt his first task was to ensure he could get all the required planning permissions. At that time they were handled by the London County Council (LCC), so he called in on the LCC engineer's offices in Spring Gardens. Due to the tight deadlines, Kearney needed to get the LCC onside and agree to approve his plans piecemeal, preliminary to the building committee's monthly meeting. This was vital to the timeline. If Kearney had to wait for each monthly meeting for approval of plans, he would be facing an impossible task. As it was, the engineer's office agreed to play ball and so Leitch's chief assistant and designer had one foot in Highbury overseeing works and one foot in the Spring Gardens offices completing plans and getting them passed. One can only suspect that again the influence of Henry Norris continued to stretch into all the nooks and crannies.

The first job in the development of Highbury was to get the pitch laid out. Just as with the Manor Ground in Plumstead, the site was not level and so this needed to be addressed. The College End of the ground was around six feet higher than the Laundry (Gillespie Road) End. And so a level trench was cut into the Aubert Park surface across from one side to the other, with the soil taken from the College End and used to build up the Laundry End. Of course this was being done in the days before mechanical diggers, JCBs and the like: all work was undertaken manually with shovels and spades – a monumental task. Kearney hired some 200 navvies who were supplied with shovels from the local council offices in Liverpool Road. A degree of drainage was added during the levelling of the pitch, as well as clinker. Cumberland turf was used to create the first Highbury playing surface.

The areas around the pitch had to be raised to form embankments, but there was not anywhere near enough hardcore on site to complete the project. Word went out and there was a never-ending stream of trucks driving down Gillespie Road and dumping their 'muck'. The muck was mostly yellow London clay and it left the local streets stained for many weeks. An earthen ramp had been created to allow the trucks access in and out of the site. Beyond that, people in their dozens started arriving bringing all sorts of fill.

The first objection that Kearney received from the LCC offices was when he submitted his proposal to build a high retaining brick wall at the College End. The wall would form the back of the College End terrace and also cordon off a grassed area between the ground and the college that would ultimately be used by the team for training. The LCC office effectively passed the buck by referring Kearney to a Parish council office in Holloway Road. The reasons are not known; maybe because it was directly affecting the college they felt the Church needed to be in on the decision. One can only guess. Kearney's meeting was with a committee of three which he described as the 'father and son' type. Nevertheless the Parish Council Committee could not make an immediate decision and so Kearney turned to Norris, who pulled some strings, and the wall went ahead. There is actually no record of an approval, so it is not known whether it was verbal or whether Norris just decided to tell Kearney to get on with it and he would deal with the fallout.

With the College End wall in place, work was started on another high embankment-retaining wall along the length of the Highbury Hill side of the site. Work was already well under way on this when a number of the Highbury Hill residents issued a letter via a solicitor threatening an injunction on the basis that the wall was being constructed on their side of the building line. Kearney was adamant his lines were correct and suggested this was simply a ruse to hold up proceedings. Some weeks before, a Highbury Hill resident had tried to gather local support to stop the ongoing building and only the strong intervention of Norris within chambers had squashed a rally that had given Kearney cause for serious concern.

BUILDING WALLS

Kearney's response to the solicitor's letter was to instruct his workers to tear the wall down and build a new one six feet in from the line of the original structure. Given that the residents had defined their line, it would be impossible to question it again – a simple solution that allowed the project to continue apace. The wall can clearly be seen in early pictures of Highbury and is indeed a huge structure running down the entire length of the west side of the ground and ultimately extending into Gillespie Road. With construction of the wall continuing, the west side embankment was completed, rising in height as it opened out towards Gillespie Road. It then swept around through 90 degrees at its widest point and continued along the Laundry End of the ground where it joined with the narrower east side of Avenell Road. On the Avenell Road side of the ground a simple grandstand was under construction which would also house the club offices and changing-rooms. The height of the Laundry End terrace immediately meant it was allocated the distinction of being the stadium's Spion Kop. However, the embankment around the ground was largely that – a large earth mount without the concrete terracing steps that are generally familiar.

Before the wall could be completed at the Gillespie Road end, Kearney had to complete the purchase of two houses which would be knocked down to serve as a large entrance directly opposite the Gillespie Road station. Large wooden gates were secured across the new entrance.

Messrs Humphreys Ltd continued with the engineering work on the site but the general feeling was that the gods were against them as time ticked on and progress appeared too slow. 'A proper Fred Karno' was a phrase in common use on the site, revealing the kind of chaos in which builders were working. Fred Karno was a theatre impresario at the time, working with the likes of Charlie Chaplin and Stan Laurel.

With just a couple of weeks to go before the opening fixture against Leicester Fosse, it was clear that the project was not going to be finished in time. Kearney took the decision to make haste with some temporary measures so that the stadium would be usable whilst continuing the building works between games. In fact, work on Highbury would continue right through the season.

Establishing spectator entry points was begun but never finished to satisfaction before the opening. The various gates were secured but there was not enough time to establish the pay boxes. Kearney was concerned about safety and so had hundreds of feet of rough timber delivered and employed a small army of carpenters to create rails and vomitory-style constructions that would funnel spectators in and out of turnstiles. Offices on the Avenell Road side and dressing-rooms were well under way but not really ready for use. Players' baths were installed but not plumbed in. Army field kitchens were brought in for heating water for use in the sinks.

In the final week before the start of the season, Norris was on the war path because the stadium was a long way from completion. It was always going to be an impossible task and Kearney had performed miracles given that everything was being done on the fly. Norris was after Leitch's blood, but the Scot made himself scarce and could not be found in the final days before the opening match. According to Kearney, Norris was 'beside himself' with anger. Late on the Saturday morning of the opening game Norris, wishing to acknowledge Kearney's superhuman efforts, took him and a Humphreys' representative to lunch at an Italian restaurant next to the Finsbury Park gates. On their return to the ground Kearney found large queues already forming outside the ground. The gates themselves were still wide open and it was only the honesty of the spectators that stopped them simply walking into the ground and taking their places on the terraces. Kids were another matter, though: they were sneaking in and hiding behind the wooden rails before whipping out onto the terraces after paying customers started to make their way in. This became a common practice in those early days. Only around 30 of the 100 terraces were actually completed for the first game and only afterwards were crush barriers actually erected. The grandstand was only half-roofed – although some spectators watched the first game from its vantage point by sitting on planks. According to reports of the time Mr Norris looked 'very tired'. That first Highbury pitch was prepared by Alex Rae, the stadium's first groundsman.

At this stage the club hadn't given much thought to a name for the ground: simply Gillespie Road Stadium was being touted by the local newspaper, the *Islington Daily Gazette*. However, locals started to use Highbury and the name stuck despite pleas in the local paper to use the suggestion put forward by the 'Candid Critic', one of its reporters.

MATCH DAY ONE

The *Matchday Programme* for that opening fixture with Leicester Fosse acknowledged that Highbury was incomplete and made the point that the club had only actually been in possession of the site for some 60 working days! The cost of the stadium to that point had been around £30,000 (according to the *Islington Daily Gazette* at the time, although other sources rate a figure two or three times this value), raised by Norris through bank loans and guarantees. The builders working on the East Stand, which would seat 9,000 supporters on its completion, were paid a percentage of the weekly gate receipts until the debt was settled.

Although Arsenal had never played in Woolwich, that aspect of the club's name was not dropped immediately with the relocation, so it was Woolwich Arsenal that hosted the opening fixture at Highbury that famous afternoon. Historically the most celebrated story of that opening day encounter was about an injury to George Jobey. The Arsenal centre-forward sprained an ankle and had to be helped off by trainer George Hardy. As the dressing-rooms were still unfinished and there was no running water, Hardy took Jobey to players' lodgings nearby. Such were conditions in those early days, that to do this he commandeered a milk cart from local milkman David Lewis who lived on Gillespie Road.

An amazing 20,000 packed into the sparse surrounds for that opening game and the patience of the crowd had to be admired: they were all admitted through 25 'turnstiles'. Many fans watched the game for free by simply standing on Highbury Hill – which quickly led the club to erect some hoardings to obscure their view – whilst many youngsters were able to do the same by scaling trees in the area. The Underground proved to be a very popular method of reaching the stadium, officials on the Metropolitan Line reporting that they carried 5,000 extra passengers to Drayton Park on that Saturday.

Interviewed a couple of days after the game, Norris told local reporters that his ambition was to provide an Arsenal Stadium capable of holding 90,000 people in comfort, who could watch to the very end and be able to depart the ground within very few minutes. Before the season ended the club dropped the 'Woolwich' from their name, so that when Bristol City arrived in north London on the afternoon of 4 April 1914 to play out what would be a one-all draw, they were facing Arsenal.

By the time the second home game of the season kicked off – against Notts County – the East Stand was partially completed and around 4,000 fans managed to be seated there for the game. Arsenal won 3–0 and went top of the table in front of 25,000.

Kearney stayed on site for a further five weeks helping to move things along. A local area official was appointed as clerk of the works along with a foreman to finish the job Kearney had started. As for Kearney he returned to Manchester, his job done, but returned to Highbury 50 years later as an official guest of the club to celebrate a half-century at Highbury.

As for Leitch, he continued to impose his influence on grounds right around England and, despite developments, there are still aspects of his work to be admired, not least at Fulham's Craven Cottage. He died in April 1939, two days short of his 74th birthday.

There was much work still to be completed in that first season. The club came up against Islington Council who placed 'a prohibitive value' on the ground, making rates and taxes difficult to meet. Norris battled on behind the scenes directing his efforts at the Assessment Committee in an effort to reduce costs.

Supporters' main complaint during those early days was the lack of on-site refreshments: there was simply nowhere to get a drink. Local entrepreneurs were quick to take advantage of the situation, often creeping into the ground to sell sweets and newspapers – a practice the club tried hard to stamp out by requesting supporters not to encourage them by making purchases. But it would be many more years before the club erected refreshment stalls of their own.

PROMOTION BATTLES

The first season at Highbury proved a success through the gates. Despite the sparse conditions and the dubious state of the embankments, which became dangerously slippery whenever rain fell, on average 23,000 flocked to games. This was two and a half times what the club had drawn in the final season at Plumstead and they were by far the best numbers in the Second Division. Norris had, through a variety of means, ploughed some £125,000 into the club to create the fledgling stadium. On the field, the quest for First Division status was paramount: it went right to the final day of the season when the battle for the final promotion spot was between Arsenal, Leeds City and Bradford. With three games to go, Arsenal faced a tough local derby encounter with Clapton Orient. Some 35,000 packed into Highbury to witness a hard-fought 2–2 draw. The draw was to prove decisive because although Arsenal won their final two fixtures (both 2–0 at home to Grimsby and then away to Glossop) Bradford held on to pip Arsenal on goal average and claim the second promotion spot.

The final table made devastating reading for Norris. Gates were, in reality, the only way for him to recoup his investment and the best opposition was required at Highbury, not to mention the interest and bumper crowds First Division games with Chelsea and Tottenham Hotspur would bring.

Things didn't get any better the following season with the outbreak of the First World War. Although the 1914–15 season took place, in the grander scheme of things it was irrelevant. By the time of Arsenal's first game of the season on 1 September 1914 at home to Glossop, Great Britain was already at war. Many of the Arsenal players were still employed in the munitions factory in Woolwich and were working long hours to help the war effort, others simply signed up to fight and were unavailable.

The season however was played out and apart from the grudge game against Orient which attracted a full house, attendances for many other games were well under the 10,000 mark. Arsenal finished fifth in the table that season whilst Chelsea and Tottenham Hotspur occupied the bottom two places in the First Division. With no end to the war in sight, the League competition was shut down for four years. By the time plans were in place for the competition to get under way, the club was £60,000 in debt. Norris was desperate and about to undertake one of the most outrageous pieces of political manipulation that had ever been seen, and would probably ever be seen, in Football League history!

THE GREATEST VICTORY

Highbury was literally bulging at the seams when the 1919–20 League season got under way. Newcastle United were the visitors and they won by the only goal of the game. Newcastle had been Arsenal's first-ever Football League opposition at the Manor Ground all those years earlier. That initial game took place in the Second Division; this encounter was in the First Division. Norris had completed the first part of his task – to get Arsenal back into the First Division. But the club's promotion to the top flight had not been as a result of their exploits on the field, rather the exploits of Norris and Wall in the lobby rooms. It was perhaps Arsenal's greatest ever victory!

By now Norris was a man of very considerable influence. He was now Sir Henry Norris, having been knighted in 1917 for his work as a recruitment officer during the war. Indeed, in this role he managed to assemble three artillery brigades from south-west London who were sent to Belgium and played a significant role in the Battle of the Somme. This achievement had Norris promoted to the rank of colonel. His profile in Fulham was now at stratospheric levels and it was no surprise when he won a place on the Tory benches in Parliament in 1918 to serve Fulham East as an MP. He was increasingly a man of influence and he used this status to canvass and convince members of the League Management Committee to vote his way – aided by the other major Arsenal shareholder, Hall, who was still a serving member of the LMC.

DIVISION EXPANSION

As the start of the 1919–20 season approached the LMC was voting on the new make-up of the First Division. As part of the re-launch plans they had decided to increase the number of clubs in the top flight from 20 to 22. Although there were no hard and fast rules about how the expansion should take place it was generally accepted that it would be done by either not relegating the clubs that had finished bottom of the 1914–15 season or by promoting additional clubs from the top of the final Second Division season prior to the war, and most likely a combination of the two. The clubs in question were Chelsea and Tottenham Hotspur, who had finished 19th and 20th respectively in the First Division. Derby County finished top followed by Preston North End, Barnsley and Wolverhampton Wanderers in the Second Division, and Arsenal finished fifth ahead of Birmingham City on goal average.

Exactly what Norris said to the committee of chairmen will probably never be known, but there was much unrest at the end of that final pre-war season and also some curious results, including a 12–0 defeat of Liverpool by Manchester United which allowed United to finish above Chelsea. It may well have been that Norris used suggestive abilities in these areas to good cause.

The first stage of the election saw Chelsea confirmed in the First Division. There was no vote on this process. The Liverpool chairman and owner at the time was Norris's close friend John McKenna, who was also LMC president. In a similar fashion, the election of Second Division champions and runners-up Derby County and Preston North End was also taken on the nod. With one place remaining to be filled in the top flight McKenna addressed the LMC meeting and recommended that Arsenal be given the place. McKenna argued that Arsenal were more worthy of the position as they had been a member of the League 15 years longer than Tottenham (although Wolverhampton had been League members for four more years than Arsenal). Tottenham, along with Barnsley, who had finished third, were up in arms over the suggestion; however, the LMC opted to put it to the vote. Curiously Nottingham Forest had also lobbied their way into the vote – they had finished 18th in the Second Division – perhaps as the result of a pay-off somewhere along the line. The voting was resolved as follows:

TEAM	VOTES
Arsenal	18
Tottenham Hotspur	8
Barnsley	5
Wolverhampton Wanderers	4
Nottingham Forest	3
Birmingham City	2
Hull City	1

So, Arsenal were elected to the First Division and Tottenham were relegated to the Second Division, with it being said that the chairmen cast their votes largely on McKenna's recommendation, believing he had good reason to suggest they do so. The fallout from this occasion surrounded the two clubs for many years to come with it often spilling onto the pitch and onto the terraces. Local rivalry was strong enough: this just fuelled it further. The election result probably saved Arsenal from a further bout of liquidation, although ironically one has to assume that Norris would have preferred Tottenham Hotspur to have remained in the First Division, in preference to, say, Preston North End, because of the sell-out crowds they would have generated at Highbury in those very cash-strapped post-war years.

The next few seasons brought Arsenal little success on the football field. With Leslie Knighton now in charge as secretary-manager the club skirted dangerously close to relegation on a number of occasions. The club finished 10th and then 9th in those first two seasons and then 17th and 19th in two of the next three. The crowds continued to come through the gates, though, and attendance averaged at around the 30,000 mark. Norris was able to get additional revenue by persuading the FA to host the England v. Wales game at Highbury in 1920 and then England v. Belgium in 1923. (See Chapter Nine: International Venue for details on these and other international encounters at Arsenal.)

BUILDING CONTINUES

Back on the terraces works continued to move forward, albeit slowly, under the guidance of new clerk of the works Jack Campbell. The terraces were completed to their full height at the Laundry End and along the west side. The terrace steps themselves were finished, with concrete replacing the earthen embankments. These adjustments made room for some 5,000 extra spectators. Concrete steps were also erected at the Gillespie Road entrance to allow people to walk to the top of the terracing from the rear rather than having to filter through and walk up the steps. Indeed, additions like these allowed the club to squeeze in more people: many had simply refused to move around the ground into the spaces as it filled from only a couple of entrance points on the north-west end. There were no access points on to the west terracing from Highbury Hill in those days, the length of that side of the ground being enclosed by houses whose gardens backed onto the west-side wall.

The East Stand had also been completed with distinctive multi-span arches. This was laid partly to terrace but included a large enclosed area of seating for club officials, dignitaries and season-ticket holders. For a while its nine distinctive arches hosted the word 'Arsenal' painted in big red letters. The stand cover embodied the distinctive style of the time and was not dissimilar to those at a number of other London grounds where Messrs Humphreys were also employed as builders. The club name remained on the front of the East Stand for only a short time and had been removed by the start of the 1927–28 season. This was probably just for financial reasons, as the paint had to be reapplied each year.

The changing-rooms and club offices were also complete, although rather sparse in nature, whilst a number of turnstiles allowed access in and out of Avenell Road. The College End of the ground didn't change at all: it was the smallest section of terracing beyond the boundary of which remained the training pitch and St John's College itself.

Attendances rose and fell but always maintained an average of 30,000 or so. Games in those days were played as mini-series with the home and away fixture often completed within the week. Tottenham Hotspur needed only one season in the Second Division to return to the First and the subsequent League encounters always provided 50–60,000 souls, many of whom would take their spot long before kick-off.

The tenure of Sir Henry Norris and William Wall at Highbury was nearing its end. Their exit from the game was not of their wanting but was certainly of their making; perhaps it was their previous manipulation of the LMC that finally caught up with them. Norris, though, made a couple of more significant decisions, the effect of which was going to catapult Arsenal into a dynasty and also take Highbury through a stage of development the likes of which had never been seen before.

THE CHAPMAN DYNASTY

In 1925 Herbert Chapman was appointed manager of Arsenal. Around the same time Sir Henry Norris completed the outright purchase of the Highbury site by paying around £64,000 for the 10-acre enclosure. In these two actions Norris had secured the future of Arsenal Football Club pretty much for all time. Norris himself did not stand for re-election to Parliament in 1924 as he'd become embroiled in a libel case with a rival Tory MP (which Norris eventually won). Sir Henry, a long-standing Freemason, became Grand Deacon of the Grand Lodge of England.

At the end of the 1924–25 season Arsenal parted company with manager Leslie Knighton. As described in Chapter Five: Managing Influence, the split was not on the best of terms, with the outgoing manager calling foul of Norris. The Arsenal chairman had placed an advert in the *Athletic News*, a weekly sports publication of the time, requesting applicants for the vacant position. Legend has it, though, that preliminary talks had already been completed with Herbert Chapman long before that point.

Early results of the new manager's first season didn't look good: a 1–0 home defeat by his former employer, Tottenham, wasn't taken well and a few games later Arsenal suffered a 7–0 thrashing at Newcastle. But a change in tactics brought about by his major signing of the time, Charlie Buchan, helped matters and the club quickly moved up the table finishing in their highest ever League position as runners-up to another of Chapman's previous employers, Huddersfield Town. It proved to be a bit of a false dawn, though, as the club struggled in mid-table for the next few years; however, Chapman was already making improvements to his surroundings.

Norris had been Arsenal chairman and majority stakeholder for some 15 years and, given his ambition, he was desperate for success. That was literally just around the corner, but a turn of events would mean that some of Norris's old wheeling and dealing would return to haunt him and leave him watching what was about to unfold from the stands rather than the boardroom.

In 1927 Arsenal reached their first FA Cup final and Norris and Wall found themselves facing charges for financial irregularities. Given the blatant manipulation of the League by Norris after the war these charges seemed trifling (we can probably assume that the powers that be had gone full circle and had simply had enough). The revelations behind the charges were published by the *Daily Mail* newspaper and became a matter of public interest that perhaps the Football League simply couldn't ignore any more.

Amongst the charges levelled by the authorities were that Norris paid for his chauffeur with club funds during the period 1921–24 and that he had personally pocketed a £125 gain from the sale of the team bus. In addition Norris was also charged with making illegal payments to Charlie Buchan to persuade him to leave his business in Sunderland and move south. Norris and Wall were banned from the game but took their appeal right through to the Lord Chief Justice. Despite Norris pointing out the huge personal investment he had made in Arsenal and Highbury – in excess of £125,000 – the appeal on 7 February 1929 failed. Sir Henry Norris's time was up. The fact was only acknowledged locally by a few paragraphs in the *Islington Gazette* headed 'Sir Henry Norris Loses His Libel Action.'

There were few tears shed for Norris in local circles and the irony that Tottenham Hotspur chairman Morton Cadman took over Wall's place on the League Management Committee was not lost on him. He did not deny the charges and was forced to watch Arsenal's first-ever Cup and League triumphs under the guidance of his manager, Chapman, from afar. Norris died an outcast from the game on 30 July 1934 following a massive heart attack, but sound in the knowledge that his beloved work was moving in a forward direction at a ferocious pace.

THREE

A Stadium Grows

With Arsenal now holding the freehold to the Highbury ground, some of the restrictions placed on them in those early days by the Church were now gone, although it would be a while before alcohol was served on site. But Arsenal were now their own boss and just as when they had arrived at the Manor Ground for the second time years before, they were now very much their own landlords.

The new Arsenal chairman was of a very different ilk to the disgraced Norris: the Hill-Wood family hailed from Glossop, where they had owned and run what amounted to a local works team, but one which had risen to the dizzy heights of Football League in the First Division for a season and had played several important fixtures with Arsenal in the Second Division. A local cotton magnate of the time, Major Sir Samuel Hill-Wood, like Norris before him, could clearly see the potential at Highbury. Unlike Norris, though, Hill-Wood was more than happy to leave the day-to-day operation of the club to Chapman, for whom he had the utmost respect. To this day the family links remain between the clubs, the role of patron at Glossop North End AFC belonging to the Arsenal chairman at the time of the move from Highbury, Peter Hill-Wood.

Changes were being effected on and off the field. Chapman was building a team that would dominate English football for the decade ahead and would become known as the 'Team of the '30s'. Off the field he had his own vision, which he set about delivering, as Highbury got ready for a transformation.

Where Archibald Leitch was an engineer who had taken advantage of the boom in football stadiums to use the skills he had learnt in the shipbuilding yard, Arsenal's choice to head up their design team for the '30s was an interesting one: the French-trained Claude Waterlow Ferrier. In partnership with William Binnie since 1927, Ferrier was a qualified architect with excellent credentials that had seen him cut his design teeth on projects such as restaurants, hotels and hospitals. After teaming up with Binnie, he moved on to grander projects and national buildings, such as the Army and Navy Club in Pall Mall and Trafalgar House in Waterloo Place.

Ferrier was an exponent of the art deco style that came into favour in the mid-'20s and it says much for his vision that the two icons of those early designs – the East and West stands – remained in their entire splendour for Highbury's duration. To say his ideas at the time were revolutionary would be an understatement. It also speaks volumes for the vision of the Arsenal board of the time that they took such a leap of faith for what would be the first non-Leitch designed or influenced facility of the time.

Ferrier examined everything from the terraces to the new stands required, not just in their exterior looks and washes, finishes and glasses, but also down to the fitments inside – the marble and the deep rich mahogany panelling prevalent in the offices and rooms of the East Stand. It was a monumental task and one that very clearly stood the test of time. Chief amongst Ferrier's priorities was to open up space to allow more people into the ground: a full house at Highbury around this time would net the club around £4,000 in gate receipts. Adding room for an extra 20–25,000 fans, and even charging them at the same price, could increase the income by another £1,500 or so.

CHAPMAN FIRST

Between the arrival of Hill-Wood and Ferrier, Herbert Chapman had made his own improvements to the ground. At the College End he erected a scoreboard, thus allowing fans to be informed of match scorers both at half-time and at full-time. It was a simple letter- and number-driven board that was far removed from the giant Sony Jumbotron screens that would dominate two Highbury corners many years later.

In 1927 a ticket system similar to that used on the Underground railways was being trialled at the Gillespie Road end of the ground. Pay boxes were installed from which supporters purchased admission tickets and these were then presented at the turnstiles to gain entry to the ground. This proved successful, cutting queues on both fronts – with only one person required to queue to purchase tickets, passage through the turnstiles was made much quicker.

For the start of the 1930–31 season, Chapman had been given the go-ahead by the Arsenal board to set another of his innovations in motion: erecting a 45-minute clock 12 feet in diameter at the Laundry End of the stadium. In September 1930 the *Islington Gazette* reported: 'The huge clock starts functioning immediately the whistle starts the ball rolling. It can be seen all over the ground by the players and spectators.' The *Matchday Programme* of the time went to lengths to explain to fans that the clock was purely to give spectators a 'rough idea' of how far the game had progressed and not to 'abuse' or consider the referee a 'fool' if he does not signal time when the clock reaches the 45-minute mark. There are some things that the passage of time does not change!

If the clock was a success with the fans it was not with the powers that be, who simply did not like it, and within a month the FA had ordered the club to effect its immediate removal. With a brief appeal rejected, Chapman authorised the £180 it would cost to have the clock converted to an ordinary mechanism and thus the seeds of the Clock End were sown; although it wouldn't be relocated to what became the College End of the ground for several years when the Laundry End was roofed. Indeed, it might never have found a home there had the club gone ahead with a plan to roof the College End. In May 1930 they accepted a quote for £3,800 from Boulton Paul Limited to roof and extend the area, only to decide against it and abandon Chapman's project a month or so later when discussions were already under way to appoint an architect to redesign the ground. An icon of football and Highbury might never have been born.

Chapman had his own ideas as to the development of the ground, which he felt should be shaped like a huge bowl with a cycle track running around it. Cycling was a popular sport in those days. In Chapman's view this would have needed the club to purchase all the houses in Highbury Hill and also to shuffle the ground itself towards St John's College and take advantage of the natural hill that ran up the Aubert Park road (the park itself had long since gone).

FOUNDATIONS LAID

The building work that Ferrier demanded was immense and in 1931 he turned his attention to the terraces, which were both extended. The College End, at this stage, was less than half the height of the Laundry End: the new plan called for it to be extended to around three-quarters of the height. The Laundry End terrace required a lot of re-working, especially in its foundations, which, to that point, had been largely clay. The club called on locals to bring their waste to act as landfill to create the new foundations. Legend has it that as a coal merchant parked his horse and cart to tip in his contribution, he lost control and the horse and cart fell into the void. Some stories say it took place at the Laundry End; others say the College End. Subsequent clearing of both terraces for the new North and South Stands decades later failed to prove the myth one way or another.

Builders W.J. Cearns Ltd were employed to undertake the works, but they quickly fell behind their schedule for completion of the works – and fell foul of Ferrier and the Arsenal board of directors at the same time. The initial timetable for the job was to have the entire north, south and west terracing completed by the end of December 1931 but an extension was granted until 18 January 1932. However, as Christmas 1931 approached, work was still a long way from completion on the north and south ends. Time was everything, of course, as unfinished work rendered parts of the ground – indeed, important areas of the ground: the terracing – unable to be used and therefore potentially costly for the club. Despite Ferrier's chasing, the builders could give no reason for the delays other than they simply had not got the job done. As such, Ferrier got hard and invoked the penalty clauses. Cearns found himself out of pocket – what he *was* paid did not reach him until the following August.

The biggest headache for the club at the time was the isolation of the west terracing. The row of houses along Highbury Hill had been a dead end for the club up until that point, with fans having to make their way along the length of the terracing from either the Gillespie Road entrance or the Avenell Road entrance. Although safety issues were not necessarily top of the agenda in those early days, there had been concerns that it was often only the good nature of the crowd that prevented problems breaking out. Indeed the Arsenal programmes often commended spectators on their 'good sportsmanlike nature' at the ground.

HIGHBURY HILL ENTRANCE

Like Chapman, Ferrier saw the need to create more space on the Highbury Hill side of the site, not just to provide access but also to allow him to build his vision of the West Stand with the assistance of consulting engineer Mr H.J. Deane. The stand required not just access but also space for its footprint. The west side of the ground had narrowed down its length as the gardens at the back of the houses became progressively longer up Highbury Hill. Notwithstanding that there was still at least six foot of Arsenal land on the other side of the west wall, Ferrier sought to purchase land and properties along Highbury Hill. He did this by acquiring a couple of houses and land at the back of it at the southern end of where the West Stand would protrude most into the footprint of the gardens. The houses were demolished and used as an access point for Ferrier's builders of the time – W.J. Cearns Ltd – to lay the base for the new stand.

Ferrier was nothing if not innovative and the missing house was used as a feature still in existence today. At ground level the entrance contained three access points: a set of double gates through which delivery vehicles could come and go, as well as matchday spectators; an 'Executive Gate Entrance'; and a front door!

The front door was used as the entrance to the three floors of flats that had been built as a bridge between the two adjacent houses. Three large metal windows were set out on each floor and under them on the left and right sides were set the words 'Arsenal Football Club'. The red letters and gates looked striking set against the cream-coloured façade.

Before the Highbury Hill entrance could be completed, the West Stand itself had to take shape and this was well under way by the end of 1931. The design at that time was for a single tier of 4,100 seats at a cost of about £50,000, a great sum of money in those days, especially as it was not the club's main stand (consider that it was not far short of what the club had paid for the site itself a few years earlier).

The stand was innovative in many practical ways. First the bank of seating was created as a single level angled down under the pitched roof and supported all the way through by several columns (today these would be strongly frowned upon due to the obstruction of sightlines). Space was kept under the vast majority of the seating platform for terracing, thus providing shelter from the elements for those standing on what had previously been just the Kop area. Before this there had only been very limited covered terracing on the Avenell Road side. The pitched roof itself was also unique in that its canopy continued out beyond the leading edge of seating in an effort to provide further protection for those standing below. (It is debatable, even today, if the roofs of either stand provided anything but scant cover for those standing – or, in later days, sitting – below, and then only when the wind was in a favourable direction!) In his initial design Ferrier had not closed in two open ends of the stands, deciding that the roof would afford the necessary protection. However, after the stand was opened and in operation it soon became apparent that it also acted as a wind tunnel, so they were subsequently closed with the use of glass to give the effect well known to everyone who has seen a picture of Highbury.

The West Stand was fitted with padded tip-up 'Windsor' seats which were quite luxurious at the time. Access to the seats was via stairwells at the back of the stand. The better seats in the middle were reserved in an executive area and part and parcel of this was access to the stand via the Executive Entrance Gate in Highbury Hill. An Arsenal programme at the time said access to this area was via an 'electric passenger lift'. This led into heated lounges where patrons of the area could mingle in comfort prior to the game. The stairwells at either end of the stand were well lit with plenty of windows.

Segregation had also started at this time, the terraced area under the West Stand being fenced off from both ends of the ground to provide a complete enclosure (no other standing areas had previously been cordoned off). It was estimated that the capacity of the whole West Stand and terracing was around 24,000. The club also found that improvements to their real estate increased their rates and taxes to well over £5,000 per annum.

The official opening of the West Stand was performed by the Prince of Wales (later Edward VIII, who acceded in 1936) on 10 December 1932: a major coup by Herbert Chapman. The Arsenal manager only five weeks earlier had Gillespie Road station renamed Arsenal station – so was quite used to organising surprises off the field as well as on it! The club called for shopkeepers to hang flags from their windows along the route being taken by the Royal Family up through Camden and also produced a special souvenir programme for the day costing twopence. To mark the occasion Arsenal's special band was conducted by Mr H.J. Kitchenside with community singing included. Reports also note that the local Mecca cafés around Highbury had a full licence between the hours of 1 p.m. and 5.30 p.m!

The *Islington Gazette* paid tribute to how far Arsenal Stadium had come in such a short time:

> When one considers what the ground was like twenty years ago, Saturday's inauguration was the climax to a wonderful achievement and full credit must be given to the players who have made such progress possible, to the director, and last but not least to Mr Herbert Chapman whose sagacity, football brains, showmanship and many other qualities have done so much for the Gunners.

Arsenal had won their first League Championship the previous season but would finish runners-up, two points behind Everton, before heading off on a series of three successive League Championships. It was truly the golden age of Arsenal, which would extend right through the '30s. But tragedy struck in January 1934 when Chapman contracted pneumonia and died.

Ferrier continued with his brief and set about designing a roof for the Laundry End next. As we know, the club had originally planned to enclose the College End but instead opted to redesign the bigger North End, something that was first discussed in October 1934. No decision was made to go ahead for almost a year when Messrs Wilson, Lovett & Son Ltd were contracted to undertake the works. The first stage of this required that Chapman's clock was relocated to the College End, which increasingly became known as the Clock End thereafter. The movement of the clock did not go without incident and both it and George Elliot, the clerk of the works at the time, almost met their makers when the structure toppled over and missed him by inches. Thankfully both prevailed!

The front of the 'shed' (the term used in those days to describe a roof over a terraced area) was emblazoned with two large AFC monograms that provided a distinctive signature to the venue – just as Ferrier had hoped. The roof was one of three that would be constructed to cover the North Bank down the years, Ferrier's original construction lasting until it was destroyed in a Second World War bombing raid. Unfortunately, before the £2,000 structure could be erected at the end of the 1934–35 season, Ferrier lost his life in an accident. On its completion it provided cover for 14,000 standing souls, or Bobites. The completion of this covered area brought the total undercover capacity at Arsenal up to around 40,000!

At the back of the North Bank, in the wall structure used to support the roof, two huge sliding doors were also constructed, the main purpose of which was to allow an unobstructed breeze to run across the pitch. One of the reasons the Highbury pitch has always been one of the better bits of green down the years is because the club has always looked after the air circulation over the pitch – the four corners of the ground have never been enclosed and ventilation is as important as natural light.

With the rebuilding of the College End and the relocation of the clock there, the original scoreboard that Herbert Chapman had installed shortly after his arrival was gone. But a new system was soon installed in the north-east and south-west corners of the ground involving a series of letters on a board running at the front of the terracing by the 'running track', the narrow strip of land running around the edge of the pitch. The letters corresponded to fixtures printed in the *Matchday Programme*. Numbers representing the home and away scores at each of the matches were simply inserted into slots next to each of the letters, making it reasonably straightforward to read off half-time scores and full-time results (although half-time scores often never materialised until the second half was well under way!).

So, not because of Ferrier's death but because of initial planning, Arsenal had completed the initial building that the club, along with Ferrier and Chapman, had envisaged at the turn of the decade. The north, west and south terraces had been extended and improved beyond recognition; safety barriers had been installed and access up to the terraces completed, removing the slippery dangerous slide that had existed previously; an innovatively used access point had been created in Highbury Hill and land bought so that a state-of-the-art stand could be constructed; a roof had been added to the Laundry End and, in so doing, the Clock End had been born. It had been a massive undertaking and despite the club's success on the field and the crowds flocking through the gates, it had taken every penny the club owned and more, leaving it heavily overdrawn.

Although he never lived to see it, another of Chapman's ideas came to fruition at the end of that third successive Championship. The Enumerator was an electronic turnstile that was able to count the crowd as it came into the ground – previously cash was taken quite literally at a gate or tickets were purchased at a booth and these were handed in at the gate to gain entry. The old system was open to abuse and there was never a way in which an accurate crowd count could be provided until the cash and tickets were counted – and as cash undoubtedly went walking at times, the count was never accurate. The Enumerator changed all this and allowed the club to set a safe limit of 70,000 on the capacity and also allowed the size of the crowd in different areas of the stadium to be monitored. On 9 March 1935, before the installation of the Enumerator, an amazing 73,295 packed into Highbury for a top-of-the-table clash with Sunderland – the all-time record for the stadium.

THE EAST STAND

The East Stand, although still functioning and just over 20 years old, was becoming a liability (see page 35 for a photograph of the stand as it was in 1914). Being mainly wooden in structure it was becoming expensive to maintain and it was obvious that repair costs over a number of years would ultimately exceed the cost of a replacement. Arsenal had also completed their third successive Championship – their fourth title in just five years – and were on their way to a second FA Cup win. Crowds were buoyant – witness the record attendance for Sunderland above – and so it also made financial sense to expand the number of seats and improve the facilities to increase revenue and take advantage of the situation. So, as 1936 dawned, the decision was made to demolish the old East Stand and replace it with a new structure. In fact the planning process was already well under way with initial drawings and designs commissioned in the early part of 1935 as part of an 18-month process.

The late Ferrier's colleague William Binnie was charged with the task of creating the replacement East Stand which, not least due to the easy access directly on to Avenell Road, was much grander and would also house the club's business activities. A quick look would show the new East Stand to be architecturally almost a mirror of the West Stand; however it was in a totally new league in terms of features. First, there were two tiers – both levels offering 4,000 seats, bringing the ground's total seated capacity up to 12,100. Access to the majority of these was via stairwells at each end, as per the West Stand, but also with internal access points. Patrons had the luxury of covered toilets, canteens and access to a huge Horse Shoe Bar, purported to be one of the largest in the world at the time.

Across five floors the club fitted out its offices and boardroom, all in mahogany with huge imposing wood doors. A main entrance was created on Avenell Road, which led into a grand, tiled hallway decked in marble and with a sweeping set of stairs that led off to the right and up to the directors' domain, whilst the hall was dominated by a bust of Herbert Chapman.

From those famous Marble Halls, off the corridor to the south side, were the administration facilities, including a large general office, typist's room, the secretary-manager's private room, accountants' and cashiers' rooms, and accommodation for groundsmen and staff. Players' changing-rooms were accommodated on the north side of the entrance and 'left nothing to be desired': the dressing areas were heated by radiators and a panel running under the floor. The treatment room included the very latest electrical apparatus, and there was a private room for trainers and a large indoor gymnasium, plus a club room for the team.

In between was the small narrow tunnel that spilt onto the pitch with the players' room directly off it on the left, sloping awkwardly under the seating above (this was later referred to as the 'Halfway House' by players, who used to meet there on Monday nights to discuss the previous weekend's game). In front of the new East Stand, Binnie constructed a small area of terracing and this was closed off and would later become the Family Enclosure.

When it was opened on 24 October 1936 – coincidentally manager George Allison's 53rd birthday – it had taken just seven months to complete since demolition had started on the original East Stand. It was without doubt the most impressive stand of its type in the country and in typically understated fashion the Arsenal *Matchday Programme* of the day described it as a 'building of wonder'. Newspaper reports said the stand 'embraced the latest ideas in luxury and comfort' and that it contained 'two large luncheon and tearooms each capable of seating 200 persons at small tables, and in addition two very large snack bars for light refreshments'.

The stand was innovative in many other ways, again illustrating the progressive nature of the club. A system of loudspeakers were originally installed in the new stand but were continued around the whole stadium, the main purpose of which was to help direct and control the huge crowds that were common and to help maintain safety. In addition a microphone system was established in the new directors' box to facilitate presentations and speeches. Negotiations with the BBC also saw the inclusion of a dedicated broadcast booth from which, at a moment's notice, a broadcast could be made from any match. And typical of the forward thinking of the day, provisions were also included in the stand for the installation of television equipment.

Whilst floodlighting had not been installed at this point, it was high on the Arsenal agenda and had been in mind during the design of the stand. The club were also seeing it as a way to allow work, such as line marking, which had to be done regularly in the days of muddy pitches, to be undertaken at any time irrespective of darkness and the fogs that often descended on London in those days.

The *Islington Gazette* summed up it all up thus:

> This must be said for Arsenal. Their scheme has not been launched for profit-making purposes. Had they conducted their affairs on business principles they would not have committed themselves to an outlay which has astonished the rest of the football world by its magnitude.

The Thursday before the opening of the stand the bust memorial to Herbert Chapman in the main entrance hall was unveiled (see page 88 for a photo). In the presence of Mrs Chapman, her two sons and daughters, the two brothers of the late manager, the club directors, players, staff and many shareholders the ceremony was performed by the Revd. N.R. Boyd, vicar and rural dean of Hendon, where Herbert Chapman had been a parishioner and where he was buried.

The 51,000 who flocked to Highbury for the opening of the new stand witnessed a 0–0 draw with Grimsby. It had cost £130,000 – two and a half times as much as the West Stand. The impact of the East Stand architecturally was indeed great and several decades later a move was started by heritage parties to have the building statutorily listed. These initial applications were declined but eventually succeeded on 16 July 1997 when the stand achieved Grade II status almost 61 years after it was officially opened.

WAR AGAIN

By the time 1936 drew to a close the improvements at the ground over the previous six years had left the club £200,000 in debt. As a team Arsenal was still a force to be reckoned with and a fifth League title in eight years would again feed the coffers in the 1937–38 season, but in 1938–39 the team had to be satisfied with fifth. Then, disastrously, both on and off the field, the country was at war. Just as with the outbreak of the Great War 24 years earlier, the club had completed a massive rebuilding programme but found itself going into a period with no games, no income and huge debt.

FOUR

Team of the '30s

Look at any sport and there will be debate about just who are the best players and the best teams. How would one team fare against another from a different era? Which players from which eras would combine to form the best-ever team? The stuff of dreams for any fan. But what is evident, and this is not only clear in retrospect but was also apparent at the time, is that Highbury has been blessed with two of the greatest footballing teams of all time, not just within the bounds of our national game but internationally as well.

Arsène Wenger's Untouchables of 2003–04 are the subject matter of a later chapter as they can surely lay claim to being the most entertaining side ever to have graced the Highbury turf; however, it is the Herbert Chapman-inspired side of the '30s that must lay claim to being the greatest Arsenal side of all time. They did not play with the swagger and grace of the latter-day heroes or go through a League campaign undefeated, nor did they play as many matches or have such a travel regime placed on them, but then most of them held down second jobs and did not have the training or medical facilities of today. Almost certainly the 2003–04 team would beat the best of Chapman's era, but in terms of trophies there are no comparisons: their haul of five League Championship titles in eight seasons, a runners-up spot plus three Cup final appearances generating two wins speaks for itself. Since that third successive Championship title in 1935, no Arsenal side since has won back-to-back titles.

The job of redesigning and constructing Highbury was the tangible part of the 'Great Design': land, money, vision and a willingness to succeed were the required ingredients. All were available to the Arsenal board of directors as the '20s were consigned to history, and so the old Aubert Park site was transformed from a basic facility into a world-renowned stadium that was trendsetting, not only in design but also in the facilities it had to offer.

The second part of the Great Design was to provide a team worthy of the facilities, to bring success – and that meant silverware – to Highbury. This, as all football supporters around the world know, can be planned, but is never a certainty. Sir Henry Norris had sought Herbert Chapman as his man to do this and there can be no doubt that Norris's choice was spot on at the time – and in the long run, as history shows. While Chapman will be profiled in more detail later, suffice to say at this stage that he came to Highbury as the man who had taken Huddersfield Town from relative obscurity to the Football League Championship and created a team that would take three successive titles – something that the Chapman-designed Arsenal would emulate a few years later.

Arsenal were indeed the 'Team of the '30s' and, as the table opposite illustrates, its achievements were significant. In the days when there was no television to flatter and project, many of Arsenal's players were nevertheless household names. Some cost a lot of money, others were conjured out of minor football, but all became essential components of a side which was horribly mean in defence and decisive in counter-attack. So much so that Arsenal's football, especially during the early part of the '30s, was often described as 'smash and grab' and from this the tag 'Lucky Arsenal' was born. Arsenal was anything but lucky during this halcyon period, but opposition fans simply had no other explanation for their continued success.

The '30s – A Year-By-Year Summary

1930   Arsenal win their first-ever major honour 44 years after they were founded, winning the FA Cup at Wembley 2–0 against Huddersfield Town, Herbert Chapman's former club.

1931   Arsenal win the League Championship, the first Southern club to achieve this feat after 38 seasons of Northern and Midland domination. Jack Humble, club director and a founder member in 1886, can watch with great satisfaction from the stands.

1932   Arsenal reach their third FA Cup final, losing to Newcastle United 1–2 to end a season which promised the Double at one stage.

1933   Arsenal win their second League Championship, but experience one of the most disastrous defeats in the club's FA Cup history: Third Division Walsall beat the favourites 0–2 in the biggest upset for years.

1934   Manager Herbert Chapman dies on 6 January. Joe Shaw, Chapman's assistant, takes over until the end of the season and secures a second consecutive League Championship. George Allison is appointed to the post of manager-director during the close season.

On 14 November England play Italy at Highbury. Seven Arsenal players line up in the England team: Copping, Bowden, Moss, Male, Drake, Hapgood and Bastin. The trainer is Arsenal's Tom Whittaker. England win 3–2 in what became known as the 'Battle of Highbury'.

1935   A club record crowd of 73,295 attends the match versus Sunderland in 1935–36. Prior to this, Arsenal achieve their third consecutive League Championship.

1936   Arsenal reach the FA Cup final, beating Sheffield United 1–0.

1938   Arsenal win their fifth League Championship in eight seasons, a League record. In the close season, George Allison breaks the transfer record by paying £14,000 to Wolves for Welsh international Bryn Jones.

1939   Arsenal finish fifth in the last season before the Second World War.

FIVE-YEAR PLAN

When Chapman arrived at Highbury he told the newspapers it would take five years for him to bring trophies to Highbury and he was proved right. Just like at Huddersfield previously, he saw there was plenty of work to do and that it would take time. As with the stadium, Chapman saw it all as part of a plan. He was meticulous in what he did and many of the systems he put in place in those early days at Highbury have proved their worth down the years. Chapman had a penchant for tactical planning with an ability to transfer his designs onto the pitch. To effect those designs, he needed bright people and so he set about surrounding himself with intelligent footballers (something Arsène Wenger always championed during his Highbury years) who would form the cornerstone of the side. So the likes of Buchan, Alex James and David Jack arrived. It was a strategy that his successor George Allison would continue with people such as Drake and Mercer. Chapman respected their intelligence as Buchan wrote in his autobiography: '[Chapman] would always listen to other people and take advantage of their ideas if he thought they would improve the team in any way.'

One of the first things Chapman did at Highbury was to set Friday meetings in the diary – each week the Arsenal players would meet at midday and discuss both the previous week's performance and what they could learn from it, and then would look at the coming match and discuss opposition players and tactics. Chapman even had a model football pitch on a table with magnetic markers for players so that they could work through everything visually. Arsenal was simply becoming the most organised club in the country – on the pitch and off it, in playing and in business operation.

But it took time for the jigsaw to be assembled. Initially it was to be created around Charlie Buchan: the lad who had grown up watching Woolwich Arsenal in Plumpstead and was now revered throughout the country was in the twilight of his career and winning honours on Wearside with Sunderland. Chapman was king when it came to the art of persuasion and Buchan was soon an Arsenal player for a cut-price £2,000 down plus £100 a goal – a deal that would cost the club around £4,000 in the end.

Buchan was to be a major influence on the playing style of the team (see Chapter 5 – Managing Influence), one that would set Arsenal apart.

Tom Parker followed Cliff Bastin to Highbury, where he would captain the side, and Jack Lambert cost £2,000 from Doncaster Rovers. Lambert seemed to be the one player that Chapman was never quite happy with down the years, but despite trying he could never find a replacement for the burly inside forward. He was joined on the other side by Charlie Jones. Winger Joe Hume signed as well, reputed to be the fastest flank player in the country at that time. But it was a £200 purchase from non-League Oswestry Town that was to become the cornerstone of the side in the years ahead: Herbie Roberts's no-nonsense play would make him a firm favourite with the Highbury Bobites.

THE FIRST FINAL

The FA Cup final of 1927 marked Arsenal's first battle for the silverware and it will be remembered as the game in which the ball slid from keeper Dan Lewis's grasp against his slippery shirt and into the Arsenal net for the only goal of the game. The Arsenal keeper blamed it on his new jersey, which had a greasy sheen to it: for many years after, the Arsenal keeper's shirt was always washed prior to use to remove its slipperiness.

The route to that final was memorable for a remarkable goal scored at Highbury which came in a sixth-round encounter with Wolverhampton Wanderers. With the game tied at 1–1, Joe Hulme crossed from the right and centre-half Jack Butler headed his only goal for that Cup campaign – nothing remarkable in that apart from the fact that he was fully 25 yards out from the goal!

Arsenal's League form remained indifferent and Chapman continued to recruit. Eddie Hapgood arrived as a spindly 19-year-old vegetarian and was forced to eat steaks to improve his physique and strength. Chapman then made two signings that broke the previous transfer record at Highbury: after much persuasion David Jack was prised away from Bolton for £11,500, then, following the retirement of Buchan, Chapman swooped for Preston's Alex James who, at £8,750, was to prove an absolute bargain, if not perhaps the first 'disruptive' player of his time.

James would become probably the most important player of the Arsenal team of that era, being at the heart of everything the team did on the field, in both a physical and emotional sense. Indeed, after Arsenal had drawn an FA Cup tie in 1930 with Birmingham City 2–2 at Highbury, prior to which James had been sent home to rest because he was worn out, Chapman called upon the Scot and cajoled him from his bed, indicating he was the driving force of the side and that they could not do without him. James responded and there was a gradual turnaround in the club's playing fortunes. It was nothing as distinct as black-and-white or as throwing a switch, but it's clear many years later, as Arsenal player and later journalist Bernard Joy noted, it was a turning point in that team's fortunes. Another significant Highbury signing at that time was Bob Wall, who would become the Arsenal secretary for many, many years and who would be responsible for much of the administration in both the rebuilding and operation of Highbury.

The FA Cup run of 1930 that was to provide the first silverware for Arsenal had begun at Highbury two weeks before that 2–2 draw with Birmingham. Local rivals Chelsea had been dispatched with goals from Lambert and Bastin in front of 55,579 – the biggest Highbury crowd of the season – in the first game Arsenal had played following Chapman's decision to let James rest. Bastin's scoring partner in the first game against Birmingham (now managed by Chapman's predecessor at Highbury, Leslie Knighton) was David Jack. The return at St Andrews was a real grudge match which Arsenal won with an Alf Baker penalty. The rest of Arsenal's road to the final that year kept them away from Highbury, with Middlesbrough and West Ham United disposed of 2–0 and 3–0 respectively.

The semi-final looked easy enough: Hull City were on the verge of relegation to the old Third Division. Typically, Arsenal found themselves 0–2 down inside the half-hour. Howieson lobbed Lewis from near the halfway line (not the first time an Arsenal keeper would be beaten from that distance in an important Cup match!) and Eddie Hapgood sliced the ball into his own net. With 20 minutes to go, the irrepressible David Jack broke the Hull offside trap to pull one back and with 12 minutes remaining Cliff Bastin's wizardry saved the day. The replay was almost a formality, David Jack netting what proved the winner as Hull finished with ten men after Arthur Childs became the first player (and the last for fifty years) to be sent off in an FA Cup semi-final.

So Arsenal were back at Wembley with a chance to erase memories of the defeat three years earlier. Skipper Tom Parker ensured that Charlie Preedy's goalkeeping jersey was not slippery or greasy (Lewis was out injured) and Chapman could hardly believe he was facing his former club, Huddersfield Town, in the final. Nine of the eleven Arsenal players in that final (no subs in those days) had been signed by Chapman. James and Lambert were the scorers – James netting a goal worked out on the coach trip to Wembley and Lambert scoring a superb solo effort. The monkey was off the back and the Arsenal fans at Highbury were about to join their team on a roller-coaster ride they wouldn't witness again for another six decades.

THE BIG ONE

The confidence that was taken from that 1930 Cup run cannot be underestimated, in particular from the turnaround in the semi-final at Elland Road. The club's League form lifted immediately and they experienced only one defeat between the Cup semi-final and final. In the lead-up to that clash with Huddersfield, Highbury saw a couple of great performances with everyone on-song and looking to cement their place in the Wembley starting line-up. First Blackburn were disposed of 4–0 and then Sheffield United were put to the slaughter with an 8–1 defeat: a shame that only 24,217 were present at Highbury to see what was the club's and First Division's biggest win to date. Lambert led the scoring with a hat-trick. Then a couple of weeks later the team's fighting spirit was exemplified at Leicester, when, having trailed 1–3, they fought back to 6–6 with David Halliday – a Scot from Dumfries – netting four! Halliday only made fifteen appearances for Arsenal and scored half his goals total in that one game!

* * *

It all boded well for the season ahead. Chapman's forward line, assembled at a cost of £34,000, was starting to look ready to be set loose and in the 1930–31 season it purred into overdrive with a championship- winning 127 goals – a record that still stands today. Amazingly, Aston Villa, who finished runners-up that season, went a goal better, scoring 128 goals that same season. Arsenal managed to score five goals against them in both League encounters. The two protagonists also met in the FA Cup third round with Chapman's side winning the replay 3–1 at Villa Park following a 2–2 draw at Highbury. Chelsea ended the club's defence of the Cup, though, at Stamford Bridge in the next round.

The road to so many goals that season was probably greatly aided by a change in the offside law which reduced the number of defending players required from three to two. Nevertheless, it was still a monumental count, 67 of which were scored at Highbury. Not surprisingly Arsenal only failed to score once all season, against Huddesfield late in the campaign, the opposition gaining some reward for the previous season's Cup final defeat in a goal-less encounter at Highbury. The two teams had drawn 1–1 at Leeds Road in November.

The 1930–31 season had got under way with five straight wins: two 4–1s to start and then 3–1 and 3–2 victories over Leeds and Blackburn at Highbury. Blackburn were the first team to take a point off the marauding Gunners in Lancashire, whilst Derby inflicted the first of four defeats the team would suffer that season. The visit of Aston Villa to Highbury in early November was eagerly anticipated and the resulting 5–2 win for the home side left everyone buoyant, with Bastin and Jack scoring twice and Lambert getting the other.

Big wins were becoming the way of things, especially at Highbury. Blackpool were dispatched 7–1 – Jack and Welshman Jimmy Brain with a hat-trick each – and Grimsby hit for nine – Jack matching Halliday's achievement the previous season by scoring four. That 9–1 defeat of Grimsby remains the best League victory by Arsenal at Highbury. Leicester were beaten 7–2 away and Bastin helped himself to three of six when Derby were the visitors. When Arsenal travelled to Villa Park for their return League encounter in March, the title was still far from decided so it was a game Villa had to win – they duly did, imposing

Arsenal's biggest defeat of the season by winning 5–1. The defeat was dealt with in the best possible way as the team went through the last nine matches undefeated, including seven wins along the way, rounding the celebrations off at Highbury with the 5–0 thumping of Bolton.

Arsenal were Champions! Chapman had used 23 players during the course of the season but only Cliff Bastin had been an ever-present, playing in all 42 League games and the three Cup ties. He also weighed in with 28 League goals; David Jack hit 31 and Jack Lambert set a club record with 38, a record that would stand for a few years until Ted Drake made his mark.

DOUBLE DAZED

The following 1931–32 season offered so much but ended with double disappointment as the team finished two points behind Everton in the runners-up position in the League and fell to Newcastle United in the FA Cup final. Crazily, the ten defeats Arsenal suffered in that campaign were the fewest by any side – Everton suffering an incredible dozen, with Arsenal completing the double over them for two of those! The record at Highbury, though, was encouraging and identical to the previous year in terms of wins, losses and draws. But there were fewer goals all round – 52:16 compared to 67:27 in 1930–31. The difference between the teams was that Everton won twenty-six of their games whereas Arsenal won twenty-two, and the Gunners drew ten compared to the Liverpudlians' four.

West Bromwich Albion inflicted the first of their two wins over Arsenal on the opening day of the season: 52,478 had packed into Highbury to see the champions take the field and parade the silverware, but the visitors won and the supporters had to wait until the third home match, Arsenal's fifth of the season, to record the first win: 2–0 over Sunderland. As the end of the year approached, the Gunners had suffered four defeats. Although the season saw 90 goals fired home, only on a few occasions did the team look like the free-scoring side from the previous year.

In the run-up to Christmas Liverpool had been thumped 6–0, but less than 30,000 were there to witness Lambert's hat-trick. Then the title defence suffered a mortal blow over the space of two days: Arsenal found themselves starting a double-header against Sheffield United on Christmas Day with the return at Highbury the very next day. A 1–4 defeat at Bramell Lane was followed by a 0–2 defeat on Boxing Day in front of a bumper 55,207 crowd. The Easter holiday period was only marginally more rewarding, comprising three 1–1 draws at West Ham, Derby and at home to Chelsea. In the final run-in and with the title already lost, the home crowd displayed their apathy again with just 30,000 and then 23,000 turning up to see 5–0 and 4–0 wins over Middlesbrough and Blackburn Rovers respectively.

Of course, by this stage the club had suffered an FA Cup final loss to Newcastle United as well. The Cup run had come through Highbury in the first couple of rounds, non-League Darwen being thrashed 11–1 and Plymouth 4–2. Then it went via Portsmouth and Huddersfield before Manchester City were defeated by a last gasp Cliff Bastin goal at Villa Park, the semi-final venue. Arsenal's third Cup final saw them become the first team to lose a Wembley final after scoring the first goal. But the loss of Alex James to injury (ironically, trying to prove to photographers he was fit) in the run-up to the final robbed Arsenal of the fluency to their style of play and they never recovered when the Geordies came back from Bob John's 13th-minute goal.

The Cup final saw a number of new faces making their way into the team, namely George Male, who had made three appearances in the championship year and would replace captain Tom Parker come the next season, and Frank Moss, who made it three keepers in three finals and was to become a fixture between the posts over the next few years.

ON THE REBOUND

To say that the Arsenal team bounced back from the double disappointment of the 1931–32 season would be an understatement of gigantic proportions. The hat-trick of championship wins that was to follow was achieved with a team that was continually evolving – indeed, by the third successive title only Bastin, Hapgood and Roberts were present from that first title season. Manager Chapman had also gone and was replaced by George Allison. Talk of a potential Double was a preamble to most seasons, Arsenal getting as far as the sixth round of the FA Cup in their second and third successive championship seasons; however, it will be the Cup run of 1932–33 that will be forever remembered. The run lasted a single round and ended at Fellows Park, Walsall, in what has gone down in the history of the English game as the greatest giant-killing feat of all time.

By the time of that FA Cup third-round tie Arsenal were installed at the top of the League table and, as in the 1930 triumph, it was Aston Villa who were the main challenger. The Highbury squad had been strengthened by the arrival of players or, in many cases, talent coming through the system. Eddie Colman was signed from Grimsby in 1928 and was often used as an alternative to Lambert in the first two of the triple championship teams. Ray Bowden was signed from Plymouth in March 1934 and would play a bigger role. Brothers Leslie and Denis Compton also started to make appearances.

The 1932–33 season started with a 1–0 win at Birmingham then immediately faltered with a 1–2 defeat by West Bromwich Albion at Highbury. Sunderland were the visitors to north London three days later and returned with their tails between their legs from a 6–1 drubbing, Joe Hulme scoring a hat-trick. This clearly inspired confidence in the team, who went on a run of eleven games undefeated, dropping just four points from a possible thirty-six. The highlight of this run was the amazing 8–2 thrashing of Leicester City at Highbury – Hulme again weighing in with a triple. But that would not be the biggest result of the year at Highbury.

The winning streak came to an end at Aston Villa where Arsenal scored three but Villa managed five to inflict only the second defeat of the season on the team. Five wins on the trot followed for Chapman's team, showing that there were no hangovers; the Highbury fans were treated to a magnificent feast of football on Christmas Eve 1932 as the free-scoring Gunners demolished Sheffield United by 9–2 with the excellent Lambert scoring five goals. It was an amazing feat for the player who had struggled to maintain his place in the team all year – but his 12 League appearances for the season brought 14 goals. Having hit that high, the team entertained Leeds for a Boxing Day encounter but lost 1–2, then drew at Elland Road in the return the very next day. Arsenal's form over the next eight games was patchy with just three wins and despite another impressive mauling – this time of Blackburn Rovers 8–0 – their indifferent form continued, with three defeats and a draw from the next four games.

The title race came to a head on April Fool's Day when Aston Villa were the visitors to Highbury. Once again the capacity crowd were treated to a spectacle, Lambert scoring two of Arsenal's five unanswered goals. This was followed by four more straight wins to secure the title with a couple of games to spare. Aston Villa again had to be content with the runners-up spot – how curious that the four League meetings between them in the two championship seasons had seen the home teams scoring five goals in each of the encounters!

For the third successive season Cliff Bastin was an ever-present (the only ever-present each season) and he returned a remarkable 33 goals – still a record for a player in the traditional winger's spot. Tim Coleman hit 24 from 27 games, which was another great performance, as a replacement for Lambert, who was now not without his scoring contribution. Hulme and Jack hit 20 and 18 goals respectively.

* * *

The 1933–34 season was a more closely contested affair with Derby County and Huddersfield Town being the main challengers to Arsenal's title, although Tottenham made a late surge into third place. Both headed the table for brief periods but it was Arsenal's early season form that provided the backbone to retaining the title, despite long-term injuries to Alex James and Joe Hulme. Indeed, Hulme would only contribute in eight League games that season.

Maybe not surprisingly, the goals did not come as freely – only 75 compared to the 100-plus that each of the other titles would bring: a 6–0 late September win over Middlesbrough at Highbury was the scoring highlight of the season. Arsenal were more secure at Highbury, halving the number of home defeats of the previous season to just two. The first of these did not come until the last day of January and was unfortunately inflicted by Tottenham. This was then followed by the second against Everton in the very next game. Indeed, the whole of January was a sombre place at Highbury following the unexpected death of Herbert Chapman on 6 January. Arsenal drew 1–1 at home to Sheffield Wednesday that very day, a game played in an eerie silence and one which, according to Bastin, 'lasted 90 years'. Chapman's death hit everyone, including the team, which, as the month progressed, suffered defeats at the hands of Manchester City, Spurs and Everton. At that point Joe Shaw, the trainer under Chapman, technically became the team manager with Tom Whittaker taking over his role until the end of the season, although many books incorrectly record it as being George Allison who became manager.

A League win at Middlesbrough in mid-February put Arsenal back on the winning road and talk of a Double was again doing the rounds. Buoyed by three home FA Cup ties, the club moved to the final eight before falling to Aston Villa. Villa's two goals were the only ones conceded by Moss in the competition. In the League the Easter period was to prove decisive, as it so often does, as Arsenal played teams at the top. Derby County were first up, visiting Highbury where 69,070 saw Alex James score the only goal of the game, and after a 1–1 draw at Stoke the team went to Derby and completed a very useful double by winning 4–2. Huddersfield Town were next up at Arsenal and following that 3–1 win, the title was a handful of points away from staying in north London. Apart from a defeat at Portsmouth, the season finished unblemished.

THE CHAMPIONSHIP TREBLE

Full-back Male was the only ever-present that season, and his full-back partnership with Eddie Hapgood (who only missed two games) was a feature of the side that year. Bastin was equal top scorer with Bowden with 13 apiece. And there was a new name on the scoring list that season: Ted Drake, who hit seven goals from his ten games. Drake had been signed by

Chapman's replacement, George Allison, from Southampton where he had been top scorer for them in the Second Division for two years with twenty goals a season. His potential was much talked about but few can have imagined the impact he would have at Highbury. In an amazing first season he scored 42 goals in 41 League games – a record that remains intact to this very day as Arsenal regained their scoring touch.

Drake loved playing at Highbury and 27 of his goals that season were scored there. If the home crowd had thought they liked what they had seen at the tail end of the previous season, then they were more than certain after the first two home games of 1934–35. The season had started with a 3–3 draw at Portsmouth – Drake, Bowden and Bastin the scorers. Then a few days later 54,062 packed into Highbury for the visit of Liverpool, who were demolished 8–1, with Drake and Bowden each completing hat-tricks. Blackburn Rovers were then dismissed 4–0 and Drake hit two more. Drake scored eight goals in the first five games and went on to score four goals in a single game four times during the course of the season – there were also three 'simple' hat-tricks in there as well!

Arsenal built their challenge at Highbury: only one win came away from home prior to the New Year – 5–2 at Chelsea. They scored 75 of their 115 goals at Highbury that season, which has never been beaten. Only the first championship side in 1930–31 came close with 70 goals. The 8–1 win over Liverpool was the first of three eight-goal barrages the team would produce at Highbury – Leicester City and Middlesbrough both being emphatically seen off without reply: Drake scored seven of those sixteen goals. Equally satisfying was the 6–0 win at Tottenham in a season of continuous highlights. Sunderland were the only significant challengers in the League, taking away three of the four points on offer. They were one of only four teams to stop Arsenal scoring and their visit to Highbury on 9 March produced the highest ever attendance at Highbury.

The only disappointment was again the FA Cup: a potential Double went missing. Arsenal again made it through to the sixth round, being drawn away in all four ties and eventually losing 2–1 to Sheffield Wednesday – one of the teams who had managed to keep Arsenal goal-less in a League game.

The championship was all but secured at Highbury with a 1–0 win over Huddersfield, two days after the 8–0 humiliation of Middlesbrough, but the final game of the season ended with the visitors Derby scoring the only goal of the game. So, Arsenal recorded their fourth championship in five seasons and whilst Drake was getting the headlines, Cliff Bastin again produced another superb season by adding 20 more goals to his amazing tally.

LUCKY ARSENAL

The tag 'Lucky Arsenal' became associated with the team during these heady days. The art of game strategy in that period was very different to what it is nowadays. Back then championships were won by 'winning the home games and drawing the away games'. Today the philosophy is about winning as many games as possible – home and away – and trying not to lose any. Of course, the introduction of three points for a win, as opposed to two in the '30s, has had some effect, but the revolution has also been down to a very big change in attitude.

For this reason teams often played a very different style at home. Attack was the key and it is no coincidence that during the halcyon period the large majority of Arsenal's goals came at Highbury. In the first four championship seasons 256 of the 435 goals were scored at home – 60 per cent. Thus, in an effort to win games, Arsenal went all out for attack and this often produced a number of notable wins – two lots of nine goals and a handful of eight, whilst five- and four-goal tallies were common, as we have seen.

In away games the onus was on the home team to attack and for Arsenal to seek a point. Thus, games were invariably tight and either drawn or sneaked by the odd goal. As such Arsenal would present themselves to the home support as an attack-minded free-scoring machine, whereas the fans at other stadiums would see a much tighter team who were often 'lucky' to sneak a draw or win. This was typified in the first half of the 1934–35 season when the home crowd saw fifty-three goals before the end of the year, whereas Arsenal only scored seventeen away from home and five of those came at Chelsea!

Arsenal's popularity was clear in the gate receipt books at Highbury that season when they became the first club ever to take in over £100,000 in a single season.

THIRD TIME AGAIN

Arsenal went into the 1935–36 season looking to retain their crown for a fourth year in succession but, in truth, fell well short of the task. There was success in the FA Cup, so there was still something to polish come the end of the season. In the League, though, the most memorable point was Arsenal's 7–1 win at Villa Park – or more accurately for the fact that Ted Drake scored all seven goals, which is still a record for a League game today. The only down side was that the feat could not become part of Highbury folklore directly. Villa, one of Arsenal's main rivals during the first half of the '30s, were relegated that year. Drake suffered with injuries during the season but still managed to net 24 goals from his 26 League games, the Villa tally clearly helping his averages. On his day with destiny, he had his knee heavily strapped and both James and Hulme were consigned to the list of injured.

Drake would score eight against Villa that season – he also grabbed the only goal in their 1–0 defeat at Highbury. The game was significant first because it was the final nail in Villa's relegation coffin, and second because Drake had to come through the game after another bout of injury if he was to make the starting line-up in the Cup final at Wembley. Unlike Villa he survived and went on to score the goal that won the FA Cup against Second Division Sheffield United a week later. Although Drake had come through the Villa game, he played that final in pain and, after scoring, had to be helped to his feet because his knee hurt so much.

The 1936–37 season was to be only the second full season of the decade that Arsenal finished without a trophy. It was a season that showed up a team of ageing players, and towards the end of the year they were as low as 17th. But against the odds the side put on a run which included thirteen wins and six draws to go top in the middle of March. All of a sudden the championship was a distinct possibility when relegation had seemed more probable. Despite this run of form only an even better run of results by Manchester City saw them and then Charlton Athletic pull ahead. Manchester City's 2–0 win over Arsenal at Maine Road ended any lingering hopes. At Highbury that year Arsenal lost just one game – 1–3 to Manchester City – but ten draws took their points toll. So while the number of home defeats was the smallest tally ever during the whole of the '30s, the total of ten wins was only one better than the nine recorded the previous season. The Cup campaign went as far as the sixth round again, with West Bromwich Albion proving to be the insurmountable barrier this time. On the way, though, there had been notable victories over Manchester United (5–0) and Burnley (7–1).

The season ended with Alex James announcing his retirement – his significance to the team could not be over-stressed as one of the club's greatest ever captains. Before his arrival, Arsenal had won nothing; during his stay, they achieved the heights that had been dreamed in a stadium of dreams. James was unique, as was the team he captained. James, as simply the player, was never fully replaced either: many tried, but none could fill his skilful boots. James was always his own man and occasionally clashed with the club, notably in 1933 when he refused to travel to Belfast to play in a friendly game against Cliftonville and was promptly dropped by Chapman for what was effectively the championship celebration game. Charlie Jones, the vice-captain, received the Championship trophy from the League president, John McKenna, that year, although James would have the honour of doing likewise in 1934. Bob John retired along with James, and Herbie Roberts never really returned from injury.

With so many major influences gone (not to mention a long-term injury to Joe Hulme as well), the arrival of a fifth championship in eight years in 1938 was somewhat of a surprise to all those outside Highbury who again suggested the club was in decline. This title, though, would be the most closely fought – going to the very last day as Wolverhampton Wanderers finished just a single point behind Arsenal. The team's tally of 52 points matched the previous season when they had finished third, whilst the total of 77 goals scored was the second lowest in the decade for the team finishing top. Drake was again the main contributor, but only with seventeen goals this time, two more than Bastin, who played in all but four of the League games.

This season Highbury was the firm basis of the championship fight: 65 per cent of the points came from games at home and 52 of the 77 goals as well. The season got under way with three wins, including a 5–0 thrashing of Wolves, who had yet to announce their championship credentials. Arsenal only managed to score five goals on two other occasions that season: both at home as well, and results were much more closely fought. The use of 29 players implies that manager Allison was never quite sure of his best team as he sought the right mix. Bernard Joy was brought in for Roberts, whilst George Hunt was added, with limited results, to help Drake. In fact, only Bastin and Male survived from the guts of the treble-title team.

By the fourth round of the FA Cup the title seemed to be a straight fight between Wolves and Arsenal, although at that stage Brentford topped the table. The two clubs were drawn together and there was an added bonus in that the two met in the League the week beforehand. Both games were to be at the Molyneux. Wolves won the first League encounter 3–1, but Arsenal gained revenge in the Cup 2–1. Arsenal were then drawn against Preston North End and proceeded to lose 0–1 at home in front of 72,121 – Preston would end the season third in the table.

Arsenal made their surge to the top of the table at the start of February by winning seven of their next eleven games and losing only one. Then Brentford came to Highbury and won 2–0 and followed this up with a 3–0 win at Griffin Park. A goal-less encounter with Birmingham City sandwiched in between allowed Wolves back to the front. A 3–1 win at Preston and a 1–0 win at home to Liverpool set up a final-day decider. Wolves went to Sunderland and if they won, would be champions. Arsenal were at home to Bolton and had to win . . . and hope.

The game at Sunderland kicked off earlier and, despite being a man down, the Roker Roar prevailed as Sunderland became unlikely 1–0 winners. At Highbury Arsenal were already leading 4–0. The crowd were able to celebrate during the final ten minutes or so of the game as news from the Northeast came in.

The stats from the final season of the decade have Arsenal in fourth place and show that Chelsea sent them packing from the FA Cup in the third round. The team was certainly a shadow of the one that had graced Highbury in previous years: with the war about to set in, this was, in reality, the final full competitive season for many of the Arsenal greats – Cliff Bastin and Ted Drake to name but two. The '30s were fast approaching their end.

Highbury had witnessed a dynasty, a team without compare.

FIVE

Managing Influence

There have been 18 managers of the club since its inception in 1897, 14 of whom have held the reins at Highbury. The roles several of these men played in shaping the stadium should not be ignored as they all ultimately strove for the best facilities to help attract the best players. Ironically, it was this ambition that would ultimately prove to be the key to the club calling it a day on Highbury and the wheels being set in motion for the move up the road.

The two managers who played their own very individual roles to achieve these ambitions were Herbert Chapman and Arsène Wenger – the two greatest managers the club has seen, and will probably ever see. Despite being from different generations and vastly different backgrounds – not to mention countries – they were and are regarded as consummate professionals in all their endeavours in and around the Marble Halls. Both ooze charisma and both have been called visionary for their very clear ideas on how football should be played and how a football club should be run. A strong argument could be formed that they have both changed the face of English football in many of the innovations they have brought with them.

Chapman required that his footballers had the finest possible facilities, despite an economic recession at the time. As Arsenal players, they had to behave like Arsenal players at all times. To achieve this, he argued, the players required the finest possible stadium and so, with the support of Sir Henry Norris, Chapman was instrumental in changing the routine Archibald Leitch-designed facility into a futuristic art deco venue which became the envy of the football world. He also literally helped put Arsenal on the map by being instrumental in getting the London Underground to change the name of the adjacent Tube station from Gillespie Road to simply Arsenal.

The aspirations of Wenger were no different, but he lived in a different world to the recession-hit times of Chapman. The finest players now require the finest wages: the Highbury of the new millennium could not deliver the level of revenue required to allow the club to attract and maintain the employment of the world's best stars. The fact that Arsenal have been able to field world-class players and achieve so much in their final years at Highbury is solely down to Wenger's eye for potential and his uncanny knack in the transfer market. The success drove the need for a new stadium – demand for tickets could never hope to be met and the income from the 53 executive boxes at the Clock End was constrained because pre- and post-match facilities were limited by space. Despite leading on the field, the club has been trailing quite significantly off it in the generation of revenue streams. Whilst Wenger has been able to turn his vision to areas outside of Highbury, such as the creation of some of the best training facilities in the world, the potential to reinvent Highbury in its small footprint soon became impractical to meet the club's needs and so the search for a new home began.

But this is touching on the surface, and the story of the Highbury managers starts many years before Herbert Chapman became associated with Arsenal: with the man responsible for taking the team to the other side of London, a man who can lay claim to being the only person to have managed Arsenal on both sides of the river.

STABILISING MOVE: GEORGE MORRELL (1908–15)

When George Morrell was appointed secretary-manager of Woolwich Arsenal in 1908, he knew exactly what he was letting himself in for. The fifth appointment in the position since the club were formed, he arrived at a time when the club was in a perilous financial state and a relocation from Plumstead to Islington was certainly not even on the horizon. Morrell brought with him the experience of being a great administrator and a record of installing compliance and creating fortune. He was assigned by the Arsenal board of the time to repeat the process he had achieved just three years before with Greenock Morton: not just making the debt-ridden club solvent but assuring its election to the Scottish First Division. His exploits in curing Rangers' financial ailments prior to this were also well documented in football circles. Thus, Morrell arrived at the Manor Ground with familiar problems to solve and he started by selling off some of the club's stars to give an initial boost to the balance sheet; however, the need to build a successful club on the playing field to generate interest to secure support from a new environment was paramount.

George Morrell's Woolwich Arsenal team were going steadily downhill and attendances were dropping. By the start of 1910 Morrell, despite his best attempts, had no option other than to place the club in liquidation. Initially, the club was sold to a local businessman, George Leavey, and from there a new club was formed and shares issued. The majority of these were acquired, as we know, by Henry Norris, who was to play a major role with Morrell in moving the club forward.

Looking west down the river, the new Arsenal board started to eye the massive stadium built by Chelsea; during the season prior to Morrell's arrival over 65,000 had packed into Stamford Bridge to see the two teams play. The need for a bigger stadium that was easier to reach was more than apparent to the Scotsman. The arrival of Henry Norris on the scene was fortuitous, and the combination of the two – Morrell's administrative skills and Norris's networking and badgering abilities – ultimately led to the purchase of the land that would become the Arsenal Stadium site.

The much-needed success on the field failed to materialise as the club continued to lose players, culminating in relegation at the end of the 1912–13 season after successive seasons of finishing 18th, 10th, 10th again and finally a rock-bottom 20th. With no Cup runs in sight either, Woolwich Arsenal was about to pack up and move to a new location, not as a First Division club, but as one just relegated to the Second Division! The last season at Plumstead had been one of the worst in the club's history; in fact, one of the worst seasons by any club in the League's history: only three wins all season (one at home) and twenty-three defeats in thirty-eight matches. The south London Woolwich Arsenal was dead. Decline on the pitch was not a surprise because the team that had reached the semi-finals of the FA Cup just a year or so before Morrell's arrival had lost many of its key players as the manager had tried to balance the books.

Despite the sparse facilities for spectators and players, with a new location, great accessibility and a burgeoning new stadium, things looked to be on the move and Morrell almost managed to steer the club to promotion in their first season at Highbury. The club won its first home game, beating Leicester Fosse 2–1, and went on to finish the season in third place behind Bradford Park Avenue on goal difference. The locals of Islington flocked to the stadium with an average crowd of 22,974, two and a half times what the club had experienced the year before. But with the outbreak of the First World War, the initial enthusiasm for the 'new' club in north London was not maintained and crowds slipped to under 13,000. With the League programme halted at the end of the 1914–15 season, things were once again precarious. The future of Arsenal was uncertain, although there were far more important concerns for everyone to worry about than football. By the last game before the war, the club's *Matchday Programme* outlined the reasons for Morrell's departure as the team set about a 7–0 demolishing of Nottingham Forest.

George Morrell, for all his efforts in keeping Woolwich Arsenal alive and providing at least a (barely) solvent club to move to Highbury, will probably always be remembered as the only Arsenal manager to suffer the indignity of relegation. If history is to have a caveat, it should be that he was also the administrator who kept Woolwich Arsenal ticking over thereby allowing the move to Highbury and to where the club is today.

MANIPULATING FACTORS: LESLIE KNIGHTON (1919–25)

Although Arsenal had finished fifth in the 1914–15 season, Leslie Knighton was installed as the manager of a First Division club when organised League action recommenced in 1919. At this stage chairman Sir Henry Norris's investment in the club was looking distinctly fragile, with two years of lower division football followed by four years during the war. Success was paramount to attract the crowds with their gate money. As argued elsewhere herein, his manipulation of the Football League in promoting Arsenal ahead of those in front of them was arguably the single most important factor in the history of the club.

Knighton was charged with delivering that success, having been painted a rosy picture of Arsenal's future in the game, although he had no illusions about Arsenal's financial position. He was made perfectly aware that there was no money available for players to be signed. Indeed Norris's dominance and bullying often left Knighton suffering a confidence crisis. Amongst some of the demands imposed on him by Norris was the fact he was unable to sign players under 5 ft 8 in. in height! As well as trying to look for local players where he could save money further, Knighton (like his chairman, an extremely persuasive operator) raided South Wales to bring Alf Baker, Bob John and Jimmy Brain to Highbury. He completely reorganised the side around pre-war faithfuls Joe Shaw, Jock Rutherford, Vic Groves and Billy Blyth with the signings of Tom Whittaker, Joe Toner, John Milne, Andy Kennedy, Alex Mackie and Bob Turnball.

The potential of the club to exist and prosper at Highbury was abundantly clear as crowds of up to 45,000 appeared on the terraces, but it was still not matched with success on the field. Attendances levelled off at an average of 30,000 over the course of his tenure. The best position Knighton achieved during his six-year spell was sixth in 1919. It was also the only year in that period that Arsenal recorded more wins than defeats in a season.

With the club desperately trying to improve the Highbury facilities and cash becoming ever tighter, relegation for the club at that point would have been a death warrant. In 1925 it was avoided by just a single League position and, although the points buffer was a relatively comfortable margin of seven points over Preston North End, the impact of the struggle had been reflected through the turnstiles when the attendance occasionally dropped close to 20,000 and was sometimes even half that.

Knighton's exit was inevitable and duly came before the end of the season. Knighton himself was livid, not least because he alleged he had been promised a benefit match by Sir Henry Norris the next season, where he would get to keep the receipts from the home game with Tottenham Hotspur – around £4,000 at that time (it turned out to be the first game of the new season). Norris, of course, denied that any such agreement existed and simply pointed at the wretched record of the club under his erstwhile manager, especially in that final season.

Leslie Knighton's career as a team manager was far from finished when he left Highbury: first he moved to Bournemouth (1925–28); then to Birmingham (1928–33), which he managed to the FA Cup final of 1931; then Chelsea (1933–39). After the war his health declined, but he became secretary of a golf club in Bournemouth. He died in May 1959 following a major operation, aged 75.

As I have suggested, history seems to indicate that in the final games of Knighton's reign Norris had already sought out the services of Herbert Chapman. The 11 May edition of the *Athletic News* in 1925, however, carried the following advertisement:

> Arsenal Football Club is open to receive applications for the post of TEAM MANAGER. He must be experienced and possess the highest qualifications for the post, both as to ability and personal character. Gentlemen whose sole ability to build up a good side depends on the payment of heavy and exorbitant transfer fees need not apply.

The author of the advert (Norris) had clearly set out his stall in regard to his requirements. For the first time the club was not advertising to fill the traditional secretary-manager position: Norris was looking for someone who could deliver success on the field, through the financial benefits of which he would build up the club and stadium. How ironic that he would employ the man who would have arguably the greatest influence both on driving the team to the championship and providing the innovation, both on and off the field, that would completely change the face of English football!

THE DYNASTY: HERBERT CHAPMAN (1925–34)

Herbert Chapman was a remarkable man with an unremarkable background. Born the son of a miner on 19 January 1878 in a small mining village in Yorkshire, he demonstrated sufficient intelligence to warrant being sent to a technical college to study engineering. This was his primary aim in life; he came into football management almost by accident. He had only modest talent as a player, although his brother, Harry, became an outstanding inside-forward with Sheffield Wednesday. Herbert's playing career, mostly spent as an amateur, eventually culminated at Tottenham Hotspur, his tenth club.

Whilst at White Hart Lane, a colleague was offered the managership of Northampton Town but suggested to Chapman that he seemed to be better qualified for the post. Chapman duly applied and took up the appointment in 1907; the Cobblers were at this time in bottom place of the Southern League. He continued to hold down a job as an engineer, as he had done throughout his nomadic playing career, yet made his new club Southern League champions in 1908–09. By 1912 he had returned to his native Yorkshire as manager of Leeds City, who were in the Second Division of the Football League. Throughout the First World War he held down a responsible job in industry, managing a munitions factory, but decided to return to football at the end of hostilities in 1919.

The Leeds club had been dissolved on orders of the FA, following allegations of illegal payments to players. Chapman himself emerged unscathed and was offered the assistant manager's chair at nearby Huddersfield Town, just at a time when that club, being in a rugby league stronghold, was facing extinction. Within a month Chapman had taken over as manager and Huddersfield never looked back, winning promotion and a Cup final place. In 1924 he took the club to the first of its three consecutive League Championship titles. Chapman had displayed considerable influence in persuading star players to join his new club; on top of this, his organisational and motivational skills turned Huddersfield into the finest English team of the 1920s.

Such success had clearly made Chapman a prominent figure in the football community and he was what Norris sought for his vision of Arsenal FC, and of Highbury. Even before Knighton was sacked, it is likely that Chapman had already been 'tapped up', to use the latter-day vernacular, and the advert in the *Athletic News* was really just keeping up appearances.

Norris had got the man he wanted in terms of footballing success credentials, but Chapman was certainly not a man he could manipulate and bully in the same way he had Knighton. Chapman was very much his own man and full of confidence in his ability to do things his way. It was such positive thinking that allowed Chapman to see potential at Arsenal.

Chapman was clear about his goals: to build a team to bring success for years to come; to build a stadium fit for such a team; and to implement many of the innovative ideas that swirled in his head about and around football. It would be a triple success story! No one in football had ever had such a single-minded vision of raising people's perception of a football club and how it should be run. His ideas were way ahead of his time, but all would be introduced eventually.

He set about his first task with vigour: despite the context of that *Athletic News* advertisement and Norris's reaffirmation that there were no funds available to facilitate the transfer of players, he was still able to persuade the hitherto immovable Norris that if he wanted to own the best club in the world, he would need the best players available. This would be Chapman's philosophy throughout his reign at Highbury – everything had to be the best. With a few good players and Chapman's reputation, the rest would follow.

Charlie Buchan was Chapman's first signing and having been born in Plumstead he had grown up watching Woolwich Arsenal before moving north to Sunderland, where he had won championship honours. Ironically, Knighton had tried to lure Buchan south before he left. Chapman was obviously much more persuasive, whilst Norris sorted out a transfer fee which was based largely on performance. This single signing was hugely significant for it paved the way for other names of the period to transfer to Highbury — even at 34 and in the twilight of his career, Buchan was a magnet. How ironic that his transfer was one of several cogs in a wheel that would lead to the end of Norris's tenure as chairman.

There was also another significant change at the time which facilitated Arsenal, the players and a formation Chapman was looking to exploit: the offside law was changed. This made it necessary for only two opposition players to be nearer the goal line when a ball was played forward, rather than three. Chapman used the new law to perfection and his Arsenal championship sides scored double the tally that Chapman's Huddersfield championship sides had.

The new manager's pitch-side start, though, wasn't the best. The 1–0 home defeat by his former employer, Tottenham, wasn't taken well and a few games later the team suffered a 7–0 thrashing at Newcastle. Buchan was so incensed by the formation the team was playing that he refused to board the train back south until Chapman agreed to discuss it with the team. By the time they arrived back at St Pancras they had taken on board Buchan's idea of a free-roving anchor player to police the edge of the area. It was trialled in the next game and a 4–0 win over West Ham proved its worth, and it evolved gradually to become known as the WM formation that was to prove the cornerstone of the great Arsenal team about to be set loose.

The first season was a foundation but still a hugely significant one for the club, as they finished in their highest ever Football League position — runners-up to the Chapman-less Huddersfield Town, who were securing their third successive championship title. New players had continued to arrive, including Joe Hulme and Bob John to name but two. The fans had responded in the right way as well, averaging almost 35,000 per game. However, it was a false dawn. For the next four years the team got bogged down in mid-table mediocrity with the one highlight being their first Cup final in 1927, although they were defeated by Cardiff City.

By the start of that first Cup final season Chapman was having an immediate impact on stadium matters as well. The club had started to install a scoreboard that would stay in one guise or another until the '70s. Matches were allocated a number in the *Matchday Programme* which reflected a position on the scoreboard alongside which both half-time and full-time results could be placed. This scoreboard was located at the College End and can clearly be seen in many of the Movietone newsreels of the time, which often featured Arsenal.

As the FA Cup run got into swing, and in between a replayed fourth-round tie with Port Vale, Highbury hosted another first: on 22 January 1927 the BBC rolled their radio broadcast unit into Highbury for the League encounter with Sheffield United. Army Captain Teddy Wakelam called the game, which saw Charlie Buchan score for Arsenal and Billy Gillespie net the Blades' goal in the 1–1 draw. Although there is no direct attribution of Chapman's influence on ensuring Arsenal and Highbury were the centre of this attraction, there can be little doubt that both he and Norris had done their fair share of networking and lobbying behind the scenes. The debate that radio broadcasts would affect attendances at matches in both the short and long term was already well under way – less than 16,831 attended the game, although it was an especially miserable January afternoon.

On the matter of attendance, Chapman said at the time: 'The BBC are doing a service to countless thousands of football enthusiasts who cannot attend the big matches through illness or other causes. This extension of the activities of the BBC will be heartily welcomed by the sporting community at large and will be an important factor in adding still further to the popularity of our great national game.' Interestingly, at the time there was also comment about the lack of sound and community singing in the stadium – this was attributed to the 'decreased attendance'! No cries of 'Library Highbury' in those days though!

During this time Chapman continued to believe in what he was working towards, but in February 1929 the club was rocked when Norris received his ban from football for alleged financial irregularities. Norris said payments he supposedly transferred to Buchan had been made at the request of Chapman. The manager denied this fact and so Norris called him a liar; there was some innuendo regarding the fact that Chapman had been the manager of Leeds City when they had been suspended from the League in 1919 after being found guilty of a similar charge. As it was, Chapman prevailed and Norris's days in football were over. Years after he had retired from the game, Charlie Buchan denied that he had ever received illegal payments.

The offshoot of this was that Chapman had a new boss and the Hill-Wood family began their association with the club. Samuel was installed as the first in a long line of Hill-Wood chairmen that survive to this day, and who would oversee the growth of Highbury and the eventual move to Ashburton Grove. More significantly, the new chairman was more than happy to leave the running of the club to the manager.

The year after Norris had been banned from the game, Arsenal recorded their first success by winning the championship. In the interim Chapman had continued to recruit top names to fill his stadium: David Jack and Alex James were two of many to fall to his persuasive tongue. Off the field Chapman also recruited Bob Wall, who was to become a founding stone in the club's administration offices, taking on the role that had been dropped from that *Athletic News* advert several years before – secretary. By this stage Buchan had retired (his last game a 3–3 draw at Everton in May 1928) and so would not be part of the Team of the '30s.

The FA Cup final in 1930 was the catalyst for the success. Arsenal's 2–0 win was as pivotal to the club's bout of success as was the Fairs Cup final in 1970 and the 1989 League win at Anfield. They were matches that moulded the shape of things to come. Two more FA Cup finals followed in the decade – in 1932 and 1936 – and, more importantly, no less than five League Championships – 1931, 1933, 1934, 1935 and 1938.

When Arsenal visited Hillsborough to play Sheffield Wednesday in August 1928, the players ran out with numbered shirts – the first time this had happened in the Football League – but the FA was less than happy with the move and banned their use for future fixtures. However it did not stop Chapman, who, the following week, had the reserves wearing them at Highbury instead!

By this time Chapman had also had the 'The' from 'The Arsenal' dropped, so that the team were now known more simply as 'Arsenal' (although The Arsenal had never been the club's official name). Chapman had driven the change through to ensure that the club would be listed first in fixtures and the like: he is also credited with coining what was to become the club's nickname – the Gunners.

As we know, Chapman had been given the go-ahead by the Arsenal board to set another of his innovations into motion for the start of the 1930–31 season: the installation of a huge 45-minute clock behind one of the goals. Off the field of play, Chapman's most significant coup literally changed the face of London forever: on 5 November 1932 Arsenal became the official name of the Underground station that had hitherto been called Gillespie Road. The station itself had originally opened in December 1906. On his first trip to Highbury as manager of Leeds City in 1913 he had noted how significant it was from a sales point of view, supporters being able to reach the stadium from the centre of London in a matter of minutes. Indeed it was an observation made in the very first Highbury *Matchday Programme* for the visit of Leicester Fosse. In this it stated that the ground could 'be reached from the city and places adjacent in less time than any other ground' and would be a great attraction for the 'cosmopolitan enthusiast'.

The Underground's operators, the London Electric Railway (LER), argued with Chapman that the cost of changing pre-printed tickets, maps and timetables on stations and trains was prohibitive and would also undoubtedly lead to a barrage of similar requests from other London clubs. But Chapman was at his persuasive best. He argued that the name change would promote the LER as a means to get to the ground and would also reduce queries from passengers regarding what station to travel to for Arsenal. The crowds were also a significant factor since, by then, it was clear that the Arsenal side, who were the reigning champions, looked set for more glory. The LER originally offered the compromise of Highbury Hill (the road directly opposite the exit of the Tube station), but Chapman would not budge his ground and in the end the Arsenal manager prevailed. After the name change, the cover of the club programme – which was at that time pre-printed in bulk for the season – included a complete map of the London Underground on its outside-back page. The inside-front page described how to purchase tickets and carried the slogan: 'The most accessible ground in London'. The inside-back cover had a simple price list detailing the cost of travelling to Arsenal station from other parts of London.

Arsenal Underground station is likely to undergo a revamp when the club moves down the road and the station grows with it, but a trip to the end of the platform in the final days of Highbury will take the explorer to the old Gillespie Road sign still imprinted on the wall.

Just a few days after the renaming of the station, Chapman stood side-by-side with the then Prince of Wales to perform the opening ceremony of the new West Stand, work on which had started a couple of years earlier under the architectural guidance of Claude Ferrier.

Chapman continued to formulate ideas that have since his day become commonplace. In 1933 he added the now distinctive white sleeves to what had been a completely red shirt. Then, legend has it, he visited an old friend in Austria and returned to talk excitedly about a night match he had watched: the pitch had been lit by the headlamps of 40 cars. Not long after, the press were invited to watch an Arsenal practice match at night illuminated by dangling lanterns. Chapman got the publicity he wanted for an idea he was convinced would work. He later watched floodlit matches in Belgium and Holland – and proposed floodlights be installed at Highbury to allow midweek matches to be played in the early evening: at this time, midweek games kicked off at 2.30 p.m. or 3 p.m., and were generally sparsely attended and often ended in the early evening gloom. The impact on club revenue would have been great at that time and no doubt the atmosphere would have been quite unique in those early days. Unfortunately, it was not a development he would see to fruition given its initial rejection. Twenty years later, it became a reality.

But what Chapman had started on and off the field, he sadly did not manage to see through to the ultimate conclusion he would have liked. With Arsenal well on their way to their third successive championship in 1934, and despite suffering with a cold, he took time out in early January against his doctor's advice to watch the third team play in a cutting wind at Guildford. 'I haven't seen the boys for a week or so,' he said. Pneumonia set in and three days later, on 6 January, he was gone.

The club's greatest pre-war manager had died at the age of 55. Just as he had set Huddersfield off on a hat-trick of championships in 1924 and had not been able to see them through, having opted to move to Arsenal, this time his hat-trick was to be seen out by another, George Allison – a Chapman recruit.

Arsenal's secretary at the time said he would often hear Chapman's footsteps echoing down the Highbury halls for many years after his death. Others at the club recited similar incidents and if Chapman's ghost does indeed haunt Highbury, it is very welcome.

The significance of Chapman to everything that is Arsenal today was defined by the bust that was created by Jacob Epstein and placed in the Marble Halls – the main entrance to the club. In truth, though, the real monument to Chapman is Highbury itself.

A LIFE'S WORK: GEORGE ALLISON (1934–47)

George Allison took control at Highbury when things were good on and off the pitch: a third successive championship was looming on the horizon and an average of 41,000 fans were pouring through the Highbury gates. The funds were flowing in and the club recorded an annual profit despite the cost of the ongoing construction.

Allison was a very different man to Chapman and had a rather unique résumé which gave him an early association with the club, so when he got the chance to take over from his mentor, he was a round peg in a round hole.

Allison hailed from the Northeast and was born near Darlington in October 1883. He decided to carve out a career in journalism and worked on the local Stockton paper, writing about local football games. When he was just 21, however, he changed tack slightly, landing the secretary's job at Middlesbrough, but when the chance came to join a London daily he did not hesitate to move south. For some reason George always seemed to draw the short straw, being sent out to Plumstead to report on Woolwich Arsenal; however, he developed a great affinity for the club, often as the only London reporter to endure the tortuous rail journey from central London. Allison eventually became the club's historian, as well as editing their programme and handbook. In 1926 he was invited to join the Arsenal board, which he enthusiastically accepted, and he was a part of the BBC Radio team that broadcast Arsenal's Cup finals in 1927 and 1930.

Allison, therefore, had developed a unique knowledge of the growing club and had worked closely with Chapman in its expansion, often taking on the role of secretary that former managers had previously engaged in as part of their job description. His new position was director-manager, eventually reverting to secretary-manager. With a backroom staff of Joe Shaw and Tom Whittaker to encourage continuity, nothing changed on the pitch as they continued to develop Chapman's dream. Indeed, Allison seemed to have inherited Chapman's shrewdness in the transfer market, beginning with the signing of Ted Drake, who would become Arsenal's greatest ever centre-forward. Later wing-halfs Crayston and Wilf Copping would be added as more championships and cups filled the Highbury trophy cabinet.

As Arsenal celebrated their third title, they were hit by another death: that of architect Ferrier, his final work being to design a 'cover' for the Laundry End of the ground.

The legacy of Chapman lived on and Allison saw through the introduction of two more innovations. First, the use of a board to notify team changes to the crowd. It toured the perimeter of the Highbury pitch perched on the back of a motorised cart and was an immediate hit with the supporters, who often only learnt of changes when they saw the players run out for the game. It was soon copied across the country. And second, the introduction of counting turnstiles. In 1935 the club were the first to install electronic turnstiles so that it could get instant feedback on the numbers coming into the ground. Just a couple of months earlier, 72,295 had jammed into Highbury for the top-of-the-table clash with Sunderland, where there had been huge crushes: there had been no real way to keep a live track of the attendance or, for that matter, the cash being taken on the gate. The Enumerator, to give the device its name, changed all this and the Arsenal gates were then closed when 70,000 had poured into the stadium.

Sadly these were to be the last two of the Chapman-influenced innovations and one can only wonder what else Highbury might have seen but for his untimely death. What Chapman had instilled in Allison and the Hill-Wood family, though, was the need to keep moving forward and in 1936 the East Stand was replaced. Amazingly, demolition began in April and the new structure was complete and ready to be opened just six months later; however, the cost of its construction left the club in the red and once again struggling for funds.

ARSENAL FOOTBALL CLUB LTD.

ARSENAL STADIUM,
LONDON, N.5.

November 20th, 1945.

Dear Sir or Madam,

Season 1939-40.

As you are likely aware, Football was suspended by Royal Proclamation on War being declared, with the result that only one first League Matches were able to be played at Highbury. Since then our Ground has been requisitioned by the Public Authorities.

You will appreciate the difficulties that confront the Club. At the present revenues are comparatively insignificant and may even cease entirely in the event of the continuation of hostilities. On the other hand there is a considerable expenditure on overheads which must yet be met.

In these circumstances, the Directors, after most earnest consideration, have decided that Season Ticket Holders shall be granted free admission to all Regional Matches played by the Arsenal on the Tottenham Hotspur Club's Ground for the duration of the War, or until further notice, and when normal League Football is resumed a new Season ticket will be issued for the whole of the first Season in exchange for the present Ticket. No further charge will be made, and so far as possible the same seats or seats as those previously booked will be allotted.

It is to be hoped that this arrangement will commend itself to you, and I look forward to the time when all Arsenal supporters will be able to foregather on the Highbury Ground as they have done in the past.

Yours faithfully,

George F. Allison

Secretary Manager.

George Allison's letter to season-ticket holders after the outbreak
of the Second World War and the suspension of the League.

On the pitch Allison took Arsenal to an FA Cup win in 1936, defeating Sheffield United with one of 'his' signings, Ted Drake, netting the winner; and in 1938 he guided Arsenal to their fifth championship in nine years as they edged ahead of Wolves and Preston in the final weeks of the season.

Not surprisingly, given his background, contacts and skills, Allison was a master of publicity, making Arsenal the best-known club in the world. His knowledge of radio meant that Arsenal always received the best public image at a time when they were universally hated throughout the rest of the country. They appeared regularly in newsreels at cinemas and several of their players were household names – amazing considering that television was still in its infancy and certainly not by any stretch of the imagination a common household appliance. That was just around the corner, though, and on 16 September 1937 Arsenal became the first team in the world to be seen on television when a BBC unit made the short trip from Alexandra Palace to Highbury to broadcast live a practice game between the Arsenal first and second teams. And if that wasn't enough, Highbury made it to the big screen when it became the setting for the 1939 film *The Arsenal Stadium Mystery*. With the regular League campaign about to be forced into an extended break because of the Second World War, it was a fitting way for the magnificent stadium to draw a curtain on the Team of the '30s.

Allison would remain in charge at Arsenal until 1947. His achievements were often overlooked as a result of sniping remarks which encouraged the view that he had inherited a great team and simply completed what Chapman had started in regard to developments at Highbury. It was always going to be difficult to succeed Chapman and the comparison was inevitable, but it is also important to recognise the simple fact that Alison wanted what was best for the club – he was Arsenal through and through and he worked on the principle that 'if it ain't broke, don't fix it'. He made significant enough signings – Drake being one such example – to show he knew talent and how to dovetail it into the system, but it didn't stop there: after the war he made an inspired signing. Remembering Chapman's ethos, he looked for experience. Word on Merseyside was that Joe Mercer's knees had given out, so when Allison approached Everton for his signature, they agreed to a nominal fee, which was all Arsenal could afford. Joe would give Arsenal several seasons of wonderful service, winning two more League titles and one FA Cup. Ronnie Rooke, Fulham's veteran, was persuaded to give it one more go at Highbury and went on to top the League scoring chart in the 1947–48 season.

Despite the onset of the second Great War, Highbury was a hive of activity. The ground was commandeered for a variety of support roles and Arsenal found themselves playing wartime games at White Hart Lane, home of perennial rivals Tottenham Hotspur. Highbury stadium was a target and bombs caused substantial damage to both the Clock End and North Bank end, all of which needed repairing. In fact, the North Bank shed was totally destroyed and had to be removed after an incendiary device had pierced the roof and set fire to the wartime goods, including mattresses, that had been stored in its shelter. It was a fluke occurrence, but it changed the face of Highbury until 1953. During these torrid years of conflict Allison ran the club virtually single-handed, which would eventually have an adverse effect on his health and well-being. And any other ideas he might have had for the further development of Highbury would have been slow to implement due to the huge debt the club had taken on by rebuilding the East Stand, plus the lack of substantial wartime income and the need for ongoing repairs.

Ill health saw the journalist from Darlington stand down as manager in 1947, and ten years later he died of a heart attack at home. His place in Arsenal's and Highbury's history must not be understated, despite a generally held view that he was simply lucky to inherit Chapman's riches. He did much more than that.

* * *

In the years that followed, managers had no real direct input on the evolution of Highbury. Although change continued to take place, it was totally controlled at board and administration level. The days of the manager–secretary had long since passed as the pressures for success on the pitch continued to increase.

SIX

College to Clock

The development of the Clock End sparked what was to be a third and final phase in the evolution of Highbury as a football stadium. The impetus came from a new Arsenal arrival – David Dein, who, as a director of the club, was looking at ways to increase revenue at Highbury. Dein has had a mixed relationship with the Arsenal fans. There is no doubt that he was solely responsible for the arrival of Arsène Wenger as manager. Equally, he has used the club to build his own empire of wealth and power-broking, and whilst this is the *raison d'être* of any entrepreneur, many also hold him responsible for instigating the beginning of the end of the glorious game and its evolution into a sport where 'greed is good'; so much so that many simply stopped attending as the south and north ends of the stadium took on new shapes. One thing is certain: Highbury as it existed in the final season of its footballing life was largely down to Dein.

Arsenal's final year at Highbury was Dein's 60th in life and 22nd at the club. He first bought into Arsenal in the early 1980s at a time when football was suffering from a poor image and hooliganism within the sport seemed rife. He paid £290,250 for 1,161 unissued Arsenal shares in 1983 – then 16.6 per cent of the club – and became a director. Chairman Peter Hill-Wood said at the time: 'Some rich men like to buy fast cars, yachts or racehorses. But David is more interested in Arsenal. I'm delighted he is – but I still think he's crazy. To all intents and purposes, it's dead money.' Hill-Wood and Arsenal were clearly happy to snap Dein's hand off when he offered to purchase the shares. Money was tight in football and word is that most thought he was a fool for wasting his money.

However, buying when the market is low is something that Dein has always excelled at and as the new stadium at Ashburton Grove grew from the ground, Dein's 13,000-plus shares were valued at a massive £35 million on paper. Along the way Dein continued to purchase Arsenal shares, taking his holding up to 42.5 per cent in 1991, which resulted in his becoming vice-chairman. In 2000 he sold £7.1 million of shares to Danny Fiszman (now the club's largest shareholder) reducing his own interest to 19 per cent. So much for dead money! Interestingly, Fiszman then became the Arsenal director in charge of the new stadium development, taking a day-to-day hands-on role in its construction and evolution from the drawing board aided by former managing director and lifelong servant Ken Friar.

Dein had started his life wheeling and dealing on the streets of London's East End. In his early teens he sold cans of food that had lost their labels while helping in his parents' grocery store. From the grocery store grew a home-cooking business which supplied Caribbean foodstuffs to the local West Indian population. This grew beyond all expectations, turning over well in excess of seven figures at a time when Frank McLintock was lifting the League Championship and FA Cup in the space of five heady days. Dein was there celebrating too, as a wealthy man, but by the time he acceded to the Arsenal board he also owned an import-export business, London and Overseas Sugar Limited – although the company was having financial problems at that stage and thus the surprise many felt at his investment in those 'dead' Arsenal shares.

Dein used his position to good effect and became a major influence in the footballing world. He was instrumental in the birth and development of the Premier League, which would reshape the structure and finances of English football. He was determined to help football's metamorphosis from struggling sport into multi-million-pound industry and looked at the success the Americans had in their national games as a blueprint for development. Indeed, it was his investigation into some of the debenture schemes used by American sports franchises to extract money from fans for stadium development that directly led to the issue of the Arsenal bond scheme. Prior to this Dein had turned his attention to the lack of corporate facilities at the club and the need to correct this.

1980s RENAISSANCE

By the end of the '80s football was fast moving into its renaissance period. The structures in which fans had been watching the game at that time were still from a bygone era. More importantly, the corporate world was starting to take an interest in the game as a way of providing a new form of entertainment for wooing clients. If football was to capture business, it needed to cater to the needs of business in its facilities. At this point at Arsenal, the facilities were still just the terraces. For almost 50 years, apart from adding seating as a lower tier to the West Stand, Highbury was still a reflection of the work of Ferrier and Binnie.

Whilst some other clubs had grasped the mantle, Arsenal was comparatively slow off the mark. This was not necessarily down to any malaise but pure physics as to the best way of upgrading the facilities in the available footprint. Part of the thinking at the time was also a new stadium. Sites such as those at Alexandra Palace and even out on the M25 near the club's London Colney training ground were considered. As it was, the feasibility of the sites and the cost involved in building a new stadium were beyond most clubs' means – remember this was in the days long before the cash cow of satellite TV.

The Highbury site itself, then, came into focus. The possibility of installing executive boxes and corporate suites in either or both of the East and West stands was examined as early as 1979 and this led to an initial feasibility study in 1984; but that proved it simply wasn't feasible or, more importantly, practical to do so. Although neither of the buildings were listed at that time (the East Stand was subsequently statutorily listed Grade II in June 1997), changing the physical appearance of such landmarks would have raised many objections: one could hear the cries of 'forsaking heritage for cash' – and rightly so. Equally, even if boxes could be shoehorned in, there was certainly no space to build the infrastructure required to support and service them: kitchens, waste management, toilets and technology to name a few. Not forgetting also the club would lose huge sections of seating. It simply wasn't going to happen that way.

So the club looked at the only other two options open to it: the North Bank and the Clock End. The North Bank was the popular end for the Arsenal support – it was also the least accessible and there was little or no room around it for supporting infrastructures without massively reworking the space. The Clock End, however, was a different proposition.

COLLEGE GROUNDS

As we know, Archibald Leitch's original design for Highbury was driven through by his chief assistant and designer Alfred Kearney. The decision to install Highbury at the Gillespie Road end left plenty of space at the south end of the site. The club used the green area behind the goal and adjacent to St John's College for training. This space would ultimately be used in the construction of the expanded South Stand and other facilities which would indirectly allow Arsenal to stage UEFA Champions League games at Highbury, albeit under special permissions.

Until the late '20s, the College End, as it was called then, was little more than simply stepped terracing constructed from clinker and separated from the fields behind by a high brick wall to which the planners had originally objected. Arsenal employed the services of Claude Waterlow Ferrier in 1930 to create a new design for the stadium and as part of his master plan he looked at revamping the terraced areas right around the ground – this included the College End, which was extended, but was also given a greater elevation in 1931. Prior to Ferrier's arrival the then Arsenal manager Herbert Chapman had installed a large scoreboard at the back of the old terracing – this was now lost. In May 1930 the club had also decided not to go ahead with a shed over the south terracing.

Had this happened, it might well have altered Ferrier's design for Highbury.

With the relaying of the terracing using concrete stepping and the installation of crush barriers, Ferrier's initial design for the College End was complete. However, it was to get one more structure that would change its name and face forever. Ferrier's plans called for a shed to be constructed over the Laundry End of the stadium; however, this meant the huge clock Chapman had installed in 1929 at the back of the terracing would have to be dismantled to make way for the support structure. And rather than lose the clock, it was relocated to the College End of the ground, which slowly became known as the Clock End. The clock was moved in 1934 and for over 50 years that end remained unchanged.

Almost 30 years later the club looked to develop the space behind the stadium. The main focus here was the construction of an indoor training hall which would become known as 'The College'. The space behind the ground had existed for many years simply as a training field used by the club prior to securing the London University training grounds at London Colney. The hall was a simple structure more akin to a large warehouse containing carpet-style AstroTurf pitches along with changing-rooms. The structure, though, was very basic and resembled little more than a large school hall of the period.

CLOCK END STAND

The south end of the ground offered the only real viable option for developing the site. Access was relatively simple and direct from Avenell Road. The entrance to the ground at that end was already in place – a players' car park existed and the demolition of The College would be straightforward. The club, therefore, drew up plans with the help of architects AD Consultants and Sunley Projects Limited not just for the construction of the new stand but for a complete complex behind it, including a new training hall.

However, Islington Council were concerned about the height of the stand and its impact on the sightlines of surrounding residents, especially the Aubert Court blocks of flats which had been constructed to the designs of E.C.P Monson in the late '40s on the site of the old college buildings which had burnt down after the war. So, permission was refused on a split vote for the new South Stand on 25 March 1985 due to intrusion on the skyline, and then again on 17 June 1985 for the same reason. In reviewing the planning documentation, there seems to have been considerable confusion as to the height of the stand. Indeed, the initial specification states 19.5 metres above pitch level, however it was first designed to measure 13.6 metres and finally sat at 16 metres above pitch level on completion. In December 1984, to try to give a visual image of the impact of the construction of the stand to local residents, a series of helium-filled balloons were arranged at the proposed height of the stand.

Naturally, the club appealed the rejection. Permission was granted on appeal on 31 July 1986 and costs of £10,000 were awarded against the council! The appeal was granted by Helen Grogan, an inspector at the Department of Transport. A further application followed this, including the replacement of the sports centre within the body of the stand, and was permitted in 1988. This latter item was of concern initially, especially as local schools had used the training pitch at the rear of the ground, but in the end this proved to be a negotiating point: for the concession of allowing schools to continue to use the facility, a covered training pitch extension would be permitted.

The structure that rose from the terraces at that point is different from what ultimately stood as the club entered its final years at Highbury. What evolved on the outside looked like a two-storey corrugated tin box on stilts. The initial designs called for 48 corporate boxes – this subsequently rose to 52 and the final development actually incorporated 53 boxes, all approximately 4.5 metres by 3 metres wide. They had enough space to accommodate eight people in relative comfort, although the eight seats were actually outside the enclosed space of the boxes (anyone who has sat in one of these seats will tell you that it can be a bitterly cold experience in the winter months as they are particularly exposed to the wind). Arsenal had hoped to complete the facility in time for the 1985–86 season but the planning application rejection put paid to this.

The stand was clad in silver profiled metal sheeting on the outside with red flash gaps (the sheeting arranged either running horizontally or vertically, depending on its place in the structure; generally, though, it was vertical where it might be deemed as a wall and horizontal as part of the roof structure). Flat roof areas were completed with a single layer PVC coating (which would later provide any number of leaks into the areas below).

Internally, the facilities were excellent: the fifty-three executive boxes spread across the two levels (twenty-six boxes on first-floor level, twenty-seven on second-floor level) were well appointed and included balconies. The £6 million the club had invested in the development was soon met by the sale of the boxes, which were instantly snapped up.

Access to the stand was by way of a tight, congested area at the back, accessed via the Avenell Road gates, threading through parked cars before emerging from glass doors into a well-appointed reception. This provided access to the sports hall as well, as it ran under the stand, and also to the boxes and conference room areas via lifts.

The conference/hospitality room areas are used on non-matchdays and the executive boxes double up as meeting rooms that can be hired out: matchday hospitality for non-box-holder sponsors. When Arsenal moved the Champions League games back to Highbury from Wembley, the College training hall (the JVC Sports Centre) had a tent erected inside it and was used as a UEFA hospitality area. Kitchens to service the areas were located on the first and third floors, with the main restaurant and sponsors' lounge on the first floor and extending over the old car park at the rear of the stand. Kiosks remained under the South Bank terracing but were refurbished. The mezzanine level took in the sponsors' lounge – some 257 metres square; plus a very small bar (17 metres square); a large kitchen (122 metres square); and then various facilities, such as toilets and offices. At ground-floor level there were 100 parking spots (although many of these would be lost as the club eventually had to bring in and double stack Portakabins to provide temporary accommodation – albeit on a permanent basis – to handle practical matters such as casual staff sign-in and the like).

When the development of the Clock End was being discussed, there was naturally a lot of talk regarding the fate of Herbert Chapman's clock itself. In the end, the original mechanism was replaced and a new, smaller version – albeit an identical replica – installed at the top of the stand in the front of the grey facia. The stand itself was covered with a cantilevered roof, but whereas Ferrier stretched his West Stand roof out to provide protection to the terraces below, this structure barely covered half of the terrace below. AFC logos were mounted on the roof corners to match those on the North Bank.

Worse still, from both a supporters' and an aesthetic point of view, was the fact that the front of the stand itself was perched on two huge concrete legs. Apart from looking appalling it rendered huge sections of the terracing underneath useless because anyone standing under the structure had their sightlines severely obstructed. The clearance height of just around 2.6 metres also made it oppressive and dingy. Access to the stand was made easier in 1989 when 189 Highbury Hill was demolished at the base to provide access for supporters to the Clock End (this later became access for away supporters into the south-west corner of the Clock End when segregation at that end was added). In 1990 part of the south terracing on the east side was demolished to provide emergency vehicle access, first-aid facilities and a staff mess room.

In May 1991 the subject of Arsenal trees also became a major local debating point. As part of the approved application Arsenal were required to provide perimeter treatment and landscaping, in particular a series of trees to the rear of 109–117 Highbury Hill. The problem was that this did not take place. Soil conditions along the way were poor and the planting of large pots, which was suggested, would have meant that the television trucks would be forced to park on Avenell Road, something that the Islington police would not approve. Equally, managing trees within the stadium would have been difficult and could in itself have led to further problems should they have taken serious root! Thus the council were seeking enforcement of the tree planting, the League demanded that TV access be provided in accordance with its rules and the local police said the TV trucks could not be parked on the street. The three-way headache was eventually solved by the addition of a screen and the introduction of ivy as a visual barrier.

ALL SEATS AND POLICE

The Taylor Report (see Chapter Seven: The North Bank) required that stadiums such as Highbury become all-seater by 13 August 1994. As the North Stand was in the process of being constructed and improvements had been made to the South Stand before the Taylor Report concluded its findings, it was the terracing at the Clock End that was modified and had seats added. The addition of seats there actually made a massive improvement on what was initially produced, which was nothing short of a slap in the face to Ferrier and Binnie and their art deco brilliance. The terraces in front of the East and West stands were also transformed with seats at this time. All this severely cut the capacity of Highbury to around 38,500. The process of increasing capacity in the stands took place during the close season of 1993 and was based on a structural steel frame and pre-cast concrete. Work continued into the start of the 1993–94 season and was completed in the October.

Building works at this time also included the construction of a police control room in the space between the South Stand and West Stand. Permission for this was granted in April 1993, at the same time as the seating on the Clock End terrace. The structure was a two-storey affair and rose to ten metres in height, with the top tier being the police control room and the bottom floor being used as a conference room and also as a TV studio by Sky Sports for live games.

Arsenal, and Dein in particular, had reached their goal and instantly recouped the cost of doing so. They had provided the ongoing means for additional revenue through subsequent renewal of box contracts, and the ability to hire out rooms and boxes for functions, ranging from meetings through to weddings, during the rest of the week. When all was said and done, the new South Stand was a quick fix and in terms of what might have been achieved and developed there, it was exceptionally short-sighted, but at that point in time the way in which football in England would be restructured and refinanced – and the extent to which the money would flow – could not have been anticipated.

SEVEN

The North Bank

The North Bank as it stood during Highbury's final season was a very different beast to that which dominated the Gillespie Road end of the ground for so many years before. It was also very different to the stand the club had planned to build. The aesthetic mistakes of the South Stand and the outcry from a variety of sources when the North Bank planning process was in full swing had a big influence in both changing minds and fashioning what was ultimately built. Thankfully.

Arsenal were under the tutelage of George Graham: they had won their first League Championship since 1971 two years earlier and were just a few weeks away from winning their second under Graham, whose playing style had earned him the nickname 'Stroller', and who had been so instrumental in that very first Double. It was a new era of success, with wins at home and in Europe. As Highbury had previously seen, stadium growth was inextricably linked to on-field triumphs and, paradoxically, it was that continuing success that would lead them away from Highbury itself.

AD Consultants, who had created the much-maligned South Stand, had been commissioned to produce the club's vision for the redevelopment of the North Bank and in April 1991 the club released the design for the new 12,750-seat North Stand. There was an immediate furore from both local laypeople and more distinguished and esteemed parties. In the '30s the innovation of the developments at Highbury set Arsenal and the stadium apart. Here, with the final decade of the twentieth century in full swing, the club was being looked at as a barometer to what was possible in the wake of the Taylor Report and its indirect requirement for all new stands in stadiums. Arsenal have always stood for excellence, both on and off the field, and, whilst the latter may have lacked application during certain periods, the monuments that surrounded the on-field exploits were always a reminder of this. As such, the aesthetics and their integration, as Ferrier had so adeptly shown down the years, were of paramount importance when incorporating 'old' and new. This offering on paper was certainly not up to the job.

There was further outcry when the financing of the stand came in for criticism. Whereas the £6 million cost of building the South Stand had been pretty much paid for by the first sales of boxes and corporate entertainment, the North Stand was being built to house the 'normal' fan – incorporating more boxes would have raised objections and alienated crowds at the stadium. That said, if the space had been there, they may well have found a home: money talks. Thus, the estimated £14 million had to be found using more direct routes, which included the club itself and loans. One source of generating revenue was through the issue of bonds: those subscribing to the bond scheme could buy the rights to have first option to purchase a seat for 150 years.

At the time of the announcements emotions were running high amongst supporters on both these fronts. The plans for the North Stand led to the formation of an action group called GAAS (Group for an Alternative Arsenal Stand), whilst the bond scheme produced a number of protest groups including the eloquently named 'Stuff the Bond'. The fact that they coincided led to a louder voice of discontent and one the club and authorities simply could not ignore. The summer months of 1991 were spent celebrating a tenth Championship but there was also deep debate.

THE NEED TO BUILD

The construction of the new South Stand had been undertaken for financial reasons: the club had needed new, expanding revenue streams and the construction of an executive facility was the correct route to achieve it. The North Stand was effectively forced on the club with the publication of the Taylor Report.

The worst disaster in the history of English football occurred on 15 April 1989 when 96 Liverpool fans were crushed to death on the Leppings Lane terrace of Hillsborough, home to Sheffield Wednesday. It was the FA Cup semi-final between Liverpool and Nottingham Forest, but no football took place that day. Unlike the tragedy at Heysel Stadium in 1985, also involving Liverpool supporters, this one didn't occur because of hooliganism: this incident was due to congestion on the way to the ground and at the ground itself. Thousands of fans travelling to the game were delayed on the roads and were anxious to get into the stadium (as football supporters, we have all experienced this). There was little monitoring of the flow of people into the ground and no effort to seal off areas or redirect supporters to less crowded sections. The Leppings Lane end was fit to burst but ironically the fencing at that end, erected in response to acts of hooliganism such as that at Heysel, did its job and kept those at the front of the crush from taking a simple step to safety. Some fans made it over the top of the fence but many had their lives taken from them behind it.

English football would never be the same and the wheels were put in motion to prevent it happening again, processes that also would have the benefit of providing England with the finest fleet of stadiums anywhere in the world. The Home Office set up an inquiry under Lord Justice Taylor immediately after the Hillsborough disaster whose remit was: 'To inquire into the events at Sheffield Wednesday Football ground on 15th April 1989 and to make recommendations about the needs of crowd control and safety at sports events.'

The Taylor Report recommended a variety of changes but a pertinent one was that all top-division stadiums in England and Scotland should phase out their terraces and become all-seater by 13 August 1994. Thus

111

millions of pounds had to be spent by clubs such as Arsenal to effect this and other changes. The renovation of the North Bank and the construction of the North Stand was the outcome of the Taylor Report and in many ways was also a memorial to those who died or were seriously injured at Hillsborough – lest we forget.

The North Bank shed, which was nearing its final days at this point, had been the second on the site following the unrepairable damage to the original structure during the Second World War – some ten seasons had passed after the war before Arsenal supporters would see the return of a cover over the North Bank. Movements were afoot to have it back in place before the start of the 1946–47 season: William Binnie had drawn up plans and had estimated at the time that it would cost £12,500 to rebuild. However, for reasons almost certainly connected to cash flow, it had failed to materialise. The club had put in a claim to the War Damage Commission for compensation for the destruction of the shed but the claim was far from met, offering, as it did, the paltry sum of £48 17s 9d (about £48.85). By 1955 the cost of replacement had risen to a few pennies under £24,767, and after some powerful arguments the War Damage Commission agreed to meet this in full. Contractors Higgs Limited were given the task of reinstating the structure, which took place during the first half of 1956 and was completed in time for the 1956–57 season.

The evolution of the North Stand was a natural requirement. The Highbury capacity at this time was just 41,188 and, of that, less than half was seating – 18,095 to be exact. The fact that the South Stand had only relatively recently been built left the club few options for renovations at the Clock End other than installing seats on the terraces underneath the stand. If seats were installed in identical fashion on the North Bank, capacity would have fallen drastically – to around 32,000, in fact. The question has to be asked: if the Clock End had been developed with a more forward-thinking attitude, rather than as a quick-fix money generator, would the move to Ashburton Grove be necessary, given a possible capacity closing on 50,000? In reality, of course, the implications for the local residents of Arsenal staying at Highbury would have been even greater – and there would have had to be some form of modernisation in the East and West stands to remove the dinginess within and the poorer views at the back of the lower tiers of each. Equally, and more importantly, UEFA might not have been so forthcoming regarding the use of the undersized Highbury pitch in its competitions. The construction of the North Stand in many respects was palliative treatment as far as Highbury was concerned.

DESIGNER PRESSURE

Several months after AD Consultants had released their initial designs and the first planning application was made (and rejected) in March 1991, the debate continued to rage. It was 5 November and the fireworks were exploding at the council meeting – the protesters were in full voice in Upper Street outside Islington Town Hall. The result was that Islington council gave Arsenal six weeks to come up with alternative designs, something more in character with the existing structures. Ferrier was still turning in his grave.

Amongst those bidding for the work was Norwest Holst and, working with architects from the Lobb Partnership and engineers from Jan Bobrowski Partners, they set out to answer the call. The Lobb Partnership included in their ranks Rod Sheard, who would later lead the design team for Emirates Stadium, following on from his work at Sydney Olympic Stadium and Wembley New National Stadium with the flagship design company HOK. Norwest Holst were local, having their base in Watford, whilst Bobrowski merged to form NRM Bobrowski and have since worked on stands at Twickenham, Ipswich Town and Sandown Park.

The combined project team ultimately created what was built: a construction of modern materials that was aesthetically pleasing and looked the part juxtaposed against the 60-year-old structures to its left and right. It was a long way from the original design, savaged for its collection of ill-coordinated materials, ugly bulk and horrid wrap-around corners.

One of the early objections on which GAAS held their ground was the height of the original design. The group employed Rivington Street

Studio Architecture to put forward their case, as well as discussing the environmental factors. Speaking at a local inquiry, Charles Thomson, an architect living in the area and a representative of GAAS, made the following pertinent comment: 'The argument from Arsenal is that we have to have it this way because the Taylor Report requires it. The argument is false. The Taylor Report requires all-seater stadiums, it does not require massive, badly designed, inappropriate buildings.'

The first design by Lobb provided for a North Stand that rose to 22.6 metres (26 metres including trusses), around 3 metres lower than the first proposal. Even so, the stand was still substantially higher than the 15 metre North Bank shed that had occupied the skyline before it. This created light-loss problems for the local residents in Gillespie Road and on completion would also interfere with television reception. GAAS had also provided their own designs for the new North Stand using the services of Ove Arup Partnership and, although these were rejected, their action went a long way to persuading the local council and Arsenal to ensure something better resulted.

But it was not plain sailing. Lobb Partnership submitted their first planning application to Islington Council on 9 December 1991 with a fee of £4,600. Following meetings with GAAS, a revised version of this application was then submitted again on 6 January 1992 which included several modifications, such as a reduction of the upper tier by one row to reduce its height by 1.3 metres and the repositioning of plant material originally scheduled for the roof. The chief executive's department at Islington Council studied the design and facility all the way, resulting in a stream of correspondence and support meetings. Given the earlier outcry regarding the look and feel of the proposed new stand, it was natural that the council wanted to ensure this would be no sore thumb.

The Lobb Partnership provided a very persuasive case regarding the design and even involved the Royal Fine Art Commission in an effort to support their case. Writing to Islington Council in January 1992, Sheard outlined their case:

> We believe our design is a sensitive blend between the existing
> 1930s art deco style established by Claude Ferrier, the architect for

the East and West stands, and a true representation of the modern materials and technology we would be using for the structure of the new stand. Claude Ferrier's partner Major Binnie was responsible for much of the structure of the existing stands and I believe our design reflects exactly the same character of a solid rear core, masking an open light-steel frame towards the pitch.

In a letter to Arsenal chairman Peter Hill-Wood, the chairman of the Royal Fine Art Commission, Lord St John of Fawsley, wrote that the commission believed the new design was a great improvement over the previous one. He went on to make some suggestions in design application that were implemented by Lobb as part of the revised application.

By the end of January 1992, a third planning application had been submitted for consideration. The Lobb Partnership design, with subsequent consultation, had come up with a structure that was five metres lower than the original AD Consultants' design on the northern elevation and two metres lower at any other point. It was also around eight metres shorter in overall length and 5 per cent smaller in total volume, as well as being set further back from Avenell Road. Part of the agreement included the provision of a nursery/crèche and adherence to a code of construction.

A letter from Arsenal's solicitors, Goulden's, to the Islington Council chief executive's office prior to the hearing had an air of desperation about it, imploring as it did the council to grant permission for the construction prior to the public inquiry hearing scheduled for 4 February. They got their wish and planning was formally granted in a memorandum dated 3 February 1992.

THE END

On 2 May 1992 Arsenal were hosting their final Football League game of the season. Southampton were the visitors and they were dispatched back down the M3 with a 5–1 thumping. Ian Wright helped himself to a hat-trick and Kevin Campbell and Alan Smith weighed in with the others. It was the end of a disappointing season: the League Championship crown had been surrendered to Leeds United as Arsenal slipped to fourth place.

The crowd of 37,702 had come to pay homage to a piece of real estate, to say farewell to an icon. Despite the attendance, there were many empty seats in the ground – the North Bank, though, was packed to the rafters. It was its final game. As the whistle sounded for full-time there was a small protest from the fans, but this was beyond the power of the club to change. Some fans left, but many waited; indeed most did, aimlessly wandering, looking, searching and remembering. The crowd drifted and security guards shepherded the stragglers out. The doors were closed.

A few days later the doors reopened and the workforce appeared – not with loaned shovels, spades and picks to create an embankment this time; instead it was with mechanical diggers. Huge yellow caterpillar-treaded monsters bearing the words 'John F. Hunt Demolition Komatsu' ripped into the posts holding up the North Bank roof and sent it clattering to the ground. Panels of black corrugated iron were dislodged from their lofty position and dangled mangled, and were removed into a waiting army of trucks. Unlike the convoy of trucks which delivered Kearney's North Bank, this fleet were taking the structure away at the rate of 130 lorries a day at its peak in a demolition process that took nine weeks. The summer months were spent clearing and preparing, and by the end of August the ground beams and drainage were complete. As September approached, the superstructure of concrete columns and staircase shafts started to rise from the ground.

As the inaugural season of the FA Premier League loomed a new kind of structure was in place – the Mural. Stretching the entire width of the North Bank and several metres high was a colourful wall of faces looking out across the Highbury pitch. Not wanting to leave the 'Construction End' (as it was now called) open, the Arsenal board had commissioned the huge painting. Acting as a barrier to what was going on behind, it also provided a useful mechanism for blocking the ball – not least from wayward John Jensen shots. Away supporters often remarked that the Mural generated more noise than the normal custodians of the North Bank. For some it wasn't as colourful as required, sharp eyes noting that the images depicted only white males. The club hastily had the oversight corrected (the artist insisted he had included other ethnic images but that these had become faded in the printing process) – the revised mural included a single Manchester United supporter in one corner as well.

By the end of the first season the three-sided Highbury was starting to look more like a complete stadium again. Behind the Mural the structure had been gradually growing as paper designs became concrete reality. The angst of the protestors had more than done its job and the North Stand structure started to blend in perfectly with its environs. One effect of the building had been to reduce the ground's capacity quite drastically; indeed, the biggest capacity crowd of the season was for the visit of Manchester United when 29,739 squeezed in.

THE END RESULT

The final touches were being put in place during July 1993 as the workers, tilers, painters, plumbers, electricians and other service workers gradually dwindled in numbers. The end result of much soul-searching was one of the first newly built stadiums to comply fully with the recommendations of the Taylor Report on sports ground safety.

The completed North Stand contained 12,400 seats across its two tiers. Of these, all but 104 were on sale to supporters – these 'obstructed view' seats were used by stewards and partially sighted supporters who could also listen to the game through an audio link. In addition, it accommodated a restaurant, several bars, a museum and a club shop. The building's most apparent structural innovation was the 17.5-metre-long propped cantilever roof trusses (the longest in Europe), which were supported by a 103-metre-long 'goalpost' girder and stabilised by the reinforced concrete stair and service cores at the rear of the building. The cantilevered upper seating tier was also structurally restrained by the service cores and this facilitated unobstructed viewing for all spectators. What is more, the mechanism allowed those in the upper tier to be 'hung' much nearer the pitch than would otherwise have been possible.

Incorporated at each end of the stand were glazed fannings, symmetrical with those in the East and West stands, thus adding to the bright, airy atmosphere. The rear of the upper-tier roof was also clad in clear sheets, allowing light to flood in. At each end of the stand, direct access to the upper tier was via a zigzag staircase appended on the outside and surrounded by a cocoon of glazing in true art deco style.

The two tiers provided seating as luxurious as you might find for general patronage at any football stadium. Each flip-up seat was padded, with armrests, and coloured either red or white. Inside, as we shall see in due course, there was plenty to admire, but like everything in life, it came at a cost.

THE BOND SCHEME

As Arsenal moved towards the 1993–94 season, Highbury was a feverish throng of workers. There was plenty happening besides the approaching completion of the North Stand – for instance, the installation of seats on the terracing at the Clock End. In all, Arsenal would be spending around £20 million to complete the alterations in compliance with the Taylor Report. Around £12–£14 million of this was used to construct the North Bank.

The club had decided to follow a route born in the USA and which had been implemented at Ibrox and Twickenham. A similar debenture scheme had also been instigated successfully for many years at the All England Lawn Tennis and Croquet Club for the distribution of tickets for The Championships. In comparison with these schemes the Arsenal bond scheme offered particularly good value, while the club remained at Highbury at least. A bond could be purchased that would give the owner the right to have first call on a designated seat for 150 years, at a cost of either £1,500 or £1,100, depending on its location. Those subscribing to the scheme could pick their seat using a system where a simulated view from the seat was generated by a computer.

In addition to being guaranteed a seat, the bondholder could claim other benefits: a name tag on the seat, use of the Bondholders' Restaurant and other guarantees such as tickets for cup finals and the like. The bond was not the season ticket – this had to be purchased in addition; however, for a ten-year period the cost was very much reduced. Indeed, for the first year the season ticket was around £280 and rose only by around £37 during the 10 years. Of course, it came as a huge shock when the subsidised period ran out and bondholders got a bill for £1,200 for their first ticket outside of the period – a rise of 300 per cent!

When the bond scheme was originally announced, there was much scepticism and mistrust regarding the true nature of its purpose. One school of thought believed it was simply a ruse to get rid of the unsavoury element of the club's support. The North Bank was, of course, where the bulk of the vocal support emanated from in those days and where the rougher elements of the club's fan base congregated.

As it was, around 4,000 of the bonds were sold – not as many as the club had hoped, but nevertheless a solid start. In fact, this was only a 35 per cent take-up, and the stand could not have been bought without the bond issue having being 100 per cent underwritten by the Bank of Scotland. Subsequently, Arsenal bought the underwritten seats back from the Bank of Scotland, although details of this particular deal have never been made public. They were on sale for a limited period, thus creating demand. Over the ten-year period of discounted tickets bondholders probably saved themselves in the order of £3,000 or £4,000 in ticket prices, and a healthy market in the sale of bonds sprang up. At its height a bond could be sold for upwards of £5,500.

In the summer of 2003 there was a huge outcry when the club announced it was looking into a *new* bond scheme at Highbury which would be transferable to Ashburton Grove. Arsenal were looking to sell around 3,000 seats in the North Stand at between £3,000 and £5,000 per bond. The initial call for interest was oversubscribed severalfold and had the potential to raise some £15 million for the club.

With the initial bond providing take-up for a chunk of the North Stand seats, the club also launched a Ticket Scheme whereby Arsenal supporters could register as a member for a small fee – £20 at the start – which gave them the right to apply for tickets. The fee was deducted from their first purchase of tickets, although this would later change and further add to club coffers. Bondholders who did not take up their option to purchase a season ticket could apply for match tickets by applying before a deadline – typically nine weeks prior to the game.

OPENING DAY

The opening day of the 1993–94 Premier League season – 14 August – saw the North Stand come to life. Whereas supporters had lingered with long faces to mark the demise of the North Bank, they arrived early to herald the opening of the North Stand. The publicity had been good – every newspaper and every magazine had lavished praise on its structure for the quality of its design and its range of facilities. Bondholders rushed to seats to check that their name had been correctly fitted and correctly spelled, but were slowed down by what they saw around them. This wasn't ugly, dirty, stained concrete, smelling of piss; it was tiled and gleaming clean throughout. It had bars and food areas; it had entertainment and modern toilet facilities. It even had a museum and a crèche.

Entrance to the North Stand was either through turnstiles on Avenell Road or Gillespie Road – almost opposite the Tube station, and the same entrance that had served Arsenal supporters since 1913. When entering through the Gillespie Road entrance turnstiles, the concourse presented itself, thrusting through to the far end where the Avenell Road turnstiles were located. On the pitch side of the concourse two banks of toilets – male and female – marked the way before the concourse opened out into a circular plaza with a bar and stage area (live pre-match entertainment was one of the many things that has had a mixed reception down the years). Photographs with trophies, games and quizzes were all tried but eventually dispensed with; swigging beer from plastic glasses whilst watching the match and goal highlights on the avenue of suspended televisions was much more the norm. After more toilets and lower-tier access points, the Arsenal shop completed that side of the thoroughfare.

On the Gillespie Road side of the concourse there existed a number of food and beverage counters, video games (Arsenal were sponsored by Dreamcast for a while), plus various access points to the upper tier and back-of-house areas. One such entrance led to the Bondholders' Restaurant and the Arsenal museum. The Bondholders' Restaurant was the exclusive domain of those who had purchased said bond. It was a fitted-out area of the mezzanine floor that had no windows and little ventilation. A hot lunch from a limited menu could be purchased along with expensive beer. In truth it wasn't a bad pre-match point but access was difficult and generally required pre-booking or a lengthy queue. The museum gradually grew in the number of exhibits but was never what it should have been. On matchdays it was often under the stewardship of the 1971 Double-winner Charlie George, who lived and breathed Arsenal.

Access to the top of the lower tier could also be gained via a staircase and this made it much easier to access the seats at the rear. It also contained food and beverage areas. Only a single lift gave access to the upper tier and so for many it was the stairs – amazing how these became more difficult to negotiate as the years wore on! – the top of which opened out on to a very airy concourse. The top tier could also be accessed directly from stairs inside the Avenell Road and Gillespie Road turnstiles, which were fully glazed and provided views into the surrounding streets. The top tier on the Gillespie Road side contained toilets, beer and food outlets, and betting booths. Along the top was a string of televisions suspended from the ceiling which showed the same fare of goal and match highlights and, of course, Arsène Wenger with his pre-match comments and team line-up. The pitch side of the concourse simply contained a continuous shelf to hold beers, and spaces in which supporters could gather and meet. Despite its smaller size it was a much better environment.

The game itself on that first day was with Coventry City as opposition and the crowd hadn't come out in huge numbers: just 26,397 made it to the ground. The Sky Blues, of course, spoilt the party by taking an unexpected 3–0 win away with them. Mick Quinn helped himself to a hat-trick in the process as, despite his size, he proved to be much too quick for Arsenal on that day. Leeds United were the next visitors and finally gave Arsenal their first win in front of the new stand, but it was an own goal that marked the first home score before Paul Merson added the winner.

HIGHBURY

The North Stand wasn't officially opened until 15 February 1994. Prince Charles, the Prince of Wales, had originally been invited but declined due to prior commitments and so the honour went to the Duke of Kent – a symbol of the club's Plumstead origins.

Stadium Miscellany

The development of Highbury never really stopped. Even when there was minimal activity on the outside, there was invariably a refurbishment going on internally. For example, in the intervening years between the creation of the East Stand and the final, third phase that saw the completion of the South and North stands, the terracing at the base of the West Stand was fitted with seats to make its whole structure fully seated. The club had first looked at installing seats in this area a few years after the North Bank roof had been replaced, but the cost at the time was considered prohibitive; however, when the 5,100 additional seats were added in the summer of 1969, the cost of doing so amounted to almost £80,000, though it was a significant landmark in the history of the stand.

During the '60s, two independent organisations – Arsenal Football Club Improvement Society and Arsenal Football Club Development Association – were making contributions to various aspects of ground improvement. This included £15,000 in 1964 to pay for under-soil heating, plus lump sums for other projects, including £11,000 in 1966–67, £20,000 in 1967–68, £18,000 in 1968–69 and £10,000 in 1969–70. The Development Association ceased to operate in 1967, with all activity then channelled through the Improvement Society, who subsequently contributed £40,000 in 1972–73 for work on the North Terrace.

The Safety of Sports Ground Act 1975 had Arsenal working hard to maintain the stadium capacity at 60,000 and spent no less that £1 million during the next five years. A sign of the times and way of things to come arrived at the same time when, for the 1974–75 season, Arsenal broke with tradition and for the first time accepted advertising within the stadium. This generated about £30,000 in revenue the first year, which obviously grew significantly thereafter.

FLOODLIGHTS

Floodlighting was another major innovation at Highbury. Arsenal was not the first club to install permanent floodlights in their stadium – Southampton took that honour, lighting theirs a couple of months beforehand; however, Highbury had seen a form of floodlighting as early as 1932 when lamps had been erected alongside the college training pitch. Four years later sixteen lamps were mounted along the fascias of the East and West stands – eight on each side – again to allow evening training on the Arsenal pitch. These lights remained in place for many years and were finally augmented in April 1951 and used for the first time in the annual match played between the Boxers and the Jockeys, a celebrity event featuring sportsmen of the time. Reports are mixed but the novelty of the game and the floodlights seemed to have attracted a crowd in excess of 30,000. Given their undoubted success, manager Tom Whittaker ordered they become a more permanent fixture and looked to exploit them as an attraction to host other midweek, floodlit encounters.

So, Arsenal played a series of games under floodlights as they sought to prove their worth to the Football Association, hoping that in due course league and cup games could be played under them, thus helping relieve end-of-season congestion as well as generating bigger midweek crowds. Whilst league games were certainly not sanctioned at this early juncture, Arsenal staged a series of high-profile friendlies to prove their worth and provide a good additional revenue stream.

On 19 September 1951 the then Israeli amateurs of Hapoel Tel Aviv travelled to London for the first official Arsenal game under Highbury's floodlights. The 44,385 crowd was boosted by a good turn-out from London's Jewish community as Arsenal cruised to a 6–1 win. Cliff Holton hit a hat-trick and half-time sub Reg Lewis notched two with Arthur Milton adding the sixth. The biggest cheer of the night, though, was reserved by the home crowd for Strodinsky when he hit Hapoel's consolation goal. Hero of the night was Hodorov in the visitors' goal, however, who performed heroics to keep the score down to manageable levels.

Highbury's next floodlit occasion was against Hendon in the London Challenge Cup. The side from the Athenian League (which would nowadays be below the Conference South Division) had the honour of being the first team to defeat Arsenal under lights, winning their LCC encounter 1–0 on Monday, 8 October 1951. Arsenal pretty much fielded a reserve side but the novelty of the night game attracted 13,548 to the ground and produced gate receipts of £846! Phebey, a cricketer with Kent at the time, scored the only goal of the game a few minutes from full-time. By this stage Arsenal had been reduced to nine men, having lost Grimshaw and Shaw to injury in the second half. These were the days before one, let alone five, substitutes!

On 17 October 1951 Glasgow Rangers completed Arsenal's floodlit season at Highbury, with 62,000 cramming into Highbury to witness what was the official inauguration of the lights. Arsenal won a best-of-five-goals encounter. Ray Daniel was the star of the evening with Arsenal, according to the *Islington Gazette*, being the 'slightly quicker side'. Unfortunately the report failed to give any details of the goal-scorers but concluded that the local supporters could expect to see a host of Continental sides arriving at Highbury for fixtures in due course, and that is exactly what did happen, a variety of high-profile European sides booking tickets for north London. Although their fixtures had a mixed reception in terms of attendance, floodlit football was here to stay.

UNDER-SOIL HEATING

Arsenal installed an electric under-soil heating system in 1964 at a cost of £13,936, which was paid for by a donation of £15,000 made by the Arsenal Football Club Improvement Society and the Arsenal Football Club Development Association. The under-soil heating had some success and often allowed games to go ahead at Highbury when others in London fell prey to the ice and cold weather. Indeed, on one occasion a Combination fixture (reserves) between Arsenal and Spurs attracted a crowd of over 25,000: the match marked the return of Jimmy Greaves from injury, and being the only local fixture to have beaten the cold snap was also the main feature of ITV's *The Big Match* the following Sunday afternoon.

By the time Arsenal were setting out on Double glory six years later, the electric system had been replaced by a hot-water system at a cost of some £35,000. This consisted of a series of pipes that were laid under the surface of the pitch so that when cold weather was forecast hot water could be pumped through them, thus heating the surrounding earth and ultimately defrosting the surface and preventing a build-up of ice. The success of the system was graphically illustrated when the 1970 Boxing Day fixture between Arsenal and Southampton was one of the few to take place despite horrid conditions that meant the Clock End had to remain shut.

However, it didn't always work to save the day. Not long after the Boxing Day fixture Arsenal were involved in a fourth-round FA Cup tie with Portsmouth. After a 1–1 draw at Fratton Park, the replay at Highbury was called off by referee Jim Finney just 90 minutes before kick-off, a huge downpour having drenched grounds throughout the country, throwing the sporting calendar into disarray. The system had been designed to drain, aerate and thaw frozen soil, but it simply couldn't handle the amount of rain that had fallen. While many of the home supporters abandoned their journey to Highbury when news reached them on the radio, about 7,000 Pompey fans were not so lucky and turned up only to be disappointed and sent back to the south coast. The system was overhauled again in 1986 at a cost of almost £100,000.

A more advanced system called PAT was installed, as at many stadiums around the world. This not only circulates hot water and hot air under the pitch, but a vacuum can also be created within the pipes to drain off excess water as a result of heavy rainfall or melting ice.

PRESS LIAISON

Working in conjunction with the Football Writers' Association (FWA) arguably some of the best press facilities to be found in any club stadium in the country were developed at Highbury. The press-boxes, as such, were situated in the East Stand adjacent to the directors' box and in reality reflected the age of the stand itself. The addition of telephone lines and ADSL connections in the final years of the stadium have at least given reporters direct access to their employers. However, it was with the expansion of the press area in the bowels of the stadium that the greatest changes came, in the creation of individual booths where journalists could complete and file their stories, interviews and reports in relative comfort.

The construction of a press conference room was also a major improvement at the turn of the millennium. It was, in effect, a small theatre, almost cinema-style, with several rows of seats sloping towards a platform containing a presenter's desk and behind which was a screen on which videos could be projected.

Off the side of the main tunnel leading on to the pitch the old Halfway House was converted into a TV interview room and it was here that post-match interviews took place. Further down in the basement of the stadium was the photographers' room where digital images could be uploaded by direct ISDN connections.

COLOUR CHANGE

Despite all the ongoing improvements at Highbury, if the club had stayed put something would ultimately have had to be done about the decay that was setting in, in both the West and East stands. By the end of the 1980s the club was regularly spending in excess of half a million pounds per year simply on the upkeep of the stadium, whilst continual improvements, such as those to the press rooms and turnstiles, cost the club well over £3 million in 1990. Part of this process included the repainting of the East Stand in the summer of 1989, which went from the curious cream and green to a more Arsenal-like magnolia and red!

Indeed, by the end of 1993, over £30 million had been spent on Highbury in just five years.

VIDEO VISION

In May 1984 Arsenal became the first British club to install a large screen in their stadium. Just as 50 years earlier Chapman had erected the scoreboard at the back of the College End, Arsenal were looking to try a new kind of innovation.

In June 1983 the club applied for planning permission to erect a Diamond Vision screen. This was rejected on the grounds of the amount of additional noise that would be created from it, the loss of light to surrounding residences and the potential intensification of use of the stadium. The club appealed and in May 1984 permission was granted – after a petition, the local residents' groups decided not to object to the appeal, having come to a compromise directly with the club. The residents' groups took the view that if Arsenal were granted permission on appeal, then the restrictions for the screen's use would have been less limiting than those agreed between the club and local residents.

The screen itself was only a temporary structure, being inserted into a scaffold frame that had been erected behind the Clock End. This was set on top of a permanent platform contained within the height of the south terrace. The screen was erected on a Friday night for a Saturday afternoon game and removed the following day.

The screen provided pre-match, half-time and post-match entertainment in the form of interviews, highlights from recent games, pop videos and cartoons. The screen also proved popular for advertisements and public-service announcements. At this time no live transmission during the game was permitted, neither was there any replay technology to show goals from the current game – this would have been difficult anyway, as at this stage games were not covered in anything like the depth they are today. The club were given permission to show three live games beamed back to Highbury. The screen was unveiled for the first time for the visit of Sunderland on 20 October 1984 and proved an instant hit with the fans.

In 1993 Arsenal secured another first when they became the first club in Britain to install two DVD-quality screens at Highbury, larger and clearer than the 8 mm Cine screen installed earlier. The giant Sony Jumbotron screens occupied pride of place in diagonally opposite corners: one was sited between the South Stand and East Stand, the other between the North Stand and West Stand. Each screen measured 37 metres square, but neither were these permanent fixtures. The displays were rented from ScreenCo and removed from their casings on a regular basis to be used at other events. During the summer of 1994, for instance, they were dispatched for use in the Citrus Bowl Stadium in Orlando.

CHARITY EVENTS

Highbury has staged a number of charity events down the years – the most popular being the aforementioned Boxers v. Jockeys games. These took place in the 1950s and were in aid of the Sportsman's Aid Society. As the name suggests, these were games played between a team of boxers and a team of jockeys – the boxers traditionally wore the red-and-white of Arsenal, whilst the jockeys wore Spurs' colours. The games were refereed by a member of Arsenal's first-team squad of the day, with a leading name from the boxing or horseracing world running the lines. The Compton brothers, Denis and Les, were among the referees of the day. Crowds of 30,000 or more were not uncommon, individuals paying seven shillings to stand on the terraces.

Highbury has also staged the FA Charity Shield game on occasion (now called the FA Community Shield). Originally known as the 'Sheriff of London Shield', it was a fixture that had been played annually between a leading professional club and a leading amateur club. It later evolved into the competition it is today, where the previous season's League champion plays the FA Cup winner in a new season curtain-raiser. The profits from the event are distributed to a number of charities.

Highbury staged the first of its five FA Charity Shield games in 1934, when, as champions, they beat Manchester City 4–0. The crowd were far from charitable on that cold November afternoon, with just 10,888 attending. Arsenal lost their next game as hosts – 0–1 to Sheffield Wednesday the following season – but the next three encounters were all won – 2–1 v. Preston North End (1938), 4–3 v. Manchester United (1948) and 3–1 v. Blackpool (1953).

Since Arsenal were champions in 1970–71, Highbury should have hosted the game at the start of the 1971–72 season (the match did not move to Wembley until 1974); however, the FA did not invite the club to participate since it had won the Double that year, and instead Leicester City (Division One champions) got the call to face Liverpool.

FA AMATEUR CUP

Highbury has twice been used to stage games at the pinnacle of what would now be called 'non-League Football'. In the days before the FA Vase and FA Trophy, the game outside the professional ranks was indeed amateur and the highest honour any such player could achieve was to win the FA Amateur Cup. On 11 April 1931 Highbury staged the final between Hayes and Wycombe Wanderers. Hayes had battled through to the final, having played all nine of their ties away from their west London home.

A crowd of over 32,000 paid £2,222 in receipts and were treated to a close game. The only goal of the match that went Wycombe's way came ten minutes from time. Hayes defender Bill Caesar handled the ball while he lay on the ground in a goal-mouth scramble and a penalty was awarded. Bill Brown took the kick, but hit it straight at the Hayes goalkeeper; however, the ball rebounded to Alf Britnell, who fired home the winning goal.

Wycombe would pay another visit to Highbury some five years later, this time to play Casuals in the semi-final of the same competition. This time it was Casuals who were the victors and, like Wycombe before them, they went on to win the trophy. In 1939 Casuals would merge with Corinthians to form the famous club, Corinthian-Casuals.

WORLD CHAMPIONSHIP BOXING

Down the years Highbury has been the stage for many events that do not relate directly to the sport. Beyond football, the stadium has been used to stage everything from hockey (England Ladies beating USA Ladies 6–1 in 1955) to World Championship boxing fights – not least the incredible match-up between Muhammad Ali and Henry Cooper in 1966. 'Highbury Gets Into Trim for the Battle of the Century' was the *Islington Gazette* headline on Friday, 20 May. Highbury would play host to one of the biggest boxing matches for many a year as Muhammad Ali and 'Our 'Enry' got ready for a re-match of the 1963 encounter which had captivated the world.

In the days leading up to the fight, Highbury was a hive of activity as an assorted army of engineers, carpenters, electricians, scaffolders and sundry helpers raced to get the stadium into boxing configuration. By midweek the workmen had erected the stage with a square of canvas in the centre of the pitch. The ring looked insignificant as the labourers got down to the task of laying boards across the rest of the Highbury turf and installing seats around the ring to help house the 40,000 all-ticket crowd. Around 80,000 square feet of timber was laid in all. George Elliot, Arsenal's clerk of works at the time, commented, 'I've been here 30 years and never seen anything like this.'

One bonus for local residents in Highbury staging the fight was that the telephone services in the area were improved with the installation of the latest technology to ensure the fight could be beamed live back to the USA via the recently launched Early Bird satellite. Key to this was the local Cannonbury telephone exchange that had to lay a special high powered cable from the exchange into the stadium to help facilitate the broadcast and also to provide the line capacity for the phones required by the world's press.

HIGHBURY

On 21 May 1966 Highbury staged London's first heavyweight championship fight in 58 years. Residents in Aubert Court were in prime position, with a free peep show of the title fight. Henry and Minnie Harries, who lived on the sixth floor, became minor celebrities for the night as they held a party for friends and relatives and were featured in the broadcast that evening.

Cooper was a 32-year-old challenger who came into the match-up with a 32–11–1 record and a good left-hook. Cooper had almost beaten the then Cassius Clay in 1963 by knocking him down with a solid left-hook in the fourth round. The bell and a cut glove, which delayed the start of the next round, may have prevented Clay from being knocked out. As it was, that fight marked the only defeat of Cooper's career to that point.

In 1966 Ali paced himself for the first five rounds, skipping around in counter-clockwise circles and staying ahead of the slower challenger. Near the end of the second round, Cooper landed a hard two-left-hand combination to the champion's head to stir the crowd. This was the high mark for the challenger and while Cooper did deliver several more solid hits, none were in combination and none appeared to have any effect on the champion. Cooper received several warnings from the referee for hitting low, as did Ali for pushing and holding.

Things changed quickly in the sixth round as Ali looked to have woken up and decided to make more of the running to devastating effect. He quickly pressured Cooper into a corner and landed a stiff right-left to his head. This opened a wound over the challenger's left eye, resulting in a steady stream of blood. After an initial inspection the referee waved fight-on, but Ali continued to work his punches to the affected area of Cooper's head and, as the flow of blood increased, the referee signalled a halt and gave Ali victory.

THE BIG SCREEN

Highbury made it to the big screen in 1939 when *The Arsenal Stadium Mystery*, directed by Thorold Dickinson, was released, based on a book of the same name written several years earlier by Leonard Gribble. The

London-born author was prolific to say the least, having written almost 100 novels under his own name and many others under a variety of pseudonyms. Gribble was fascinated by sport at the time and many of his stories reflected this, for example *They Kidnapped Stanley Matthews*, published in 1950. The premise for the book and the film was no doubt the great success of the Arsenal side of the time, the Team of the '30s.

The central character of the film was Superintendent Anthony Slade of Scotland Yard, who had featured in 45 of Gribble's novels and who was played brilliantly by Leslie Banks, who portrayed him as mischievously eccentric. He worries about his hat and his up-coming appearance in the police show as much as he does about the murder he is investigating.

The murder itself seems to occur on the Highbury pitch. Arsenal are playing a top amateur side called the Trojans who have caused ripples throughout the English footballing world, having beaten a host of other top clubs. The game against Arsenal is deemed their ultimate test. At half time Arsenal are leading by the only goal of the game but as the second half gets under way the amateurs equalise from the penalty spot. As the game restarts, one of the Trojans' players collapses and is found to be dead.

The movie itself is quintessentially British and very tongue in cheek, and whilst it lacks any real twists it is certainly a curio for football fans, especially those following Arsenal.

The action on the field was taken from shots from an Arsenal versus Brentford game, which turned out to be the Gunners' last home game before the outbreak of the Second World War.

Disappointingly, the film doesn't use Highbury as well as it could or should have. The opening ten minutes feature the players from both sides, introducing many of them as they watch a film used to promote the charity game around the cinemas. The scenes in the dressing-room and the Marble Halls are fascinating; following this there is a lot of play, but aside from that Highbury fades into the background. Very little else occurs in the stadium itself, although there are scenes inside the various offices. There are the usual doses of staged action, including players on mazy runs, slipping past defenders without skill or effort and the scene in the treatment room underlines Herbert Chapman's far-sighted, scientific approach to caring for his players – this film coming several years after his untimely death.

George Allison and Tom Whittaker appear as themselves, and Allison is featured lecturing his team at one point, using immortal lines such as, 'Now, the Trojans will be unfamiliar to you, since they play an attacking game . . .' and 'It's 1–0 to the Arsenal. That's the way we like it.' Wonderful!

THEMED MATCH DAYS

As part of the countdown to closure of Highbury, the club staged a number of themed match days during the final season. It was perhaps fitting that the last one of these, against Wigan Athletic, was designated 'Goals Day' – on an afternoon that saw six flash into the net. Shots, a free-kick, a penalty and a hat-trick ensured a good assortment for the fans that afternoon: the only item missing to complete the set was a header.

Other themed days are listed below – unfortunately, there are a couple of serious omissions from the list: Herbert Chapman Day and Team of the '30s Day might have been expected inclusions.

THEME	OPPOSITION
Players Day	Newcastle United
Goal Celebrations Day	Fulham
European Night	FC Thun
Doubles Day	Everton
Internationals Day	Birmingham City
Wenger Day	Manchester City
European Night	Sparta Prague
Memorial Day	Sunderland
49-ers Day	Blackburn Rovers
League Cup Night	Reading
Boxers v. Jockeys Day	Ajax
Great Saves Day	Chelsea
Hat-trick Heroes Day	Portsmouth
Back Four Day	Manchester United
FA Cup Day	Cardiff City

STADIUM MISCELLANY

1913 Day	Middlesbrough
League Cup Night	Wigan Athletic
London Derbies Day	West Ham United
Home Grown Players Day	Bolton Wanderers
Managers Day	Real Madrid
Captains Day	Liverpool
Junior Gunners Day	Charlton Athletic
Decades Day	Juventus
David Rocastle Day	Aston Villa
Dennis Bergkamp Day	West Bromwich Albion
Records Day	Villarreal
Kits Day	Tottenham Hotspur
Goals Day	Wigan Athletic

NINE

International Venue

Highbury has hosted many matches that haven't involved Arsenal Football Club directly. While it has welcomed FA Cup semi-final games and European Cup replays (these particular encounters are covered in the chapters that follow), and games in the old Football League representative format – a side selected from players playing in the Football League, irrespective of their national allegiance, and matching their skills against representative teams from the likes of the Scottish and Italian Leagues. It has also set the stage for full England international matches. There have been Over-30 v. Young (typically under-23) England match-ups as well, featuring greats like Matthews, Greaves, Haynes, Flowers and Gascoigne.

ENGLAND'S HIGHBURY

Highbury staged twelve England international games in all and ironically the first three of these games contained not a single Arsenal player. In the fourth, a classic encounter known as the Battle of Highbury, there were no fewer than seven from the host club. It is therefore difficult to say that any one particular Arsenal player was the first to represent the team in an England side at Highbury. If the question needed an answer, then perhaps it should be Eddie Hapgood, since he was England captain that famous day and so would have been first onto the pitch at the very least!

The use of Highbury as an international venue was first promoted while Sir Henry Norris continued to exert his influence over the FA. He was determined to secure a game at his still relatively new stadium and many reports at the time suggest that it was simply another case of Norris using his old-fashioned business-deal mentality to get a fixture; however, in that post-Great War era England did not have a specific stadium to use as a home venue. In the immediate pre- and post-war years England had played significantly more away games than they had at home, and those home games had been at venues such as Ayresome Park (Middlesbrough), Ashton Gate (Bristol) and Stamford Bridge (Chelsea). Playing a game in north London, at that time, therefore seemed a perfectly natural extension of this policy – the fact it was at Highbury rather than White Hart Lane would certainly have been regarded as one-upmanship by Norris.

England's record at Highbury was exceptional. After having lost the first match against Wales, they went on to win nine and draw two of the dozen fixtures played there, scoring a massive forty-seven goals in the process and conceding fifteen.

Highbury welcomed Wales on 15 March 1920 as its first post-war visitors – indeed it was only England's second game after the war, having drawn 1–1 against Ireland at Windsor Park in Belfast the previous year. There were no Arsenal players in the England team and just two from London, ironically both from Tottenham. The Welsh side that day included some of the best of the time, amongst them the great Billy Meredith. Wales won the game with goals from Stanley Davies (penalty) and Richard Richards. The England goal came from Charlie Buchan – then a player with Sunderland – who would return to Highbury some years later to sign for Herbert Chapman. A near-capacity crowd of 21,110 witnessed the game. Wales went on to win that year's Home International Championship. England gradually moved north for its other two home games that season, which were staged at Hillsborough (Sheffield) and Roker Park (Sunderland).

Arguments abound regarding the selection of Highbury as an international venue again in 1923 because the date of the match was just six weeks before Wembley Stadium opened. However, Wembley was never built as a home for English Football internationals and, indeed, during the next six years only two England games would be played there. Stamford Bridge and Selhurst Park were amongst the London venues for games that continued to be taken around the country and in particular to the north of England. It wasn't until the 1952–53 season that England started to play all their London games at Wembley, and it was a few more years before all England fixtures were at the Empire Stadium.

The game on 19 March was the first in England against a 'foreign' side, more specifically one from outside the Home International countries. Belgium were the visitors on this occasion, only the second meeting between the teams. England ran out very easy winners in front of just 14,052. The amateur player Kenneth Hegan from Corinthians scored twice as England's more professional side took advantage of their fitness in the second half to cruise to a 6–1 win. Belgium had managed to equalise Hegan's early opener but his second secured a half-time lead and four more were added in the second period. The England side that afternoon still had a heavily Northern bias of players, Tottenham's James Steed being the only other Southern player in the team.

England's third game at Highbury in December 1931 pulled in a full house for the first-ever visit of Spain and again only the second fixture between the two sides. It proved to be a savaging by the Three Lions, who ran up a 7–1 scoreline. Again, it was a team without any Arsenal players.

England had cruised to a 3–0 half-time lead, helped by two goals in the opening three minutes from John Smith and Thomas Johnston. Smith added England's third and his second shortly before the interval to pretty much ensure the spoils for the host side. There was no letting up in the second half, however, as Johnson added his second. Samuel Crooks also notched a brace and Dixie Dean scored a final seventh in the dying minutes. Spain did pull one back during the second half, winger Guillermo Gorositiza the scorer.

BATTLE OF HIGHBURY

With the Team of the '30s approaching their full potential and many Arsenal players already household names, Highbury was once again chosen to host an England international encounter and the home side was full of local talent. This time Italy, recent winners of the 1934 World Cup, would be the opponents. It was the time of Mussolini, Fascism and the FA's refusal to acknowledge the World Cup as a competition of any note; as such it was a game that was a clash of arrogances: England believing they were very much the best side in the world and Italy as World Cup holders, the country's dictator claiming the victory as a triumph for his beliefs. In fact this was Italy's first game since lifting Jules Rimet and they had been beaten only four times in the thirty-four matches they had played since Vittorio Pozzo took over as manager in the second half of 1929. The two sides had played out a 1–1 draw in Rome eighteen months earlier – the only previous meeting between them.

The English press were already sounding their downfall as Mussolini's Azzurri arrived. The selection of no fewer than seven Arsenal players for the game (this was still an era devoid of substitutes) heralded the headlines 'Highbury Occasion' from the *Daily Express* and 'Arsenal Armada' from the *Daily Mirror*. The Italians, resplendent in their designer suits, were on bonuses to win: £150 a man, a brand-new Alfa Romeo and exemption from national service. By contrast the England match fee was £2, at a time when Ted Drake was still using white ribbon as a belt to maintain the position of his trousers around his hips. The game was as much a contrast of social styles as of political beliefs. The Battle of Highbury was already being played out.

The England side that took to the pitch that evening was very inexperienced at international level – there were just 38 caps across the whole team. Manchester City's Eric Brook was the most experienced player despite only winning his tenth cap that evening! Two players were making their international debuts, Arsenal's George Male and centre-forward Drake, whilst four others were making just their second England international appearance: Cliff Britton (Everton), Jack Barker (Derby County), Stanley Matthews (Stoke City) and Ray Bowden (Arsenal).

Male got his chance after Derby County's Tom 'Snowy' Cooper withdrew and Drake won the first of, amazingly, just five caps, after he took the place of original centre-forward choice Sam Tilson of Manchester City and his initial replacement, George Hunt of Tottenham Hotspur. Injuries took their toll even in these early days. As such England, through circumstance, would take the field with seven Arsenal players – at the time of writing, still a record for one club – led out by Eddie Hapgood, who was given the captain's armband for the first of 21 occasions in his career.

The Italians were at full strength and made only two changes from the team who had beaten Czechoslovakia in extra-time of the 1934 final. Carlo Ceresoli replaced veteran Giuseppe Combi in goal, returning from an injury which had sidelined him from the FIFA competition, and Pietro Serantoni replaced Angelo Schiavio. Serantoni would become a regular in the side that went on to retain the trophy in 1938. The Italians kept their three *oriundi*, South Americans with Italian nationality – Luisito Monti, Raimondo Orsi and Enrico Guaita. The Italian team was based mainly on players from two clubs – Juventus supplying five of the line-up and Ambrosiana-Internazionale three players.

Before the game the teams were presented to Prince Arthur, Duke of Connaught and Strathearn whilst the Italian Ambassador, Count Grandi, was also present. The 56,044 in attendance witnessed an incredible first few minutes – latecomers would have been livid as the two sets of players tore into one another. In the very first minute of play, Ceresoli brought down Drake and England were awarded a penalty. Eric Brook stepped up and hit his shot well enough, but the returning keeper produced a magnificent save to deny the Manchester City forward; however, within moments, Brook had redeemed himself by heading home from Britton's free-kick.

With just two minutes of play gone, Italy were reduced to ten men when Wilf Copping challenged centre-half Monti for the ball and left the naturalised Italian nursing a broken bone in his foot that forced him to leave the field. With no substitutes, Italy were facing an uphill task. The Italians were incensed and the game started to deteriorate. As the Italians lost their heads, England added two more goals inside the ten minutes that followed. Brook added his and England's second, driving home a free-kick from outside the area, and Ted Drake completed a perfect debut when he made it 3–0 just two minutes later, hooking the ball into the net and completing a fine move down the England right.

Drake's goal came whilst Hapgood was receiving treatment on the touchline following a flailing arm to the face that left him with a broken nose, which inflamed team and clubmate Copping further. The Arsenal hard man was already a cult figure amongst the Highbury faithful and legend has it that he had deliberately removed Monti from the equation, although there was no footage of the tackle at the time. The game was being covered on BBC Radio and the commentator at the time, no less than the Arsenal manager, George Allison, made light of the matter (even then managers did not see their players making mischief!).

Copping went on to give as good as any of the visiting Italians, both in a footballing and physical sense, in what was arguably his best display of his 20 appearances for his country. The game left him with a reputation that would see him christened as the ultimate football hard man. Hapgood and Monti weren't the only players to suffer broken bones that day – double goal-scorer Brook also ended the game with a broken arm and several others finished with bandages more befitting wartime action.

At 3–0 and with a man advantage England looked to be home and dry but the second half saw a more composed performance by the Italians who had obviously used the half-time interval to re-focus, although not remove, their attentions away from physical retribution. In this respect they started to show their real pedigree, more akin to their designated standing in world competition.

Italy scored twice through their Ambrosiana-Internazionale centre-forward Giuseppe 'Peppino' Meazza. With the first-half fog now replaced by heavy rain, Meazza's goals came four minutes apart around the hour mark. Skilful play by Guaita set up his first and he then headed home Attilio Ferrari's free-kick for the second. Indeed only the crossbar prevented him from a hat-trick, although there was also a string of fine saves by England keeper Frank Moss, who was making his last international appearance.

In the aftermath of the game the FA considered withdrawing from all internationals. The 19-year-old Stanley Matthews considered this 'the roughest match I ever played in'.

SETTLING DOWN

It was almost two years before England returned to Highbury, where Hungary were beaten 6–2 by a side which included three Arsenal players – Male, Bowden and Drake. Centre-forward Drake was the star of the day, notching a hat-trick in what was to be the last of his five England appearances. Brook opened the scoring midway through the first half and Jeno Vincze produced a short-lived equaliser, but Drake scored twice more before half-time to see England go 3–1 ahead at the interval. Hungary reduced the deficit to a single goal seven minutes into the second half through Laszlo Ceh, but Cliff Britton and Raich Carter scored either side of Drake's third.

It was almost another two years before the England side were back again, against a FIFA Rest of Europe side, at Highbury in October 1938. With relationships within Europe starting to deteriorate and the Second World War fast approaching, the European side was missing many of the big stars of the time. The England team featured just two Arsenal players – Hapgood and Copping – perhaps a clear indication that the Team of the '30s was nearing the end of its reign as the dominant force in English football. Two first-half goals from William Hall and Tommy Lawton in front of over 40,000 put England in the lead, and another late in the second half from Leonard Goulden secured a 3–0 victory.

International football was made virtually obsolete for a period of over six years during the war and it was approaching ten years before England returned to Highbury in May 1947 where the French were the opposition. It was the sixth international played by the England team inside six months – the game provided a good outlet for energy and was an opportunity to celebrate the return of normal competition in Europe. A national side including Tom Finney, Tommy Lawton and Wilf Mannion drew another big crowd. Full-back Laurie Scott was the sole Arsenal representative, an ever-present in the England side since international games resumed. After a goal-less first half Finney provided the lead five minutes after the restart and goals by Mannion and Carter gave England their ninth win in ten games over the French.

Later that same year Sweden were the November opposition in Islington, the side including star names such as Gunnar Nordahl and Nils Liedholm. With Arsenal's Laurie Scott continuing his impressive run at right-back, Stan Mortensen and Tommy Lawton had fired their country into a 2–0 lead inside 18 minutes, Lawton's goal coming from the penalty spot. Mortensen added a third on thirty-five minutes and England looked to be cruising until Nordahl reduced the deficit two minutes before the break. A penalty on the hour converted by Gunnar Gren brought the Swedes right back into the game and it wasn't until four minutes from time, when Mortensen completed his hat-trick, that England ensured victory with a 4–2 win. Incidentally, Thomas Nordahl, the son of Gunnar, would grace the Highbury pitch 23 years later, being a vital member of the Anderlecht team who would face Arsenal in the European Fairs Cup final in 1970.

The England side that took to the field against Switzerland in December 1948 was competing in a return fixture, having lost 0–1 in Zurich just over six months earlier. The result at Highbury, though, showed much more confidence on the English side: the eventual six-goal rout took just five minutes to get under way, with John Haines starting the scoring. The West Bromwich Albion player added his second of the night within a minute of John Hancocks's on 25 minutes to give the home side a 3–0 advantage at the interval. John Rowley made it four on fifty-five minutes and a second burst of two goals in a minute – thanks to Hancocks and Jackie Milburn – completed the rout midway through the second half. The England side that night didn't include any Arsenal players but Alf Ramsey and Stanley Matthews were in the team.

The summer of 1950 saw England take part in the World Cup in Brazil and bow out after just three games, including the embarrassing 0–1 defeat to the USA in Belo Horizonte. When the national side returned with their tails between their legs, they embarked on a series of international games that were as much about restoring pride as anything else. The third of these was at Highbury, following emphatic wins over Northern Ireland

(4–1) and Wales (4–2) in the Home International Championship. Yugoslavia were the visitors in the winter of 1950 and played out the first-ever international draw at Arsenal Stadium. The England side was captained by Alf Ramsey and from Arsenal there was just Leslie Compton, who got on the score sheet at the wrong end. This was the second of only two caps won by Compton, who had become the oldest ever England debutant when he started the aforementioned game against Wales the previous week. England took a 2–0 lead thanks to strikes from Nat Lofthouse, but five minutes before half-time Compton put through his own goal to allow the Yugoslavs back into the game. Midway through the second half Todor Zivanovic produced the equaliser.

France became the only team to feature in two England matches at Highbury when they returned to north London for a friendly international fixture in October 1951. The first game had ended in a 3–0 win for the home side but this was a much closer affair, ending all-square at 2–2. England, devoid of any Arsenal players, took the lead after just four minutes when Abdelkader Firoud put through his own goal. But after eighteen minutes of play, two goals inside a minute turned the game around, René Alpsteg and André Doye giving the French a 2–1 lead. Tottenham's Leslie Medley hit the equaliser shortly after a half-hour of play and that's the way the game ended.

It was almost ten years before another England match would be staged at Highbury and it would be the very last one hosted there. It was a World Cup preliminary-round tie as Luxembourg made their first visit to play a full international in England. The total amateurs had already lost the first leg of this tie 9–0 in Luxembourg City and the 33,409 in attendance were expecting another big score – but it didn't quite turn out that way. England cruised into a 3–0 half-time lead with Ray Pointer, Dennis Viollet and Bobby Charlton scoring the goals, although the second and third didn't materialise until shortly before the break. Then Camille Dimmer pulled a goal back for the visitors (a goal that remains, at the time of writing, the only one ever scored by Luxembourg in England!), and it wasn't until ten minutes from time that Bobby Charlton struck his second and England's fourth of the evening to give the home side a 4–1 victory.

So, Highbury closed its doors on the England full international for good with Arsenal players absent from the final two games.

* * *

Matthews, Mortensen, Lawton, Ramsey and Frank Swift took to the Highbury field on 6 May 1955 for perhaps the first match between an Over-30 England squad and it's Young version, featuring Haynes, Ron Flowers and Ronnie Clayton in its line-up. Another occasion in 1959 saw Greaves, Charlton, Haynes and Jimmy Armfield on the pitch. This game ended three-all, Young England playing in Arsenal shirts in the second half after a rainstorm in the first left their shirts sodden. Trailing 3–1 at the interval, the team's comeback must surely have been inspired by the Arsenal kit! The two sides met again in May 1962 at Highbury.

In April of 1988 the England Under-21 side staged a European Championship final game at the stadium, drawing 2–2 with France, England's goals coming from Paul Gascoigne and an own goal from Silvestre.

ARSENAL'S INTERNATIONAL GAMES

Arsenal has also played against various international-flavoured sides down the years, although these have been a little scarce to say the least. In November 1965 the Brazilian FA presented a side at Arsenal which, after much confusion, turned out to be leading club side Corinthians and not the Brazilian Select XI the organisation had promised. However Corinthians were arguably the best Brazilian club side at the time and as such represented their country well as a select side. As it was, the South Americans who turned out looked as though they could barely be bothered to go through the motions on a night where 17,789 suffered the almost intolerable cold for a match described in reports as 'pure purgatory'. A young Jon Sammels made his name with two drives to record the win.

In early August 1969 a pre-season encounter saw the Italian Under-21 side win 1–0 at Highbury. The Arsenal side that evening included Sammy Nelson, Ian Ure, John Roberts, David Court, Jon Sammels, Ray Kennedy, Eddie Kelly and George Armstrong in its ranks, although only Ure, Court, Sammels and Armstrong were first-team regulars at the time. The Arsenal team were unlucky to lose to the Italians for whom AC Milan goalkeeper Villiam Vecchi was in unbeatable form. The only goal of the game came eight minutes from full-time from substitute Guido Magherini.

In early winter 1984 Australia were on tour in Europe, and visited Highbury on 27 November. The game saw the return of John Kosmina to the ground as the Socceroos' skipper. The player from Adelaide had played three first-team games for Arsenal before returning to Australia and was playing for Sydney City when he made his return as Australia's most experienced player with 65 caps; however, it was the limited experience of Arsenal's Ralphe Meade that grabbed the headlines not just because he scored a last-minute winner but because it was his third goal in his second of two games that day. The Arsenal youngster had earlier scored twice in a win over Crystal Place in a Football Combination fixture when he came on nine minutes from time, replacing David Court, with the sides tied at 2–2. With the game in its final minute Meade latched on to Charlie Nicolas's lofted-through ball which he volleyed home.

For most of the Highbury game, the Socceroos had the better of the encounter, which barely attracted a crowd of 4,000, despite a strong Arsenal line-up. The visitors took the lead early in the half but Ian Allinson levelled things two minutes later following up Cork's shot that the keeper couldn't hold. As the game neared its final stages, the Australians again went into a lead only for Allinson to equalise within a minute.

Perhaps Arsenal's best performance, though, came in 1989 when they took on and beat France 2–0 at Highbury. The goals from Alan Smith and Martin Hayes came against a talented French side that featured Eric Cantona amongst others. The French manager that evening was Michel Platini, who was assisted by the future Liverpool boss Gérard Houllier.

REPRESENTATIVE GAMES

Highbury has seen a variety of representative games down the years, many of them being of Football League inter-league status. The first of these was held on 12 March 1921, three days short of a year since the first England international game at Highbury. This time out fans gathered to see the Football League take on the Scottish League, with players belonging to each of these two leagues selected regardless of their nationality, thus a Scotsman playing in the English Football League would have been eligible to represent the Football League team from England. The Football League side won the encounter with the only goal of the game coming off the head of Charlie Buchan.

Buchan was still a Sunderland player at this point and the lone Arsenal representative in the team was Dr James Paterson, who was ironically a Scot. The game itself was largely uninspiring for the 35,000 or so gathered, so much so that the newspapers of the time picked up on a story quite unrelated to what was happening with the scoreline: 'Dr Paterson got the cheers of the people over an unusual incident in which he was concerned when the Arsenal outside-left was presented with a bunch of daffodils by a "bright little maiden" who ran onto the pitch.'

Almost 39 years would pass before Highbury hosted another Football League fixture. Scotland were the visitors again and once more left the losing side after the only goal of the game was scored by Birmingham City's Harry Hooper. The home side had a more Southern bias this time, featuring as it did five London players: Jimmy Greaves, still a Chelsea player at this point; Dave Mackay and Cliff Jones from the other half of north London; and the great Jack Kelsey in goal and Jimmy Bloomfield the only Arsenal players in the starting line-up. Indeed it was a pretty useful-looking side, with Bobby Robson in its ranks as well. It was also quite cosmopolitan with Kelsey and Jones being Welsh internationals and Mackay a Scottish international.

On 11 March 1953 over 55,705 people turned up at Highbury to see a representative encounter between the London FA and the Berlin FA (it says a lot about the post-war pulling power of football). The Highbury floodlights were on and the crowd got full value for money in a highly entertaining encounter that saw London run out emphatic 6–1 winners.

Two Arsenal players were on show that night in the form of Jimmy Logie and Holton and they made significant contributions in both play and scoring – Forbes, who would have been a third home player, was withdrawn from the match through injury.

London took the lead straight from the kick-off when the Arsenal pair combined perfectly to present Charlton's Kiernan with the chance to powerfully drive home from just inside the area. Kiernan added a second and then his club teammate Vaughan added a brace to send London four goals to the good at the interval. Two second-half goals from Holton were split by a consolation effort by Ritter. Receipts for the game that evening totalled £30,443.

HIGHBURY'S ENGLAND GAMES

15 March 1920 England 1 Wales 2 (21,110)
Home International Championship (121st full England
  international)
Scorers: England – Buchan; Wales – Davies (pen), Richards

19 March 1923 England 6 Belgium 1 (14,052)
Friendly International (132nd full England international)
Scorers: England – Hegan (10, 26), Chambers (55), Mercer
  (77), Seed (80), Bullock (85); Belgium – Vlaminck (16)

9 December 1931 England 7 Spain 1 (55,000)
Friendly International (180th full England international)
Scorers: England – Smith (2, 44), Johnson (3, 70), Crooks
  (50, 85),
Dean (60); Spain – Gorositiza

14 November 1934 England 3 Italy 2 (56,044)
Friendly International (174th full England international)
Scorers: England – Brook (3, 10), Drake (12); Italy –
  Meazza (58, 62)

HIGHBURY

2 December 1936 England 6 Hungary 2 (36,000)
Friendly International (207th full England international)
Scorers: England – Brook (25), Drake (32, 43, 80), Britton
(52), Carter (87); Hungary – Vincze (29), Ceh (48)

26 October 1938 England 3 Rest of Europe 0 (45,000)
Friendly International (220th England international match)
Scorers: Hall (20), Lawton (39), Goulden (73)

3 May 1947 England 3 France 0 (54,389)
Friendly International (232nd England international match)
Scorers: Finney (50), Mannion (64), Carter (77)

19 November 1947 England 4 Sweden 2 (44,282)
Friendly International (238th England international match)
Scorers: England – Mortensen (15, 35, 86), Lawton (18
pen); Sweden – G. Nordahl (43), Gren (60 pen)

2 December 1948 England 6 Switzerland 0 (48,000)
Friendly International (244th England international match)
Scorers: Haynes (5, 26), Hancocks (25, 65), Rowley (55),
Milburn (66)

22 November 1950 England 2 Yugoslavia 2 (61,454)
Friendly International (261st England international match)
Scorers: England – Lofthouse (29, 34); Yugoslavia – Own
Goal (Compton, 40), Zivanovic (72)

3 October 1951 England 2 France 2 (57,600)
Friendly International (265th England international match)
Scorers: England – Own Goal (Firoud, 4), Medley (32);
France – Doye (18), Alpsteg (19)

INTERNATIONAL VENUE

28 September 1961 England 4 Luxembourg 1 (33,409)

World Cup Preliminary Round (349th England international
  match)

Scorers: England – Pointer (35), Viollett (37), Charlton (45,
  80); Luxembourg – Dimmer (67)

TEN

The FA Cup

The most famous cup competition in the world provided Highbury with some memorable games over 90 years or so. From thumping ten-goal victories to painful defeats in the final seconds of a pulsating tie, the FA Cup has rarely failed to deliver to fans who have turned out in their droves to experience some of the magic on which the competition prides itself. Much of this has been manifest in unbelievable comebacks, goal feasts, humdingers, punch-ups, last-minute penalties and, of course, Arsenal being on the receiving end of humbling Cup shocks at the hands of lower league opposition. Often Cup runs have gained momentum or spurred on the Gunners in their march towards the twin towers of Wembley or to the Millennium Stadium in Cardiff.

But Highbury has been host to other memorable Cup ties which haven't involved Arsenal – supporters of 19 clubs will remember it as the neutral semi-final venue from where they were catapulted into the final at Wembley, whilst for others it will be where they made their exit at the penultimate stage. Portsmouth and West Bromwich Albion have played in four and three Highbury semi-finals respectively with very mixed fortunes.

In addition, Highbury staged two games of the ill-fated play-offs experiment, where the losing Cup semi-finalists came together, and down the years the ground has also acted as a neutral venue to settle ties that have gone into a second replay.

No matter how the season is progressing for the sides paired together, one thing is certain: when a Cup tie has been staged at Highbury a certain magic filled the air and this seems to have intensified if it was a replay or evening game, the floodlights adding an extra flavour in themselves.

SEMI-FINAL VENUE

The selection of an FA Cup semi-final venue is often ruled by geography. This has certainly been the case down the years, and in the modern era Highbury has been used less and less as a result of its decreasing capacity and the trend to maximise revenue at national stadiums such as Wembley and the Millennium Stadium. Indeed, the days of club grounds being chosen for semi-finals now look consigned to the history books, the new National Stadium at Wembley looking to host all semi-finals from 2007.

The following table lists the FA Cup semi-finals that have taken place at Highbury. West Bromwich Albion had the most to fear from semi-final ties at the north London ground, having lost all three they played there. Portsmouth, who won two of their four ties at Highbury, drew the penultimate match at the stadium in the only tied semi-final at the ground. The last tie, Chelsea v. Wimbledon, was the only all-London encounter.

Highbury's FA Cup Semi-Finals

YEAR	TEAMS	SCORE
1929	Portsmouth v. Aston Villa	1–0
1937	Preston North End v. West Bromwich Albion	4–1
1939	Portsmouth v. Huddersfield Town	2–1
1949	Leicester City v. Portsmouth	3–1
1958	Manchester United v. Fulham (replay)	5–3
1978	Ipswich Town v. West Bromwich Albion	3–1
1981	Tottenham Hotspur v. Wolverhampton Wanderers (replay)	3–0

1982	QPR v. West Bromwich Albion	1–0
1983	Brighton & Hove Albion v. Sheffield Wednesday	2–1
1984	Everton v. Southampton	1–0
1992	Liverpool v. Portsmouth	1–1
1997	Chelsea v. Wimbledon	3–0

Arsenal greeted the news that they would stage the 1929 Portsmouth v. Aston Villa FA Cup semi-final with mixed feelings. Villa had knocked Arsenal out of the Cup in the sixth round just two weeks beforehand and reports suggest that Arsenal deserved a replay at the very least. Of course, had Arsenal prevailed in the sixth-round tie then Highbury's first semi-final would have still been some way off. As it was, Villa went into the semi-final as overwhelming favourites to make it to the final – but the Cup is about upsets and so Portsmouth prevailed with a much-disputed penalty. Smith scored from the penalty spot after the kick had been awarded when Kingdom was adjudged to have handled the ball – to most observers it looked accidental (this was in the days when a handball had to be intentional to be given).

The first half belonged to Aston Villa who did everything but score against a nervous-looking Pompey side; however, as the half progressed the 'naval side', as the press of the day described them, grew in confidence and this culminated in the penalty just before the interval. The goal clearly rattled Villa, who were a shadow of themselves in the second half. Pompey continued to grow in confidence and well deserved their win at the final whistle. The crowd of 37,147 produced receipts of £4,904 10s.

It would be another eight years before Highbury would host another FA Cup semi-final and once again one of the teams had been Arsenal's conqueror in the sixth round: this time it was West Bromwich Albion who had beaten Arsenal 3–1 at The Hawthorns a month earlier. The Baggies' opponents at Highbury were Preston North End. The Lancashire side proved much too strong in what amounted to a reasonably easy victory by four goals to one. The match was won and lost in the first twenty minutes as Preston surged on to a three-goal lead. O'Donnell scored Preston's first and third goals, with a strike from Dougal sandwiched in between. A free-kick by Robbins was touched in by Burns for Albion's goal before O'Donnell set up Dougal for the fourth.

Two years later Highbury hosted one of the last two semi-finals before the outbreak of the Second World War. Portsmouth took on Huddersfield Town, Pompey recreating their earlier semi-final success at the ground. After going behind, it took two late goals, one from new signing Bert Barlow and the other by Jock Anderson, to take them through 2–1 to their third final.

In 1949 Leicester City were just a moderate Second Division outfit struggling to escape relegation when they embarked on their historic first-ever trip to Wembley. A wonderful semi-final performance inspired by Don Revie saw them defeat League champions elect Portsmouth 3–1 to deny Pompey their own crack at the Double.

The 1958 FA Cup semi-final was a nostalgic one. It was the first time Manchester United had played in London since they had won by the odd goal in nine against Arsenal in February earlier that year. That nine-goal thriller had since been dubbed one of the great Highbury games (see page 243). Much had happened since that day, the Manchester United team having been decimated by the tragic Munich air crash.

Fulham were the opponents for the replay tie and a 68,000 capacity crowd had been expected; however only 38,000 turned up since the game was being screened on television. Given United had a depleted side, Fulham had been the favourites to progress, but the 'Busby Babes' had other ideas. Teenager Alex Dawson was the hero of the day, scoring a hat-trick – he remains the last player to have bagged three in an FA Cup semi-final – as United eventually won a see-saw game 5–3.

Twenty years later it was Ipswich Town and West Bromwich Albion who were competing for a place in the 1978 final. As Arsenal were beating Orient at Stamford Bridge, Ipswich were booking their place in the showpiece event of the year at the Gunners' home ground. It was the Baggies' 18th semi-final appearance, while Ipswich had made the last four for the first time. It was the Tractor Boys who took an unexpected lead after just eight minutes. A flowing move culminated in Mick Mills whipping in a shoulder-high cross that was headed into the roof of the net by a diving Brian Talbot. Skipper Mills himself doubled the advantage when he seized on a miscued clearance from a corner to swivel and score. A superb defensive performance by the East Anglian side seemed to have secured victory, but with ten minutes left the game burst back into life when Tony Brown reduced the deficit from the penalty spot. With West Bromwich Albion throwing everything forward in search of an equaliser, John Wark rose highest in the dying seconds to send a towering header into the back of the net and his club to Wembley and a Cup win over their afternoon's hosts.

Three years later and it was Arsenal's neighbours and bitterest rivals, Tottenham Hotspur, who would be celebrating a Highbury victory. A last-minute penalty at Hillsborough to pull the scores level at 2–2 four days earlier had denied the north London club a place in the 1981 Cup final – but they were not to be denied a second time and put on an impressive display to dispose of Wolverhampton Wanderers. An early goal by Garth Crooks did little to settle the nerves of the Spurs' fans who had made the short trip up the road. Wolves went forward in search of an equaliser only to be denied by the woodwork. The match-winning moment for the Lilywhites came just before the break when Glen Hoddle seized on a defensive error to send Crooks scampering through on goal to smash the ball past an exposed Paul Bradshaw. At last the Tottenham fans could relax in the alien surroundings of the North Bank. They even sang 'We kind of like it here' as Wembley beckoned. The match was sealed by a rasping 20-yard effort that swerved into the net from the inspirational Ricky Villa. The Argentinian would go on to light up Wembley with two goals in the 3–2 Cup final replay win over Manchester City.

In 1982 the competition saw West Bromwich Albion make their third Highbury semi-final appearance but unfortunately for them it was not third time lucky. The victors that day were Terry Venables's Queens Park Rangers side. West Bromwich Albion were the bookies' favourite but it was the hunger to prove them wrong that gave the west Londoners the edge. There was a sense of irony about the eventual match winners for QPR.

Glenn Roeder and Clive Allen had mixed views about playing the semi-final at Arsenal's ground. Both had been dubbed 'Highbury rejects' following short, unsuccessful spells at the club, none shorter than Allen, who had spent just 62 days in north London before becoming an expensive £1 million pawn in a transfer deal which took him to Crystal Palace. But any bad memories of the ground were soon forgotten as the pair combined in the 72nd minute to see the ball eventually cannon off Allen's leg straight into the back of the West Bromwich Albion net for the only goal of the game.

It was a memorable clash the following year with Brighton Hove Albion enjoying a thrilling Cup run on their way to the 1983 final. While Arsenal were at Villa Park taking on Manchester United, their home ground was awash in blue and white as the Seagulls brought 26,000 fans to town. It was a welcome relief for the south coast side who were languishing at the bottom of the First Division. Their opponents Sheffield Wednesday, meanwhile, were high in the Second Division and were relishing the chance to reach the final. Brighton took the lead through former Liverpool star Jimmy Case who was on hand to rifle Tony Grealish's back-heeled pass into the corner of the net off the underside of the crossbar.

The lead lasted just six minutes. Sheffield Wednesday equalised through Anton Mirocevic. As the Owls piled forward in search of a winner, Steve Foster, whose headband was the symbol of the Cup campaign, kept Jimmy Melia's side in the game with a superb defensive performance. It was to be Brighton's day and they grabbed the winner 14 minutes from time when Michael Robinson fired the Seagulls to the Wembley final their fans had dreamed of.

Highbury played host to its fourth successive FA Cup semi-final in 1984. In a dramatic, thrilling performance Southampton and Everton matched each other blow for blow over 90 minutes. The Saints piled forward but Steve Moran, Danny Wallace and Frank Worthington were all denied by a world-class performance by Neville Southall. The Wales international goalkeeper was equal to everything Southampton threw at him to take Howard Kendall's men into extra-time. With the match entering its 118th minute, Reuben Agboola handled outside the Southampton penalty area. Peter Reid floated the free-kick into the box, substitute Graeme Sharp nodded it on and Adrian Heath headed the ball into the far corner to provide Everton with the Wembley experience, by a single goal.

It was not until 1992 that Highbury would again host an FA Cup semi-final, but this time there would be no celebrations for either set of fans as Portsmouth and Liverpool played out a 1–1 draw. Portsmouth had arrived at Highbury with the omens (if not a League position), the south-coast side having been victorious in their previous Cup semi-final staged at Highbury, albeit many years beforehand. The game proved to be a cagey affair over ninety minutes as the two sides failed to break the deadlock. Into extra-time and the Pompey chimes rang out as Darren Anderton fired them into the lead. With time running out, Ronnie Whelan slipped home a dramatic equaliser when he was on hand to pick up the spoils after John Barnes's free-kick rebounded to him. The replay saw Liverpool win through to Wembley.

The final FA Cup semi-final ever to be staged at Highbury came in 1997 and was fittingly an all-London affair between Chelsea and perennial Cup fighters Wimbledon. Chelsea, wearing yellow on the day, ripped into the Wimbledon defence in the opening exchanges and raced ahead when Mark Hughes scored in front of the North Bank. Then came a moment of pure magic from the diminutive Italian Gianfranco Zola. In one move, he flicked the ball back and turned Dean Blackwell inside out before turning and scoring in the right-hand corner. It was one of the truly great FA Cup goals. Hughes added his second as Chelsea cruised to a 3–0 win. They would go on to beat Middlesbrough 2–0 in the final.

THE EARLY YEARS

Arsenal supporters have experienced all sorts of highs and lows down the years when it comes to the FA Cup, but Highbury's love affair with the competition took a few years to develop, the competition initially failing to produce ties of any note. Highbury staged its first FA Cup tie on 9 January 1915 when 9,000 turned up to see Merthyr Tydfil. In fact, the tie had originally been drawn as a Merthyr home game but the club had moved it from their small Welsh venue to north London. Arsenal won the match 3–0 with Henry King scoring a hat-trick.

In the early days it seemed to be the same old story for Arsenal at their new ground: they only played at home by arrangement – or rearrangement – and were unceremoniously dumped out of the competition on their travels. It was not until 1922 that Arsenal finally got to play a 'proper' home tie, which ended goal-less against QPR; however, they won the replay and a crowd of 39,421 saw John Rutherford and Henry White (who would claim two goals) score in a 3–0 third-round win over Leicester City. White bagged another goal at Highbury in the 1–1 draw with Preston North End in the next round, but Arsenal were beaten in the replay.

Arsenal fans had to wait until 1927, more than 40 years after the club's formation, before they were treated to an FA Cup run which ended with an appearance in the final. After winning by the odd goal in five at Sheffield United, Arsenal earned a home replay against Port Vale following a 2–2 draw in Burslem. A crowd of 35,781 saw Charlie Buchan grab the winner and then make the next tie at home to Liverpool safe by heading in the second in a 2–0 win.

Indeed, it was the Bs who bagged the goals for the Gunners during the 1927 Cup run: inside-forward Buchan grabbed five goals, while Jimmy Brain, who scored the first goal against the Scousers, plundered four in five appearances. And it was Billy Blyth and Jack Butler who took centre stage in the quarter-final tie against Wolverhampton Wanderers. In a close match Butler proved the unlikeliest of match winners as the centre-half powered a header from all of 25 yards into the back of the net, following Hulme's cross. It was his first and only goal in the famous Cup competition over his ten years at the club and proved enough to send the Gunners on their way through to a semi-final victory over Southampton at Stamford Bridge before falling at the last hurdle 1–0 to Cardiff City at Wembley.

By now, Arsenal, led by Herbert Chapman, had had a taste of what success might be like. They made the semi-final in the following season, losing to Blackburn after handsome Highbury victories in every round which suggested they might have gone the whole way again.

In 1930 the team finally lifted the trophy, beating Huddersfield 2–0 – under the shadow of the uninvited giant German airship Graf Zeppelin 2,000 feet overhead. They had won more on their travels than at home,

25 August 1913 and the building of the Laundry End terraces is under way. The system of rakes and risers that will form the basis of the terraces can be seen. (photo by Topical Press Agency/Getty Images)

Arsenal forward Ted Drake (centre) takes a shot at goal during a match against Sunderland at Highbury on 18 September 1937. Arsenal won 4–1 in front of a crowd of 65,635. (photo by Fox Photos/Hulton Archive/Getty Images)

Arsenal's first trophy: the FA Cup. Pictured are many of the players who would launch the club on its first Championship, led by the great Herbert Chapman. (photo courtesy of George Old)

Highbury's greatest night – 28 April 1970: Arsenal's John Radford (centre) heads to salute the North Bank after scoring the second against Anderlecht in the Fairs Cup final. (photo by Dennis Oulds/Central Press/Getty Images)

Stoke City goalkeeper Gordon Banks looks on as Charlie George celebrates with Eddie Kelly (number 12) after their victory at Highbury in the last home game of the season. (photo by Roger Jackson/Central Press/Getty Images)

Viewed from the landing, the Marble Halls of Highbury make for a magnificent sight. Central is the bust of Herbert Chapman.

The captains from three Double seasons have lined up at the top of this tunnel, waiting to take Arsenal out onto the Highbury pitch.

 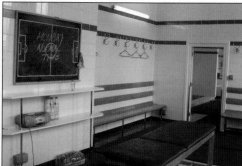

The home changing-room retains its original design and would have been an inspiration to the Team of the '30s. Its under-floor heating and huge baths have always made it popular with the players.

The West Stand was the pride and joy of Claude Ferrier. In the original design, seating was only available in the upper tier.

The delightful Highbury Hill entrance to the West Stand upper tier, housing club accommodation above. Designed by Claude Ferrier, it is pure art deco.

The entrance to Arsenal's famous Marble Halls in the stadium's East Stand. In days gone by, this would have been policed by an Arsenal commissionaire.

Match day and the North Stand dominates the local streets. Note the use of the glazed fannings to tie in with the original designs for the West and East stands.

After the debacle of the South Stand, the design of its opposite was closely monitored. What emerged was something much more in keeping with the works of Ferrier and Binnie.

All quiet on a non-match day: the East Stand can be seen in all its external splendour (this time looking up Avenell Road towards Aubert Park).

Bruce Smith outside the Highbury gates as the farewell gets under way.

Arsène Wenger: the man who has had the biggest impact on Arsenal and the club since Herbert Chapman.

As Arsenal's time at Highbury drew to a close, the emerging form of the Emirates Stadium dominated the North Bank skyline.

The North Bank rises as one to salute the final final whistle at Highbury as 93 years of memories are completed. (photo by Mandy Mead)

Red-and-white T-shirts with the slogan 'I was there' printed on them were handed out to fans making their way into Highbury for the final game. The result was amazing and set the scene for a sight never to be forgotten.
(photo by Mandy Mead)

having been drawn away in every round and won all their games at the first attempt. Cliff Bastin – who would remain Arsenal's top FA Cup scorer of all time at Highbury – became the youngest player to appear in an FA Cup final at the time, being just a month past his 18th birthday.

The holders got off to a fantastic start the following season back at their north London home: a huge ten-goal victory over Lancashire Combination side Darwen set the tone as the Gunners attempted to defend their trophy. A crowd of 37,481 saw Arsenal legend Cliff Bastin hit four, David Jack grab a hat-trick, and Jack Lambert and Joe Hulme bag a brace each as Arsenal ran out 11–1 winners. This marked the biggest FA Cup score at Highbury and Bastin's four in the game has never been bettered by a subsequent Arsenal player in the competition on his home turf. Plymouth Argyle were next at Highbury for a fourth-round tie and were dispatched 4–2 in front of a near-capacity 65,386 crowd. Wins over Portsmouth, Huddersfield and Manchester City led to a final against Newcastle, which the Magpies won.

A sensational 2–0 defeat at Walsall in the third round of the 1932–33 season will remain forever part of FA Cup folklore as the ultimate giant-killing act.

A 1–0 win at Luton the following season was the forerunner to three successive home ties. Arsenal went on to dispose of Crystal Palace before losing 1–2 at home to Derby County in the fifth round. The ties against Palace and County attracted over 65,000 paying customers each – halcyon days indeed!

Arsenal faced away draws in succession again during the 1934–35 season, the Cup run ending in Sheffield with a 1–2 defeat to Wednesday in front of almost 67,000 fans at Hillsborough. In 1935–36 Sheffield would provide the finishing point, but this time in the form of United, as Arsenal swept to Wembley and beat The Blades by a goal from Ted Drake. The highlight of the run was a three-goal replay win over Newcastle United at Highbury in the fifth round.

The defence of the Cup in 1936–37 lasted until the sixth round, where West Bromwich Albion knocked the Gunners out 3–1. When Arsenal crashed out of the Cup to Preston North End the following season in front of 72,121 fans, they could never have imagined that a barren spell of some 12 years was to follow before Highbury would see another Arsenal FA Cup tie.

By the 1947–48 season Arsenal were in the hunt for silverware again as they headed for another Championship victory. But expectations of a then unprecedented League and Cup Double were to be short-lived. A home draw against Second Division Bradford Park Avenue saw 47,738 fans packed into Highbury to watch the start of a hopefully successful Cup campaign; however, Arsenal's humble opponents had other ideas and 22-year-old winger Billy Elliott notched a first-half goal for the visitors to silence the home crowd. The visitors put up a stirring defensive display – led by centre-half Ron Greenwood, who would later manage England – to hold on for a memorable win.

SOOTHSAYER SWINDIN

Two years later and it was a much happier FA Cup experience for the home fans in a campaign focused on keeper George Swindin's predictions that seemed to keep coming true as the final approached. He started off by predicting Arsenal would go all the way to Wembley and do so with a home tie in each round. Accordingly, Sheffield Wednesday were the first visitors to north London in the third round and looked certain to get a replay, but with just 13 seconds left on the clock Reg Lewis dispatched the winner. Second Division strugglers Swansea City were next in town but proved classic underdogs on a frosty pitch as Arsenal struggled to a 2–1 win. Burnley were drawn at Highbury in the fifth round and goals by Lewis and Compton proved enough to send the 55,458 fans home happy.

Now Swindin predicted a home tie with Second Division strugglers Leeds United and so it was drawn. It was the first FA Cup encounter between the sides and was settled by Lewis again. The Gunners were through to a semi-final clash against London rivals Chelsea. Despite trailing 2–0 at White Hart Lane, Arsenal drew level and won the replay, and went on to lift the Cup, beating Liverpool in the Wembley final with a brace from Cup favourite Reg Lewis.

Once again the holders' defence of their FA Cup title was to be dashed the following season, this time at Old Trafford in the fifth round, but only after 72,408 had crammed inside Highbury to see an enthralling five-goal thriller with Northampton Town in the previous round. A Lewis double and a single strike from winger Don Roper proved enough to send the Gunners through 3–2. The following season – 1951–52 – Arsenal were beaten finalists, playing only one home tie in the process. A Lewis hat-trick and a goal from Doug Lishman (who hit three consecutive Highbury hat-tricks earlier in the season) ensured a 4–0 win over Barnsley in front of yet another bumper 70,000 crowd.

Despite clinching the League in 1952–53, the Gunners were to crash out of the FA Cup at home to Blackpool in round six, and the following season to lowly Norwich City, 2–1 in both ties. It was an unhappy time for Arsenal's FA Cup ambitions at Highbury. Throughout the late 1950s and early 1960s they were invariably knocked out of the competition on their own patch.

By 1966 the League Cup had been introduced and the Gunners enjoyed two trips to Wembley, in 1968 and 1969, but returned beaten finalists in that competition. It was not until 1971 that Highbury was to bear witness once more to the magic of the FA Cup – as part of a unique Double.

DOUBLE TIME

Arsenal would make two trips to the FA Cup final at the start of the '70s. In 1971 they reached the second leg of the Double in a Cup run that became famous for Peter Storey's penalties. Following a 3–0 scoreline at non-League Yeovil, Portsmouth were beaten in a replay at Highbury with Storey scoring the winner from the spot with just a handful of minutes remaining – he had scored Arsenal's only goal from a penalty in the original 1–1 draw at Fratton Park.

A Charlie George brace was enough to beat Manchester City 2–1 at Maine Road before Arsenal travelled to Filbert Street to slog it out with Leicester City. They had Bob Wilson to thank for escaping from the Midlands with their FA Cup hopes intact. Back in north London,

Leicester put up a steely resistance in front of 57,443 – Highbury's biggest crowd of the season. The game was settled by Charlie George, who climbed highest to head in George Armstrong's corner.

In the semi-final against Stoke City, Arsenal were trailing by two goals. A thunderous volley from Storey reduced the deficit and he held his cool to convert from the spot with the final kick of the game after McLintock's goal-bound header had been handled on the line. Arsenal won the replay with relative ease 2–0 and the players of 1970–71 secured immortality with an extra-time win over Liverpool in the final.

Arsenal would reach the 1972 final but fall short of defending their 1971 trophy win; however, the Gunners were drawn away from Highbury in each round of the Cup and only made one appearance at the ground: 63,077 witnessing a goal-less draw in a replay with Derby County. The fifth-round replay was played at the height of the three-day week and, with an energy crisis on hand, the midweek replay had to be staged in the afternoon. Thus, the crowd swelled. The gates were closed long before kick-off. Perhaps those most unfortunate that day were inside Highbury: they witnessed a thoroughly boring FA Cup. To make matters worse, they were subject to extra-time and no goals, Arsenal winning the second replay 1–0 at Leicester.

The 1977–1978 season saw another great Cup run, inspired by Malcolm Macdonald. 'Supermac' was to score in every round up to the final during that competition and opened his account with a brace in a 5–0 win at Sheffield United. Wolverhampton Wanderers were the next opponents at Highbury. It was a tense Cup-tie on a drenched, heavy pitch, but it proved to have a dramatic climax, MacDonald heading the win in the dying seconds after his marker, Bob Hazell, had been sent off seconds before.

The draw for the next round opened up memories of 1933, the Gunners' opponents being Third Division Walsall. In the days leading up to the game, the newspapers predicted a Cup upset, but it was hot air on a freezing afternoon as Arsenal won 4–1. A 3–2 win at Wrexham was followed by a 3–0 semi-final win over Orient at Stamford Bridge. It was not to be a winning year for Arsenal, despite making the final. But Highbury could still claim some credit for the eventual winners of the trophy. Ipswich Town, who would defeat the Gunners 1–0 at Wembley, played out their semi-final at their opponents' home ground.

THREE IN A ROW

The 1978 final marked the first of three FA Cup final appearances in a row for Arsenal – though sadly only one of those would result in a Gunners victory. The 1979 final with Manchester United would provide perhaps the most dramatic Cup final of all time – and the competition also saw an extraordinary start for the eventual Cup winners.

A 1–1 draw at Hillsborough in the third round saw Sheffield Wednesday make the long trip south. Wednesday were then in the Third Division and it was assumed that Arsenal would make easy progress through to the next round; however, Liam Brady had to come to the Gunners' rescue to ensure a 1–1 draw. The two sides played out three more ties at Filbert Street sharing ten goals in the second and third replays before Arsenal finally ran out 2–0 winners. Fans at Highbury had no such drama in the next round where goals from Willie Young and Brian Talbot defeated Notts County 2–0.

A 1–0 victory at Nottingham Forest was followed by a 1–1 draw at Southampton, which meant Highbury was to stage another quarter-final replay, which the home team won 2–0. Having disposed of Wolves by the same score in the semi-final the clash at Wembley seemed to be destined to a similar finish with just five minutes remaining. Opponents Manchester United, who had been outplayed, found a second wind and with just a minute remaining, squared the game at two each. Then, in a final dramatic play, Brady pushed Rix wide on the left and his cross was met at the far post by Sunderland, who steered it home to take the Cup back to Highbury.

Arsenal would make the twin towers again in the following season. Alan Sunderland started the new campaign where he had left off in the previous one, scoring against Cardiff City inside two minutes of the third-round Highbury replay. Then came one of the best goals scored by a visiting FA Cup team at Highbury as the Bluebirds launched a thrilling break that saw John Buchanan curling the ball over the oncoming Pat

Jennings. But Alan Sunderland ensured Arsenal progressed safely by converting Rix's pass to secure the win.

After seeing off Brighton, the Gunners found the steely resolve of struggling Bolton Wanderers harder to overcome, needing a replay at Highbury after a 1–1 draw at Burnden Park. A 2–1 sixth-round win at Watford set up a marathon against Liverpool in the semi-final – no fewer than four games were needed to separate the two teams. Despite all that effort, Arsenal went down to West Ham United in the final, falling to a Trevor Brooking header of all things!

It was quite a different story five years later in the 1984–85 competition. In another great FA Cup tale, Fourth Division Hereford United held the Gunners to a 1–1 draw on an icy pitch at their famous Edgar Street ground – the scene of an incredible FA Cup win over First Division Newcastle United at a time when Hereford were a mere Southern League side. Hope of an upset at Highbury was short-lived as Arsenal cruised to a 7–2 win. So, Arsenal had safely negotiated their passage. But the Gunners were soon humbled at the hands of Third Division leaders York City who won 1–0 in the next round.

GRAHAM'S CUP KINGS

When George Graham took over the reins at Arsenal, his early success was in the League Cup. He then led two title-winning sides and narrowly missed out on the coveted League and FA Cup Double when Arsenal were subjected to Wembley semi-final heartache at the hands of arch-rivals Spurs. Ironically, as Graham's side, built on solid foundations at the back, began to lose the consistency which had stood them so well en route to lifting the First Division trophy twice, the cup competitions took on huge importance for the fans and the team. With a striker who could produce something out of nothing in Ian Wright and the ability to cling on to a one-goal advantage, Arsenal were to be dubbed 'cup specialists' during the early '90s.

In 1992 a hugely embarrassing third-round exit in the Cup at the hands of lowly Wrexham brought back all the memories of Arsenal's great defeat at the hands of Walsall back in 1933; however, all this was to be banished to the past the following year. The 1993 competition started with a visit to Yeovil. This time it was to a new stadium and Ian Wright grabbed an impressive hat-trick topped off with a 30-yard chip in a 3–1 win.

Arsenal then found themselves drawn with Leeds United at Highbury where the visitors swept to a two-goal lead and the home side appeared to be crashing out of the competition. A half-time roasting saw the Gunners fight back to earn a draw and win another thriller 3–2 at Elland Road in the replay. Having disposed of Nottingham Forest in the League Cup thanks to two Ian Wright goals, the Arsenal striker repeated the feat in the FA Cup in front of the Mural. A win at Ipswich and then FA Cup semi-final revenge over Tottenham Hotspur at Wembley earned Arsenal a final spot. Their opponents in the Cup final were Sheffield Wednesday, whom they had beaten a couple of months earlier at the same venue to lift the League Cup. The FA Cup final was probably the most boring ever played and ended in a draw. The replay at Wembley failed to sell out and it needed a last-minute goal in extra-time by Andy Linighan to give Arsenal a unique Cup Double.

The following two seasons held a much different kind of FA Cup drama for fans at Highbury. Following all the slices of luck and the momentum Arsenal had gained on the north London turf during the cup runs of 1992 and 1993, the next two campaigns belonged to the underdog. A victory for the Premiership outfit at Millwall was followed by a tricky tie at First Division Bolton Wanderers. An epic tie finished 2–2 and many fans and pundits felt the chance had gone begging for the north-west side, but Bolton were inspired at Highbury to win 3–1 after extra-time.

The next season threw up a repeat of the previous third-round tie, though this time Arsenal were held to a goal-less draw at the Old Den and Millwall relished the chance for a crack at the mighty Gunners at Highbury. Arsenal succumbed for the second year, losing to lower league opposition. Two cracking strikes gave the south Londoners a 2–0 victory and bragging rights long into the night and the '90s.

THE TIE THAT NEVER WAS

By the time Arsène Wenger took over at Highbury Arsenal had suffered a few barren years in the FA Cup competition. Wenger was about to change that and the club would become almost regular participants in the final for a number of years. In fact, there would be four FA Cup wins and one losing finalist appearance in just eight years! In his first full season Wenger took Arsenal to the Double and a 2–0 win over Newcastle in the club's last Cup final appearance at the 'old' Wembley Stadium. On the way there Arsenal had been drawn at home to Port Vale and West Ham but both games were drawn and so the Cup that year was won very much on the road.

Wenger would have to wait until the fifth round of the 1999 competition before he tasted a home victory in the FA Cup and it would be one that would create FA Cup history. Sheffield United were the visitors on 13 February, and they were putting up stern resistance. Patrick Vieira headed in for Arsenal early on and after the home side had struck both posts, Sheffield United plundered an equaliser. The score was tied at 1–1 with time running out when Sheffield United goalkeeper Alan Kelly kicked the ball into touch to allow one of his players to get treatment. But when Ray Parlour threw the ball back towards the Blades' goalkeeper, Arsenal's new Nigerian striker, Nwankwo Kanu, chased the ball and managed to keep it in play before squaring to Dutch winger Marc Overmars. As Highbury stood shocked and stunned, Overmars rolled the ball into the empty net and pandemonium ensued. Manager Steve Bruce threatened to take his players off and abandon the tie, and players stood bemused by what had happened. Order was restored, the goal was awarded and Arsenal held on for a 2–1 victory. Kanu claimed he was not aware of the tradition of returning a ball after it had been kicked out to allow for treatment.

However, minutes after the full-time whistle Wenger made footballing history by offering to re-play the tie. The FA agreed to the request in the interests of good sportsmanship. The purists suggested the game should be replayed in Sheffield but it was in fact the original game that was being *re-staged* rather than replayed. Ten days later the two sides met again at

Highbury for an eerily similar game. Once again Overmars struck but this time Arsenal did manage to pull further ahead through an exquisite Dennis Bergkamp chip and, while the visitors did pull a goal back, Arsenal went through by the same 2–1 scoreline.

A 1–0 win over Derby County – the goal scored by Kanu – set up a classic FA Cup semi-final with Manchester United, which Arsenal's rivals won in a classic replay at Villa Park which saw Arsenal denied a win when Bergkamp's last-minute spot kick was saved, setting up Ryan Giggs's spectacular extra-time winner.

MILLENNIUM SUCCESS

Having entered the new millennium, the FA Cup final was soon given a new venue – the Millennium Stadium in Cardiff. Chelsea had been the last club to win the trophy at the old Wembley and they were drawn against the Gunners at Highbury the following year in the fifth round. Indeed, Chelsea would become regular visitors to Highbury and in the competition over the next few years as Arsenal became the FA Cup side of the new century.

The FA Cup campaign began in Carlisle, with the Gunners victorious 1–0, followed by a 6–0 thumping of QPR at Loftus Road. A home draw provided holders Chelsea as the opposition and after a goal-less first half, Thierry Henry opened the scoring from the penalty spot. The goal seemed to wake up the visitors and ten minutes later Jimmy-Floyd Hasselbaink beat David Seaman with a superb right-footed shot from the edge of the box. Arsenal substitute Robert Pires broke the deadlock as the second half entered its final phase, flicking a long ball from Igor Stepanovs past the advancing Carlo Cudicini. Five minutes from time Sylvian Wiltord wrapped up the tie.

Wiltord was on target again as the Gunners saw off Blackburn 3–0 at Highbury; Tony Adams and Robert Pires grabbed the others in a comfortable victory. A semi-final win over rivals Tottenham Hotspur gave Arsenal a place in the first final held in Cardiff. The Gunners seemed to be heading for a winning start courtesy of Freddie Ljungberg's goal until they were left heartbroken by two late strikes from Liverpool's Michael Owen.

But 2001 signalled the start of Arsenal's love affair with the Welsh stadium, which would prove much kinder in the following years: the club won the Cup three times in four years. Some form of revenge over Liverpool was forthcoming as a rare headed goal by Dennis Bergkamp proved to be enough to knock the holders out of the competition in the fourth round. Gillingham were dispatched 5–2 and a Dennis Bergkamp master class saw Arsenal past Newcastle in a sixth-round replay at Highbury 3–0. Arsenal went on to defeat Middlesbrough with an own-goal in the semi-final at Old Trafford before lifting the FA Cup – days before clinching the Premiership title – with a 2–0 win over Chelsea in Cardiff.

Amazingly, Chelsea were drawn against Arsenal for the third successive season as they attempted to retain the trophy in 2002–03. This time it was at the quarter-final stage and Arsenal again proved to be Chelsea's FA Cup nemesis in a pulsating tie at Highbury shown live across the nation on a Saturday night. First blood went to Chelsea when centre-back John Terry headed home Jesper Gronkjaer's cross in the third minute. The home side's response was instant and they soon had a penalty when Cudicini was adjudged to have fouled Francis Jeffers; however, the Italian made up for his error by saving Henry's spot kick – perhaps remembering the one he faced two seasons before. The Gunners drew level on the 36-minute mark when Jeffers pounced to bundle the ball home after Ljungberg had his shot blocked.

Despite his spot miss, Henry was in breathtaking form and scored a remarkable goal in the last minute of the half. A hopeful punt upfield saw Henry scampering through as the visitors failed to catch the charismatic forward offside. He turned to receive the ball and as it landed at his feet he spun 180 degrees around the on-rushing goalkeeper before guiding the ball into the empty net.

Chelsea were not to be defeated, however, and grabbed a late equaliser when Campbell's attempted clearance struck Frank Lampard and rolled into the net. The Gunners won the replay 3–1 at the Bridge and advanced to the semi-final where they saw off Sheffield United – this time in less controversial circumstances. A Pires goal from close range settled the final 1–0 over Southampton and the FA Cup returned to Highbury.

For the 2003–04 season there was much talk about Arsenal possibly becoming the first team to win three successive FA Cups and, given the form of the Untouchables, as they became known, it looked a distinct possibility; however, it was not to be. A week of inconsistency in both FA Cup and Champions League saw Arsenal relinquish their Cup crown to Manchester United in the semi-finals.

After hammering Leeds United 4–1 at Elland Road, next the Gunners took on a Middlesbrough side that came to London in the fourth round hoping to revive their season. But they found a record-breaking Arsenal side in an unforgiving mood and were similarly disposed of. Almost inevitably Chelsea would be FA Cup opposition and were once again dispatched at Highbury. Adrian Mutu hit an exquisite curling shot past Jens Lehmann to send Chelsea in with a half-time lead, which was pegged back early in the second half when José Antonio Reyes, a recent signing from La Liga club Sevilla, unleashed a rapier-like drive which arrowed into the far top corner of the net. Within five minutes the Spaniard had doubled his account and sent Chelsea out of the Cup as he ghosted on to a Patrick Vieira pass. Arsenal destroyed Portsmouth 5–1 at Fratton Park in one of the performances of the season but finally fell to a Paul Scholes strike at Villa Park against Man United in the last four. And so ended a sequence of almost three years without a defeat in the competition.

However, the circle came around again as Arsenal inflicted revenge on the Red Devils by defeating them in the 2005 FA Cup final – the first ever to be decided by a penalty shoot-out. Skipper Patrick Vieira ensured the Cup was on its way back to Highbury with the winning spot kick after Lehmann had saved from Scholes. The shoot-out ended 5–4 after a goalless 90 minutes and extra-time.

Stoke City had been beaten at Highbury in the third round and Wolverhampton Wanderers were similarly dismissed. That year it was Sheffield United's turn to be reunited with Arsenal. The Championship side earned a draw at Highbury and Arsenal needed penalties to get through the replay. A win at Bolton was followed by a 3–0 defeat of Blackburn Rovers in the semi-final to set up the final showdown with Manchester United.

Arsenal completed their penultimate year at Highbury with yet another trophy in the boardroom cabinet. It marked the tenth time the world-famous Cup had made the journey to north London and made sure that one trophy would be on show during the final year of the stadium's life.

Any hopes, though, that the fabulous old trophy would find its way across the road into the Emirates Stadium were dashed after just two rounds of the competition. Given that it was a Welsh team – Merthyr Tydfil – that provided Arsenal with their first FA Cup opposition at Highbury in January 1915, it was perhaps fitting that the final Highbury opposition in the competition should also be from that part of the world.

Two early goals by Robert Pires helped to see off a stubborn Cardiff City side 2–1. The game was Arsenal's 142nd in the competition at Highbury, with 92 having been won along the way.

A trip to Bolton to face a rejuvenated Wanderers proved to be the end of the road though: with Arsenal having to field a side devoid of players due to injury, suspension and players off on African Cup of Nations duty, the club's amazing run in the competition was extinguished by a late winner from the home side.

THIRD PLACE PLAY-OFFS

For some strange reason, in the early '70s the FA decided it would be worthwhile staging a third-place play-off game between the losing FA Cup semi-finalists. The original concept was for the game to be a curtain raiser for the FA Cup final itself, played on the Friday night. Needless to say, the concept didn't last too long. However, the games are part of FA Cup history and the first-ever third-place game was staged at Highbury. Barely 15,000 turned up to see Brian Kidd score twice as Manchester United beat Watford.

Highbury was the venue for the 1973 play-off game, though it had now been transformed into a curtain raiser for the season as Arsenal took on Wolverhampton Wanderers. Arsenal were seeking their third final in succession in 1973 but had come unstuck to Sunderland. They didn't fare any better in the play-off, Wolves winning 3–1.

ELEVEN

European Encounters

For many, the first taste of European football in north London came in the immediate aftermath of the Second World War. The fabulous Dynamo Moscow side of that era were embarking on a tour of England and generally demolishing the teams put in front of them with an amazing mix of skill and power. One of the aspects of the tour the Dynamoes had insisted on was to have an encounter with the world-renowned Arsenal – a testament to the incredible reputation of the Team of the '30s. Sadly, the famous side was no longer available and many of the Arsenal players had yet to return to British shores, let alone get back into competitive football. Equally disappointing was that, contrary to the beliefs of many, the game did not take place at Highbury but at Arsenal's wartime home of White Hart Lane: Arsenal Stadium was still far from ready to resume its normal routine. It is a great shame because accounts of the 4–3 Russian win prove it was a game that would certainly have made a fitting start to the quest for Europe.

As it was, a series of fixtures against European opposition didn't take place for several years, and many of these were staged under the new and increasingly popular Highbury floodlights. Many European teams have since visited Highbury outside UEFA competition, some to support testimonial fixtures and pre-season knockarounds, such as the Mikita tournament, but these early encounters were as competitive as non-competition football could be at that time and there was a mystique about the visitors which gave the club the opportunity to generate some extra cash. Indeed, it was not unusual for the *Matchday Programme* to cost twice as much at these encounters. The public's attention to these matches quickly waned and attendances were little more than average; however, those who did attend often had the opportunity to see some of the greatest names in the game, many of whom were already legends.

Herbert Chapman's forays into Europe to investigate new ideas and methods led to a number of early European encounters at Highbury. As early as 4 December 1933 Arsenal played against a first Vienna XI at Highbury in front of a capacity crowd; however, it was after the war that matters became more serious. One of the first to display their skills were Spartak Moscow: the game was settled on a cold November evening in 1954 with a much-disputed penalty, ending the game 2–1 in the Russians' favour. The home team deserved a draw, but despite big gaps in the visitors' defence Arsenal couldn't find the back of the net. The main talking point after the game was the visitors' level of fitness, which was more than apparent on the evening, although Arsenal manager Tom Whittaker countered this in post-match reports, saying that his side's fitness was every bit as good as Spartak's and describing the Gunners' first-half performance as possibly the best of the season to date.

In October 1959 London was celebrating Swiss Fortnight – a festival of all things Swiss – and Arsenal hosted Grasshopper to mark the occasion. As it transpired, the Zurich-based side had a defence with more holes in it than Swiss cheese and Arsenal won both halves 4–1 to accrue an emphatic 8–2 win. Len Julians – a stand-in for normal centre-forward David Herd – took his chance with five goals, two coming in the first half. John Barnwell scored in each half and Gordon Nutt completed the Arsenal rout. Volanthen and Robbiani scored for the visitors in a game that attracted 18,006.

Dynamo Kyiv provided more Russian opposition in late November 1961, but despite their having recently won the Russian championship, only 17,500 turned up for the game, which ended one-all. Arsenal were dominant in the first period and George Eastham put the home side into a 25th-minute lead with a drive from outside the area. The second half was a complete reversal, as the Russians dominated play with Lobansovsky, a six-foot-four winger, giving Arsenal right-back David Bacuzzi a torrid time. The inevitable equaliser came on 55 minutes, when Trojanovsky curled the ball in off the upright. The visitors had plenty of opportunities to win the game, but could not find the net.

Real Madrid came to Highbury on 13 September 1962 for an encounter that saw some of the greatest names in European football on display, including Alfredo Di Stefano, Ferenc Puskas and José Santamaría. The *galacticos* had an easy win, with Terry Neill given a roasting by an ageless Di Stefano who inspired his club's 4–0 victory. Real skipper Francisco Gento scored twice, Puskas was credited with the third after a series of deflections and Davaik scored the fourth.

It was lined up as the 'Old Pals Reunion', as Dynamo Moscow returned to north London in November 1965, this time for a prestige friendly at Highbury. Fresh from having humbled both Newcastle United and Stoke City, Dynamo found Highbury a different matter as Alan Skirton emerged the star performer in Arsenal's 3–0 win. According to the *Islington Gazette* report, Skirton was 'shooting, dashing and tumbling to warm the cockles of 20,000 hearts'. Skirton opened the scoring with a blistering 20-yard drive before John Radford headed home a brilliant second just before half-time. The Russian side didn't threaten the Arsenal goal and it was left to Peter Storey to add his first senior goal a minute from full-time to complete the rout.

With UEFA gaining strength and the bigger clubs seeing the potential rewards of competitive European football, the days of the high-profile 'friendly' were soon consigned to the past and a variety of cups, then leagues came into being.

EUROPEAN REPLAY

For most Arsenal fans the first competitive European encounter at Highbury came when the amateurs of Staevnet Copenhagen arrived in the autumn of 1963 to play in the first-round second leg of the Inter

Cities Fairs Cup, as it was then called (later to become the European Fairs Cup and then the UEFA Cup); however, whilst this was Arsenal's first competitive encounter in Europe at home, it was not the first played at the stadium. Indeed, Highbury had staged games in both the Inter Cities Fairs Cup and European Cup prior to the arrival of the Danish team – or the Arsenal team for that matter!

The original concept of the Inter Cities Fairs Cup was not the dynamic moneyspinner that evolved into the UEFA Cup many years later, but one to promote commerce and fellowship between European cities that held trade fairs. At the time London was staging the motor show and radio and television show, along with a multitude of industrial exhibitions, and was naturally included. It was in 1955 that the London Football Association put forward an entrant for the Inter Cities Fairs Cup competition, as did Birmingham. However, you will not find any winners of the competition that year: it made a slow, somewhat discouraging start. It was three seasons before the second leg of the final was completed, not least because the major club sides had first call on their players and so getting a team together was often a problem. London reached the finals of that inaugural competition but lost out to Barcelona 8–2 on aggregate.

Of course, the London side – which in many reference books is shown erroneously as Chelsea – invariably contained Arsenal players. The semi-final of that first competition pitched London against Lausanne and was played at Highbury on 23 October 1957, thus making it the first European competition to be staged at the stadium. The first leg had seen the Swiss win 2–1 at home with the London team winning the return 2–0 and progressing to the final 3–2 on aggregate. The team at Highbury for the second leg of the semi-final featured four Arsenal players – Jack Kelsey, Stan Charlton, Bill Dodgin and Cliff Holton. Chelsea's Jimmy Greaves opened the scoring for London after just ten minutes, levelling the tie on aggregate before home favourite Holton fired in the aggregate winner after seventy-six minutes.

Barcelona won the final, with the London leg of the tie being staged at Stamford Bridge. Arsenal players in the first leg included Jack Kelsey and Vic Groves. Kelsey was still in goal for the second leg, where he conceded six goals. His other Arsenal teammates in the side that night were Bowen,

Groves and Jimmy Bloomfield. That London side also included Jim Lewis, an amateur player with Walthamstow Avenue (now many times merged to form Dagenham and Redbridge).

RANGERS REPLAYS

A few years later, in the 1959–60 season, Highbury staged the first of two European Cup games, neither of which involved Arsenal. In those fledgling days of the competition results were settled by games and, as such, any matches tied on aggregate went to a third deciding game. That is what happened in the quarter-final tie between Glasgow Rangers and Sparta Rotterdam. Rangers had travelled to Rotterdam for the first leg with Wilson, Baird and Murray scoring the goals that gave the Gers a 3–2 advantage to take back to Ibrox, and with a semi-final place looking a formality. It wasn't to be. A goal from Van Ede secured a 1–0 win for Sparta to level the tie 3–3 on aggregate.

Highbury was chosen as the venue for the replay on 30 March 1960 and drew 34,176 – the majority being Rangers supporters. Sparta took the lead after just seven minutes of play, Verhoeven heading home from a corner kick. He then equalised 26 minutes later, slicing the ball into his own net while trying to clear a free-kick from Wilson. Rangers took the lead 11 minutes into the second half when Baird drove home from all of 25 yards after a headed clearance fell at his feet. Midway through the second half the Sparta keeper was again beaten by one of his own players when Van der Lee deflected the ball from a cross – this time the goal was credited as an own goal. Cosselaar converted a penalty kick to reduce the deficit with less than 15 minutes remaining and although Sparta looked to force the game into extra-time, the Gers held out and progressed to the semi-finals.

UEFA also chose Highbury as the venue for another Rangers replay – this time against Red Star Belgrade (or Crvena Zvezda Beograd to give them their Serbo-Croat name) in a preliminary-round replay of the 1964–65 European Cup. Rangers had won 3–1 at Ibrox but went down 4–2 in Belgrade. Tied at five-all, the replay at Highbury went the way of the Glasgow side, 3–1, with two goals for Forrest and one for Brand.

GETTING COMPETITIVE

It was perhaps fitting that Arsenal should celebrate their 50th anniversary at Highbury with their entrance into European competition, although the club's first two encounters at home did little to indicate what was to follow a few years later. A seventh-place finish in the League in 1962–63 was enough to qualify the club for the forthcoming Fairs Cup, where, as we have seen, they were paired with part-timers Staevnet. The side was a combination of amateurs drawn from various Copenhagen clubs playing under the one name. Staevnet was the organisation of the then International Football Combination in Copenhagen and Arsenal had played them many times as part of pre-season tours in Denmark. Arsenal's association with this Danish side came from Herbert Chapman, who first took the Huddersfield Town side he managed there in 1922 and continued the tradition when he moved to manage Arsenal. As for the match, it went the way of 14 of the 15 previous games between the clubs (there being a single 1–1 draw in 1931). Around 15,000 crammed into the Copenhagen stadium as Arsenal swept the home side away 7–1.

The return at Highbury almost a month later at the tail end of October was a formality and only 13,569 turned up to see the foregone conclusion. But whilst the tie was never in doubt, the Danish concoction of 'office, factory and shop workers' played out of their skins to draw 2–2, then secured their first-ever win over Arsenal with a third goal just two minutes from time!

Arsenal nevertheless moved on to the first leg of a second-round tie with Standard Liège at home. Once again the home support wasn't overly enthusiastic, with just 22,003 turning up to see a game that had Bob Wilson in goal. The would-be Scot was in his first season at Highbury and was playing as an amateur at the time – little did he know then that his next run out in goal would lead to European glory. Arsenal's goal that night was hit by Terry Anderson after 67 minutes (Anderson would only ever score two goals for Arsenal in his three-season career at the club) and cancelled out an 11th-minute strike by Kilola, which had given the Belgians the lead.

Jim Furnell, who had recently signed from Liverpool for £15,000, was in the Arsenal goal for the return leg, which Arsenal lost 1–3. Furnell was the third keeper Arsenal had used in European ties that season – Iain McKechnie being the other. As an aside, McKechnie had been signed from Southend United a couple of seasons beforehand as an outside-left, but after dominating in goal in practice matches, he got his chance in between the sticks thanks to George Swindin! McCullogh had given Arsenal the lead on 32 minutes, but the Royal Football Club was simply too good and hit three without further reply.

EUROPEAN GLORY

It would be six years before Highbury fans would get another chance to experience European competition again, but the wait would be well worthwhile. This time there was a new manager in charge – Bertie Mee – and for the first time in many years there was a degree of expectancy about the club. Much of this was simply down to the organisation that Mee installed and also the fact that a number of useful-looking youngsters were coming up through the ranks.

Cup glory had looked a distinct possibility for the side. Having reached two League Cup finals and lost both, Mee's team had a real sense that this was a make-or-break year. Smarting from a 3–1 defeat by Swindon Town in the 1969 League Cup final, the side had seen their form go from strength to strength and fourth place in the League in 1968–69 saw Arsenal up for a European Fairs Cup place. (UEFA rules at the time only permitted clubs from the top division to participate in the Fairs Cup, so Swindon – then from the old Third Division – were excluded.) Arsenal's season was about to unfold through six single games at Highbury as the ghosts of seventeen years were laid to rest. Many, including ex-players, said these games laid the foundations for the Double that was to follow on the back of it.

Arsenal's first opponents were not exactly 'European', playing as they did under the Union flag; Glentoran would have argued, though, they had a greater European pedigree than Arsenal, having played in top UEFA competitions for several years. The only players to remain from the

Gunners' previous European encounters were George Armstrong (v. Staevnet) and David Court (v. Liège), and both were in the starting line-up that September night in 1969. Amongst the Glentoran players appearing that night was the striker Tom Morrow, but thoughts of another day were dismissed quickly enough as Arsenal cruised to a 3–0 win and, although they lost the return in Belfast, went through 3–1 on aggregate.

In the second round Arsenal were drawn against Sporting Lisbon. It was a tight goal-less affair in the Alvalade Stadium – partly thanks to a great penalty save by reserve keeper Geoff Barnett – and Arsenal returned to Highbury confident but also in the knowledge that they had never won the second leg of a European tie to that point. The game was pretty much over by half-time, as the side recorded a second 3–0 home win. Rouen provided the third-round opposition and a 0–0 draw in northern France put minds at ease for the return leg. Supporters arrived at Highbury buoyed by the recent signing of Peter Marinello, who was making his Highbury debut. The crowd of 38,018 witnessed a tense affair that was settled in the last minute of play by a rare headed goal from Jon Sammels.

In the quarter-finals Arsenal drew Dinamo Bacau, possibly the weakest team of the remaining eight, and a 2–0 win in Romania virtually settled the tie. The second leg at Highbury didn't draw the biggest crowd, but the 35,342 there were tingling with anticipation with a semi-final berth in a European competition just 90 minutes away. That evening the home side produced one of the best performances of the season and hit the visitors for seven. John Radford, Charlie George and Jon Sammels all scored twice, with George Graham netting the other.

That Arsenal were now in the European big-time could be in no doubt. On 8 April 1970 Ajax arrived at Highbury for the first leg of the semi-final. They had been losing finalists in the European Cup the previous year and were themselves on the verge of greatness. Their starting line-up that night included Johan Cruyff, Ruud Krol, Dick Van Dijk and Piet Keizer; in fact, the side featured six of the Dutch side who had drawn 0–0 with England at the start of the year. The crowd of 46,271, with a large contingent from Amsterdam, was as fired up as any to be visiting Highbury, not least for the opportunity of seeing the 23-year old Cruyff, who had just been the subject of a £200,000 bid by Barcelona.

Arsenal knew that they needed the right result in north London and with fourteen goals scored and just one conceded at home in the previous rounds, confidence was sky high. Playing in a changed strip of yellow and blue, their prospects received a boost after just 16 minutes when a speculative long-range effort by Charlie George ended up in the back of the net. It was a lead that didn't look too solid when Cruyff slipped around Wilson to push the ball goalwards for the equaliser, but as the brilliant Dutchman turned away, arm aloft in triumph, Frank McLintock appeared from nowhere to collect the ball and bring it out.

In the second half Highbury rose as Arsenal sought a second goal. It came when Sammels broke free on the right and in front of the North Bank hit his first shot off the keeper's legs and then drilled the ball into the far corner of the net. Within three minutes George Graham was tripped in the area and Charlie George stepped up to score low to the keeper's left in what was his first-ever Arsenal penalty. With a 3–0 advantage for the second leg, the tulips of Amsterdam never really had a chance to bloom as Arsenal defended heroically and, despite a 17th-minute goal by Gerrit Murhen, the lead never looked like being overturned. Ajax were beaten 3–1 on aggregate. But the Dutch side would have revenge on an even bigger stage in just a few years.

Arsenal were in their third final in three years and the pubs around Highbury that night were full of belief that this would be third time lucky after League Cup final defeats. Belgian side Anderlecht were to be their opponents and the draw gave Arsenal the advantage of staging the second leg at Highbury. The first game quickly turned into a nightmare with Anderlecht taking a 3–0 lead. With eight minutes remaining eighteen-year-old Ray Kennedy, a substitute for Charlie George, headed home a George Armstrong cross to reduce the deficit and give Arsenal a vital away goal.

THE GREATEST NIGHT

Tuesday, 28 April 1970 was the team's date with destiny. It was to be Highbury's greatest night. It wasn't a full house, but it was close: 51,612, the biggest gate of the season. Highbury had never been as loud and noisy as it was that night, nor has it since. Ask anyone who was there: it will bring a shiver to his spine. The *Matchday Programme* for the final included a half-page picture showing Joe Mercer with the FA Cup and a banner that read: 'The last major Cup trophy to come to Highbury'. The away goal meant that Arsenal needed two goals without reply to make the caption obsolete.

The game lived up to the occasion, the setting and the noise. George Armstrong – who never had a bad game – played his best ever. Time and time again his jinks down either flank of the Highbury pitch left Belgians in his wake. The first goal was important and it came on 25 minutes when, following a cleared corner, Eddie Kelly took a pass from McLintock, transferred the ball from his left to his right foot and then hit a long-range effort high into the net. It was not dissimilar to the opening goal by Charlie George against Ajax at the same Clock End.

The second half began where the first had left off. Thomas Nordahl's shot early on hit the post and was a timely warning. With less than 20 minutes remaining and the seething mass of the North Bank trying to suck the ball forward, George Graham fed it wide on the left to the advancing Bob McNab who crossed the ball deep into the penalty area. Racing in with arms widespread either side of him, John Radford met the ball high above the defence and powered it down into the net. Radford then set off on his trademark air-punching run as he and Charlie George led the celebrations in front of the North Bank, releasing years of pent-up frustration.

The goal meant that Arsenal were ahead on aggregate. Anderlecht had to score. In reality this meant that Arsenal could do with a third goal to at least ensure they couldn't lose if the visitors managed a goal. And almost from the restart, with the stadium still buzzing from Radford's header, Arsenal won the ball and Charlie George held it deep on the left before delivering the pass of the night. Sweeping the ball 50 yards or so across the pitch, he found Jon Sammels racing forward – the quality of the delivery was superb, taking the defender out in the process. The Arsenal number 8 controlled it brilliantly high on his chest before advancing in from the angle and in almost a perfect replica of his third goal in the semi-final nestled the ball in the back of Jean Trappeniers' net. Two goals in a minute made it 3–0 and the Belgian side didn't know what had hit them. What followed can only be described as delirium, as fans and players alike celebrated with unbridled joy as 17 barren years without a trophy were swept away at the sound of a single whistle. To have produced a display of such style, dedication and passion in N5 simply added to the occasion.

DEFENDING CUP WINNERS

Had Anderlecht scored to level the tie at 4–4 that night and had it remained that way after extra-time, then a replay would have taken place at Highbury on Tuesday, 5 May. At this stage in European football, when no team could be named winner after two legs, away goals and extra-time, it was decided by the simple toss of a coin.

The penalty kick rule was introduced the following season – when Arsenal set out for their Double and also looked to defend their precious trophy – however it would be another rule that would bring their aspirations to a quarter-final end.

Arsenal's first opponents in 1970–71 Fairs Cup were Lazio. The first leg was played in Rome and was an ugly affair that led to a lot of press talk about the return at Highbury. Arsenal had led 2–0, thanks to John Radford, but some curious refereeing and in the last few minutes a ludicrous penalty decision for handball – after McLintock had clearly headed the ball clear – saw the game end 2–2. Disputes between the players continued long after the game had finished and it was a surprise that the return was a sedate affair settled with strikes by Radford and Armstrong: Arsenal were through 4–2 on aggregate.

Austrian side Sturm Graz were the next opposition and proved to be as hard to dispose of as Rouen had been the year before. A relatively easy game had been predicted but Sturm scored the only goal in the first leg, leaving Arsenal looking for two in the return. Given that Arsenal had scored twenty-nine goals and only conceded two in their Highbury games to that point, the expected turnaround looked a foregone conclusion. But it was far from it, and although Ray Kennedy gave Arsenal a first-half lead on the night and equalled the aggregate score, in front of an increasingly frustrated home crowd Arsenal simply could not find a way past the part-timers. It was a late penalty from Peter Storey that separated the sides. Beveren-Waas were at Highbury for the first leg of the third round and in amongst the Christmas songs they didn't put up much of a fight, going down 4–0 – Graham and Sammels scoring one each and Kennedy managing two – which was the aggregate conclusion after a goal-less draw in Belgium.

In the quarter-finals FC Cologne provided the opposition. The first leg at Highbury was under the control of Hungarian referee Istcan Zsolt, who had already made his name in English football history as the referee who famously sent off the Argentine defender Rattin in the 1966 World Cup encounter between England and Argentina. The game that evening featured other players of note from that World Cup: Wolfgang Overath for one, along with Wolfgang Webber, who scored the dramatic late equaliser for West Germany that sent the final into extra-time. The German side frustrated at every opportunity over the two legs, especially at Highbury where Arsenal should have built an unassailable lead. Frank McLintock opened the scoring midway through the first half but with almost the last kick of the first half, full-back Karl-Heinz Thielen equalised and scored what was to be a knockout away goal. There was all-out attack in the second half but desperate defending limited the home team to one more goal: Peter Storey's flying volley home from the edge of the area late in the game. In the second leg Biskup converted a fourth-minute penalty. It was the only goal of the game and the Germans held on for an away-goal win.

EUROPEAN CUP DEMISE

Highbury had seen two European Cup games long before Arsenal staged their first at the stadium. Norwegian side Strömsgodset IF Drammen were the visitors and already 1–3 down from the first leg in Oslo, where Peter Simpson scored a rare goal. With the tie already in the bag, Arsenal cruised to a 4–0 win, 7–1 on aggregate overall. Goals were again easy to come by in the second round. Kennedy and Graham scored within two minutes of the start and the end to secure a 2–0 win in Zurich over Grasshopper, whilst goals either side of the interval from Kennedy and George were added to by Radford for a 3–0 win in north London late on.

The quarter-final draw paired Arsenal with their Fairs Cup semi-final opponents from two years previously: Ajax, who were the reigning champions of Europe. Arsenal returned to Highbury for the second leg in great spirits, having kept the score at 1–2, and notched a vital away goal. Indeed, Arsenal took the lead in Amsterdam with a Ray Kennedy goal and were very unlucky to lose the game. The second leg at Highbury was full of anticipation but took a disastrous turn with 16 minutes gone when a mix-up between George Graham and Bob Wilson gifted the visitors a goal and the tie. Graham, defending deep, rose to cut out a cross on the edge of the area. Unchallenged, he decided to nod the ball back to Wilson in the Arsenal goal. Unfortunately, Wilson had come too far out of his goal looking to take the cross, hesitated, and was stranded when the ball bounced past him and into the empty net. Ajax would go on to retain their trophy and indeed claim a third in successive seasons as one of the all-time great sides emerged.

It was six long years before Highbury would stage another night of European football. The 1978–79 season opened with the UEFA Cup beckoning for Arsenal. Now under the managership of former player Terry Neill, the club qualified courtesy of a fifth-place finish in the League the previous season. East German side Lokomotiv Leipzig provided the first opposition at Highbury but were dispatched 7–1 on aggregate.

The next two rounds provided late drama at Highbury with vastly different results. In the second round Arsenal were drawn away at Hajduk in the first leg and returned from the encounter in Split with a vital away goal scored by Liam Brady. Trailing 2–1, the side looked to be heading for a goal-less draw at Highbury until Willie Young headed home the 'winning' goal just eight minutes from time. Red Star Belgrade were next up and again Arsenal returned to Highbury one goal behind – 0–1 this time, without an away goal – but Alan Sunderland relieved the mounting pressure with a goal midway through the second half. Then with extra-time just three minutes away Savic fired in an equaliser for Red Star and sent Arsenal out of the competition. Lining up on the opposition side that evening was a player known as 'Little Pigeon' – Vladimir Petrovic – who would later become one of the first foreign footballers to play for Arsenal.

CUP-WINNING DISAPPOINTMENT

The following season saw Arsenal make their debut in the Cup-Winners' Cup, following a last-gasp Wembley win over Manchester United. The side dispatched of their Turkish opponents Fenerbache in the first match of the competition and went on to do likewise with 1.FC Magdeburg and IFK Göteborg in a rather uninspiring run to the final, in which they were drawn at home first in each round. Arsenal met Juventus in the semi-finals, the Italians arriving with a supreme defensive record having only conceded a single goal in the previous rounds. They also arrived in north London with a reputation for diving and shirt-pulling, and all the other tactics that have blighted the Italian game down the years. Things proved to be no different during the match in early April, and the task was made all the harder when Cabrini put Juve in front at the half-hour after Pat Jennings had saved his initial spot kick. The home crowd of just under 52,000 responded in the right way and the volume went up another level when Tardelli was sent off for a disgraceful foul. Down to ten men, Juve looked to shut up shop, and time after time fell to the floor holding shins, arms, heads and anything else in reach, quite often when an Arsenal player wasn't! With time running out and amidst incessant Arsenal pressure, a Brady cross was nodded down by Willie Young and Bettega's panicked clearance ended up in his own net. Just six minutes remained.

The return in Turin ranks amongst the greatest Arsenal games of all time. Graham Rix's cross was met by substitute and bit-part-player Paul Vaessen who could hardly miss with his header from only inches out. No British team had ever won in Turin and with only two minutes remaining Arsenal demolished another record. But there was to be no final glory. The final in Brussels – at Heysel – came just a few days after a third successive FA Cup final had ended in defeat to West Ham United.

Arsenal were better than Valencia on the night but couldn't convert the odd chance they made. The Spanish side sat back and ultimately won the penalty shoot-out for which they seemed to be playing. It was Arsenal's 15th game in 45 days and 70th of the season in all. Fatigue in the end simply took its toll.

Those two final results, combined with the fact that Arsenal had to win their final two League encounters of that 1979–80 season to qualify for Europe (which they didn't), left Arsenal in the cold as far as European passage was concerned for the 1980–81 season. Although finishing third in 1980–81 secured Arsenal a UEFA Cup place for 1981–82, they had to beat Aston Villa on the last day of the season to do so. But it was a campaign that would last just two rounds, as the team failed miserably. Having beaten Panathinaikos 3–0 on aggregate, Arsenal were expected to get easy passage to the third round when they were drawn against the part-timers of KFC Winterslag; however, the Belgian team of accountants, school teachers and dishwashers had other ideas. The first leg in amongst the Belgian coalmines was settled in favour of the home team through a second-half goal. Arsenal returned to Highbury to right matters but within four minutes Billen had scored a vital away goal and left Arsenal needing three without reply to save them from total humiliation. Hollins reduced the aggregate arrears on the half-hour and Rix scored midway through the second half, but the away goal sent Arsenal tumbling out of the competition. The newspapers the next day had a field day: 'Now is the Winterslag of Arsenal's discontent' said *The Times*.

SIMPLY THE BEST

Arsenal qualified for the 1982–83 UEFA Cup but only because Tottenham – who had finished ahead of Arsenal in fourth place on goal difference – won the FA Cup and went into the Cup-Winners' Cup. The opponents this time were Spartak Moscow, who had been visitors to Highbury years before when a series of European friendlies had been staged at the stadium. The first leg in Moscow saw Arsenal take a two-goal lead inside the half-hour with Stewart Robson and Lee Chapman scoring. But two goals either side of the interval and a late late winner gave the Russians a slender lead for the return.

The match at Highbury took place on 28 September 1982. The date is not significant for anything other than the fact that the 28,455 in attendance that night witnessed possibly the greatest ever display by a visiting team – in any competition. The Russians were coming, and they just kept on coming, with a style of turns, touches and one-touch passing that wouldn't be seen again for another 20 years as the visitors won 5–2. Never before and never since has a visiting team playing in competitive football been given such an ovation at the end of a game. Whilst a few left early, the majority of the Highbury crowd were sporting enough to wait and stand in unison to applaud the visitors off. The Russians in return acknowledged the salute that was being given to them. Arsenal had been mauled and were out of Europe at the first hurdle. But there was no disgrace this time.

ENFORCED WAIT

It was nine long years before Highbury would see European competition again, the combination of non-qualification and the five-year ban for English football in the wake of the Heysel Stadium disaster denying the club any opportunity. Arsenal returned to the competition in the 1991–92 European Cup as English champions, George Graham having achieved his second title as manager in three years. The format of the competition was changing with there being two knockout rounds followed by a Champions League stage for the teams remaining – two groups of four with the winners of each group playing in the final.

Arsenal failed to make the league stage, though: having disposed of Austria Vienna in the first round, the Gunners faced much sterner opposition in Benfica in the second. And with a 1–1 draw in Portugal, there was cause for optimism prior to the return leg at Highbury; when Colin Pates shot Arsenal into a 20th-minute lead, it looked well founded. However, as in Lisbon, an equaliser was quick in coming: the increasingly influential Isaias hit a sweet 30-yard volley to square the aggregate score at two each. The 30 minutes of extra-time were dominated by the visitors, who were not quite as devastating as Spartak those years earlier, but certainly a class or two above the home side. Goals from Kulkov and a second on the night for Isaias in each period put the Portuguese side through and Arsenal out.

Having won the cup Double by beating Sheffield Wednesday in both the FA Cup and League Cup finals, Arsenal returned to the Cup-Winners' Cup in the 1993–94 season and set their stall out as undisputed cup kings by reaching the final two years in succession. The path to the first final took them through four rounds. Danish side OB Odense were first up and provided typically gritty opposition, unlike Standard Liège in the next round, which included a 7–0 win in Belgium as the side swept to an amazing 10–0 aggregate win. The quarter-final saw Italian opposition return to Highbury, once again from Turin but this time in the form of Torino. A 0–0 draw in the first leg set up another tight encounter at Highbury that was settled after 66 minutes via Tony Adams. Paris St-Germain were the semi-final opponents. In the Parc des Princes Ian Wright raced on to Paul Davies's free-kick and headed a lead. David Ginola equalised early in the second half and set up a semi-final return at Highbury two weeks later. A goal after just seven minutes by Kevin Campbell settled Arsenal's nerves and proved to be the decisive strike in a game in which PSG did little to trouble the home goal. The only negative on the night was Ian Wright getting booked, which would keep him out of the final.

The Parken Stadion in Copenhagen might as well have been Highbury on the night of the final, given the massive support the Gunners received. Outnumbering Parma supporters two to the dozen, one end of the stadium was a mass of swirling Arsenal and England flags across two levels. The only goal of the game came early on when a quick throw by Lee Dixon, which was hacked at by sweeper Minotti, dropped perfectly in front of Alan Smith, who hit his volley sweetly and the ball swept into Bucci's net off the far post. Stephen Bould and Tony Adams were superb at the back as the Gunners held firm; Smith led the line and held the ball with skilful resilience. Parma could not find a way through and finally the long 90 minutes expired, leaving Parken Highbury free to celebrate

European success for the second time in the club's long and illustrious history.

No team had ever successfully defended their Cup-Winners' Cup title – Arsenal would come very close to achieving that feat but would ultimately lose out to a speculative lob from the halfway line. The 1994–95 Cup-Winners' Cup campaign was more charged than the previous season's victorious route and offered up similar opposition along the way. Omonia Nicosia and Brondby were negotiated in the first two rounds, the Danish side providing typically difficult opposition.

In between the second round and quarter-final Arsenal had a two-legged encounter with AC Milan for the rights to the European Super Cup – a game played between the European Cup and Cup-Winners' Cup holders. The first leg at Highbury in February didn't capture too much imagination as only 23,953 attended what was a fairly typical 0–0 draw. The return game at the San Siro ended 2–0 in Milan's favour and they lifted the trophy.

Back to the Cup-Winners' Cup and this particular season's French opposition was supplied in the quarter-finals by Auxerre, a team coached for over 20 years by Guy Roux, who had taken them from a local side through the semi-professional ranks to top flight European competition – a remarkable feat – but Arsenal remained on course with a 2–1 aggregate win. Italian opposition again surfaced at the semi-final stage in the form of Sampdoria. The Italian club arrived at Highbury for the first leg without two of their biggest names – David Platt and Ruud Gullitt – but it was still a star-studded side and the north London faithful were treated to a terrific encounter. The goalscoring hero of the evening came from an unlikely source: up from a corner defender Steve Bould delivered the most delicate of touches to steer the ball past Zenga after David Hiller's shot had been parried by the keeper. Within three minutes Bould had doubled his tally for the season when his back flick from Schwarz's corner drifted into the far corner of the net. The 38,089 capacity crowd were in high spirits at half-time with Arsenal 2–0 to the good. However, six minutes after the restart the mood changed dramatically when Yugoslav Vladimr Jugovic pulled one back for the visitors. Ian Wright restored the two-goal advantage, but Jugovic was again unmarked in the area and free to score his second of the night and leave the game balanced in Sampdoria's favour at 3–2.

The return in Genoa produced a night of high tension; Sampdoria were at full strength and Mancini gave the Italians the advantage with his 16th-minute goal. In an open game Ian Wright fluked an equaliser on the hour. Then disaster came in the shape of two goals in the 84th and 86th minutes by Bellucci which left Sampdoria 3–1 up on the night and 5–4 ahead on aggregate. Then, in the dying seconds, Steffan Schwarz hit a free-kick from fully 35 yards which beat Zenga, more as a result of its accuracy than power. Extra-time failed to produce the winner and so to penalties where Seaman performed miracles to save three of the five against him and send Arsenal through to the final in Paris.

At the Parc des Princes penalties again looked likely to settle the result. In extra-time Juan Esnaider opened the scoring for Real Zaragoza (to become the first person to score in every round of a European competition) and then John Hartson fired home an equaliser. With just seconds of the 120 minutes remaining, Nayim received the ball just inside the Arsenal half and, seeing Seaman off his line, lifted the ball high and over the back-peddling Arsenal keeper for a brilliant, or flukey, deciding goal. It was Arsenal's last game in the Cup-Winners' Cup, not least because the competition itself was discarded after the 1998–99 season as a result of the reorganisation of the Champions League and UEFA Cup. The Gunners had reached the final all three times they had qualified – but sadly only won once.

That defeat, combined with a lowly League position, meant there was no European campaign the following season, which saw Bruce Rioch appointed as manager. Rioch signed Dennis Bergkamp and David Platt and took Arsenal to a UEFA Cup place, only to be sacked and replaced by Arsène Wenger, who would be looking to mastermind further European glory for Arsenal. His first two seasons fell well short of the mark and failed to produce a single win at Highbury for the home team. By the end of September 1996 the UEFA Cup sortie was over, Borussia Moenchengladbach winning both legs 3–2.

PAOK Salonika were Arsenal's next opponents at Highbury in the 1997–98 competition. The Greek side had won the first leg of the first-round tie by a single goal. Dennis Bergkamp drove home an aggregate equaliser as early as the 22nd minute and the game looked to be heading for extra-time until Vrizas scored the overall winner with just two minutes remaining.

WEMBLEY REMOVALS

The promise and potential of Arsène Wenger's side was fully realised in the 1997–98 season when the Premiership and FA Cup Double was secured. Arsenal qualified for the much-revamped Champions League and the quality of the football ensured that tickets were forever in demand. Arsenal as a club took the decision to move the home European games for the next two seasons to the old twin towers for reasons severalfold. The increased attendances – regularly capacity sell-outs – would boost the club's coffers (although in the club's defence, it cost as little as £10 to sit on the Wembley benches), while Highbury lacked the facilities required to host the games and would lose around 5,000 seats due to advertising and sponsorship requirements, not to mention the seating requirements of UEFA, which would mean East Stand season-ticket holders would have to be relocated for the games. In addition, the Highbury pitch was below the minimum regulation size required by UEFA for Champions League football. By selling the £10 and £15 tickets in blocks of three games, the club pretty much guaranteed a full house for each and maximum revenue for Group games. This, of course, ensured income even from 'dead' games, where the fate of a Group may have already been decided: clever marketing, but at that price few cared and, just as importantly, it provided a real opportunity for dads to take their sons and daughters to their first games.

The use of Wembley came with mixed blessings. While there were the financial and political requirements, the intimacy of Highbury was gone, as was the advantage of the small pitch, which suits the Wenger game. Equally, opposing teams seemed to be inspired by the chance to play at Wembley in its final days before demolition. As it was, the crowds came, but the team began a sequence of failures (in a Championship sense) in the major competition. In 1998–99 third place in Champions League Group E meant elimination. It was a similar scenario in 1999–2000, but third place this time around saw progression into the UEFA Cup and the decision was taken to move the games for this trophy back to Highbury. It came as a great relief to the fans, and probably the players as well, who had never really looked at 'home'. The proof of the pudding came when the team went all the way to the final.

Nantes, the first team to be entertained back on real home turf, was the first of three sides to be disposed of, with the free-scoring Gunners creating an aggregate of six goals as their psychological advantage returned. Into the last 16 and a tie with the Spanish champions elect Deportivo La Coruna. The first match at Highbury was set up as an encounter between two of the emerging teams in Europe (although this was the UEFA Cup not the Champions League). Arsenal won the leg 5–1 and ensured their qualification for the last 8 where Werder Bremen were felled 6–2 on aggregate. The scoreline included a rare hat-trick from Ray Parlour in the away leg.

A French side would once again be the only thing standing between Arsenal and another European final. Racing Club de Lens came to Highbury for the first leg of the semi-final confident, not least because they had defeated Arsenal in the Champions League the previous season. Equally, Arsenal were without Henry who had been sent off in Bremen. The only goal in Islington came as early as the second minute, when Bergkamp was once again a scorer. A tight game was expected in Lens and so it materialised, but Arsenal had the fillip of a goal from the returning Henry moments from the interval and ended up comfortable 3–1 winners. The Parken Stadion in Copenhagen was the scene of a very poor final against Galatasary that ended goal-less and was won on penalties by the Turkish side.

REFURBISHED HIGHBURY

Arsenal returned to Champions League action for the 2000–01 season with Wembley abandoned (it was about to be mothballed anyway, but had Arsenal decided to continue it would have remained open to them) and

Highbury taking a new look for the top-flight encounters. The normal swathe of advertising stuck to the East and West stands was hidden behind plastic silver curtains emblazoned with UEFA Champions League logos. The first five rows of seats at the front of the North and South stands were empty and largely obscured behind official sponsorship boards. The indoor training hall was draped in tents, where hospitality was provided for UEFA officials and sponsors. Lifelong, almost hereditary-style, East Stand season-ticket holders were shoehorned from their seats and despatched to other parts of the ground. These were just some of the changes caused by the arrival of full-blooded Champions League football to Highbury – not forgetting the special dispensation from the governing body to allow the under-regulation-size pitch to be used.

By virtue of the previous season's Premiership second place, Arsenal directly qualified for the league stage of the competition, being drawn in Group B with Sparta Prague, Shakthar Donetsk and old adversaries Lazio. The schedule of games was punishing, but nevertheless Arsenal secured passage to the second phase as mini-league winners. The decision to return to Highbury had been fully vindicated on results alone – the three games giving three wins and nine goals and providing the base for the qualification to the second phase where their Group C berth featured Olympique Lyon, Bayern Munich and Spartak Moscow. The inclusion of the Russian side again brought back memories for older supporters, and after a first trip due East their fears seemed founded as Spartak recovered from Silvinho's second-minute goal to rattle in four of their own for a comprehensive victory. A two-goal lead at home to Bayern was surrendered as Arsenal wobbled, but a win in Lyon boosted confidence and saw the French side earn a Highbury draw a week later.

Spartak's visit to Highbury was eagerly anticipated but the home side had to wait until eight minutes from time for a goal – thankfully from the boot of Henry to give Arsenal three vital points. The final game in Munich saw Bayern win but Arsenal qualified for the quarter-finals in second place above Lyon, courtesy of the results between the two sides. Valencia were the opponents in the last 16 and Highbury was buzzing with anticipation.

Minutes before half-time the lively Argentine Ayala produced a vital away goal to send the Spanish into the dressing-room ahead. Backed by encouraging vocal support, the Gunners came out with greater urgency in the second half and Henry had soon reduced the deficit and watched as Parlour scored a great goal to provide the lead. Then Henry found himself through with only the goalkeeper to beat, but his effort was wide. The collective groan around the four stands was as audible as any chant that evening – this was the moment a semi-final place should have been secured. The forebodings were well founded in the Mestalla for the return game. Despite a great defensive effort, the lanky Norwegian John Carew nodded an aggregate-equalling goal 15 minutes from time and sent Valencia through on away goals to a semi-final against Leeds United.

MORE OF THE SAME

Entry to the 2001–02 Champions League season was again by way of a runners-up position in the Premiership. This at least ensured direct passage to the league stage, where the opponents in Group C were Panathinaikos, RCD Mallorca and Schalke 04. Despite an opening defeat in Mallorca, Arsenal regained their composure to qualify for the second phase, where Bayer Leverkusen, Deportivo La Coruna and Juventus provided the opposition. Two first-half goals in Spain gave Deportivo an opening win and meant that Arsenal simply had to beat Juventus at Highbury a week later – the first time the two clubs had met since the 1980 Cup-Winners' Cup semi-final. Those in attendance that night witnessed one of Arsenal's best European performances for quite some time as the Gunners dominated and were well worth their 3–0 win. A 1–1 draw in Leverkusen was followed by a 4–1 win in the return home leg. Looking set for qualification for the quarter-finals, Arsenal had to face Deportivo, then Juventus in Turin. The game against the Spanish side was vital and a win would all but secure qualification. But a frustrating night saw Depo take an early lead and complete a 2–0 win late on. The trip to Turin also ended in defeat (0–1) and hopes of Champions League glory were again consigned to the dream bin.

HIGHBURY

Arsenal qualified for the competition in 2002–03 as reigning Premiership champions – in fact, Double champions for the third time. The first league phase was to prove encouraging with qualification on top of the pile, but once again results in the second league phase were below par. For the second season Arsenal would find themselves finishing third and failing to move into the knockout stage. The competition had started full of promise, though, with a home win over Borussia Dortmund, followed by a 4–1 victory in Eindhoven to dispose of PSV. A Gilberto Silva-inspired win in Auxerre meant that Arsenal had almost secured next-stage progress with three straight wins. Needing just a point to secure passage, Arsenal lost their home return with Auxerre and then lost in Dortmund. Despite this result, qualification was assured due to results elsewhere. The final Group game against PSV at Highbury was goal-less but ensured top place in the Group and a seeding in the draw.

The second Group phase reintroduced some old rivals – Valencia and Ajax. But first up, a visit to Italy to play Roma, where an early goal for the home side was eclipsed by a stunning Thierry Henry hat-trick. Valencia were Highbury visitors for the first home game and held out for a 0–0 draw. When Ajax left north London with the score at 1–1, Arsenal's qualification chances had taken a big knock and were not helped by another 0–0 draw in Amsterdam. With a visit to Valencia to end this set of Group games, a win over Roma at Highbury was a matter of necessity. Vieira opened the scoring but Roma equalised in first-half added time. Despite being reduced to ten men, the Italians held on. The result meant that Arsenal had to win in Spain but once again it was John Carew who inflicted defeat with two goals either side of Henry's hope-giving strike for an Arsenal side devoid of players through injury.

LONDON ENCOUNTER

During the 2003–04 season Arsenal gave one of their best-ever European performances, the only disappointment being that the game did not take place at Highbury but in the swirl of concrete that is the San Siro. As Highbury supporters had watched in awe during Spartak's performance at

Highbury many years before, so too did Arsenal inflict a 5–1 defeat on Internazionale that was every bit as impressive and certainly as stylish. That result was a million miles away from possibility after the first Group game, where Inter had won 3–0 at Highbury despite being without a few of their star players. Indeed, the Italians might have inflicted an even bigger embarrassment had they not eased up, given their lead had been fully established before the interval. This was Arsenal's biggest home defeat since that Spartak game in 1982. A 0–0 draw with Lokomotiv in Moscow was followed by another defeat by Dynamo in Kyiv.

Arsenal came home to Highbury with just a single point from three games and without a win in Europe for eight games. With Dynamo at Highbury for the return fixture, Arsenal had to win or face virtual elimination. Having dominated the game and had shot after shot kept out, full-back Ashley Cole managed a diving header at the far post with just two minutes remaining. The goal provided the win and visibly lifted the team, so they went to Milan believing they could win – despite several players being absent – and proceeded to do so in stunning style. The result elevated Arsenal to second in Group D and a 2–0 win over Lokomotiv ensured qualification. The three points saw Arsenal finish top of the Group, having been anchored at its base with just one point after three games.

The second Group phase of the competition had now been dropped by UEFA and that season's new format saw the two teams qualifying from each stage enter a straight knockout phase. For this last 16 stage, Celta Vigo were the opposition and a 3–2 win in Spain set up a perfect return. At Highbury, Arsenal were assured and cruised to a 2–0 win on the night. Next, the quarter-final draw that everyone wanted to avoid happened. Arsenal would face Chelsea, whom they had beaten twice in their three encounters that season to date.

Chelsea had not won against the Gunners in their previous 16 games and the first leg at Stamford Bridge ended 1–1. In the return Arsenal looked lacklustre and tired from their heavy schedule of games. However, Reyes gave Arsenal a first-half lead. Early in the second half Chelsea's excellent Frank Lampard drove home a parried save to equalise and with three minutes to go Wayne Bridge was unmarked to drive home Chelsea's winner from the side edge of the box. Once again Highbury had seen Arsenal eliminated from Europe, the club having never progressed beyond the quarter-final stage of the premier cup competition.

PENULTIMATE CHALLENGE

Arsenal went into the penultimate Highbury season with the title of the Untouchables – a side not experiencing defeat on their way to the Premiership title the previous season; one in which they had disposed of Chelsea in the FA Cup but had fallen to them in the Champions League. The questions as to why Arsenal could not carry their League excellence on to a Continental stage continued, with many possible answers, none definitive. Perhaps it was just the mix of styles and the congestion of fixtures. At least starting from season 2005–06, FA Cup semi-finals were being moved to prevent their juxtaposition with the Champions League quarter-finals. Time would tell.

The Group draw provided familiar opposition in the form of PSV and Panathinaikos. Rosenborg were the new challengers and caused a slight hiccup as Arsenal made their way through the games and into the last 16 as winners of Group D. An own goal by Brazilian Alex gave Arsenal a 1–0 win at Highbury over PSV and having taken the lead in Norway, Rosenborg produced an equaliser to gain a surprise draw. Successive draws in Athens (2–2) and at Highbury (1–1) against Panathinaikos were followed by another draw in PSV, leaving the Group open. Arsenal had to win their final game, at home to Rosenborg, to ensure qualification, and did so emphatically. Reyes, Henry, Fabregas, Pires and Van Persie were the five different goal-scorers.

Arsenal were drawn to face Bayern Munich in the first knockout phase and memories of the Gunners defeat a few years earlier were fresh in the minds of many. An inept defensive display saw Arsenal fall behind 3–0 in Munich and only a late Kolo Toure goal gave Arsenal a glimmer in the second leg. Highbury was strangely subdued in the return and the team simply didn't do enough to trouble Oliver Kahn in the visitors' goal. A lone strike from Henry gave Arsenal the win on the night this time, but in a reversal of previous fortunes, Bayern won the tie. The Highbury Champions League dream remained just that.

FINAL SHOWING

The final European campaign at Highbury almost provided the stadium with the fairy-tale ending it deserved. Arsenal supporters will remember the final in Paris against Barcelona as the one in which goalkeeper Jens Lehmann was sent off early on and left a ten-man Arsenal to perform a heroic rearguard action. The players were a dozen minutes or so away from an amazing victory thanks to Sol Campbell's header late in the first half. Two gilt-edged chances in the second half were squandered by Henry at a time when a second goal would have been even too much for the Spanish opposition. However, two late goals by Barca meant the end of a record that had been the backbone of this staggering turnaround in Arsenal's Champions League fortunes: ten successive games without conceding a goal in the competition – 995 minutes in total – beating the previous record by two full games – and all that with a defensive back four described as makeshift at the time.

The run to the final started with the club's best overall Group stage performance. Indeed, they entered they final Group game having qualified as Group winners and with a 100 per cent record. The Group draw paired the Gunners with familiar faces in Ajax and Sparta Prague, but also threw in surprise qualifiers FC Thun from Switzerland.

Ironically, Arsenal started the competition like they would finish it, having had to play the opening game against FC Thun game with ten men – Robin van Persie the expulsed culprit this time, being shown the red card for a high challenge. Arsenal won the game with a Bergkamp goal deep into injury time to snatch a 2–1 win against the Champions League debutants.

Another 2–1 victory in the next game – this time in Amsterdam against Ajax – was a more accomplished performance as Arsenal had a dream start with Ljungberg scoring inside two minutes of the start – a goal that marked the club's 100th in the competition. The Ajax goal, coming after

Pires had extended the visitors' lead, proved to be the last one conceded in the competition until late in the final.

A 2–0 win in Prague against Sparta saw Henry make an unexpected return from a six-week layoff after an early injury to Reyes forced Wenger to bring his star on earlier than anticipated. Four touches later, Henry produced a stunning strike to put Arsenal ahead. Then, 16 minutes from the end, Henry scored with a shot on the turn – it was no classic, but it did make Henry Arsenal's greatest goal-scorer. He passed Ian Wright's record with his 186th goal in just his 303rd appearance in an Arsenal shirt. The win left Arsenal five points clear at the top of Group B.

A comprehensive 3–0 result in the return encounter at Highbury ensured Arsenal a place in the knockout stages, but the relative ease with which Arsenal had disposed of the Czech side was not mirrored in Switzerland, where a penalty by Robert Pires two minutes from time allowed them past the stubborn opposition of FC Thun. It was a missed penalty by Henry in the final Group match – at home to Ajax – that cost Arsenal their 100 per cent record in the competition, the game ending goal-less but leaving Arsenal with an impressive 16 points out of a possible 18.

There was an 11-week wait until the competition resumed again with the knockout stages, and it was a mouth-watering prospect. Real Madrid were to be the opponents and it would be the first meeting in a European competition between the two sides. By the time of the first leg in the Estadio Santiago Bernabéu, the Arsenal defence was indeed looking makeshift – Eboue, Toure, Senderos and Flamini: only Toure could be regarded as a regular. Arsenal were up for the occasion though, and a wonderful virtuoso goal from Henry two minutes after the interval was enough to secure a first-leg win. But this was no smash-and-grab exercise: Arsenal outplayed their hosts for much of the game, a fact acknowledged by Madrid's David Beckham.

For the return two-weeks later, Highbury was buzzing. Although there were no goals on the night, what unfolded was possibly the greatest goal-less draw every played at the stadium (see Chapter 15 – Landmark Games).

The draw for the quarter-finals pitted Arsenal against Juventus and signalled the return of Patrick Vieira to Highbury. Naturally, it was the central point of discussion in the lead-up to the game, headlined the old master against the young pretender: Vieira against Cesc Fabregas. In this battle, youth was the victor, the 18 year old scoring the first goal and making the second for Henry as Arsenal took a deserved 2–0 first-leg lead. The tie should have been over as a contest long before the final whistle, as Arsenal squandered chances to give them an unassailable lead going into the second leg. The visitors also ended the game under-strength, as they had two players sent off for second offences late in the game. Just to add to his woe on the night, a booking for Vieira meant he would miss the second leg.

In 1972, Ajax denied Arsenal at the quarter-final stage, Valencia did the same in 2001 and Chelsea were the stumbling block in 2004: this time, though, Arsenal were not to be denied and a goal-less draw in the Stadio delle Alpi in the return saw Arsenal make it the semi-final of the competition for the first time. Arsenal were never really troubled during the game and the clean sheet was their eighth in succession in the competition — a new Champions League record as Henry recorded his 100th appearance in the tournament.

But although they were in the last four for the first time, there was still another record to put right. Arsenal were the only one of that season's eight seeded teams never to have won the competition. To make it to the final, they would have to beat Spanish side Villarreal, who had qualified for the Champions League for the first time in their history and were clearly the surprise package of the season. The two games were predictably tight, tense affairs and the tie was decided by two key moments. In the first leg at Highbury, four minutes before half-time, Kolo Toure stabbed home the only goal from Aleksander Hleb's cross – the last goal in European competition to be scored at Highbury – to give Arsenal a slim advantage.

The second leg in southern Spain at Estadio El Madrigal was equally tense as Arsenal rode their luck, Guillermo Franco and Diego Forlan both inches from scoring. But the defining moment of the tie came two minutes from the final whistle when a challenge by Gale Clichy on Jose Mari was harshly deemed a penalty. Lehmann, magnificent throughout the competition, guessed right and dived to push away Juan Riquelme's spot kick. Arsenal were in the final.

Paris was the setting and Barcelona the opposition. Arsenal returned to the city of one of their most haunting defeats: 11 years previously Nayim had scored a last-gasp winner from the halfway line. That was the Parc des Princes; the venue this time was the Stade de France in a encounter whose prospects were described by everyone as 'The Dream Final'. It was billed as a Champions League final that had every chance of being the greatest ever played.

The game that was sold as matching the two best players in the world – Henry v. Ronaldinho – but was ultimately destroyed as the footballing spectacle everyone was longing for when Jens Lehmann brought down Samuel Eto'o just out his box and was shown the red card by Norwegian referee Terje Hauge after just 17 minutes. The goal that Ludovic Giuly scored from the free ball was disallowed and the ensuing free-kick was placed wide by Ronaldinho. Both teams felt aggrieved, but perhaps it was the millions watching worldwide who were the biggest victims – but for a moment's advantage play from the referee ...

As it was, Arsenal should have already been in the lead, Henry having spurred two golden chances inside the first couple of minutes of play, the second with only Barca keeper Victor Valdes to beat. It was ironic that an English team being criticised for having few English players performed in a typically English fashion, and it was one of those Englishmen that gave Arsenal the lead shortly before half-time – Sol Campbell rising to head home unchallenged from Henry's free-kick. Against the odds, and with replacement keeper Manuel Almunia having made a number of excellent saves.

The Catalans flew at Arsenal at the start of the second half, but Arsenal held firm, with Henry again spurning a one-on-one opportunity. Barca changes came and it was the last of these that unlocked a tiring Arsenal door. Henrik Larsson made opportunities for first Eto'o and then Juliano Belletti to score in quick succession and so end the dream. It was a bitter pill to swallow and the defeat meant Arsenal had lost in three finals appearances in a row – the previous two against Real Zaragoza in the 1995 Cup-Winners' Cup final and Galatasaray in the 2000 UEFA Cup final.

TWELVE

Doubles Galore

Highbury could not have seen a better start to a home season. Despite two indifferent performances in the first two away games, which had brought just two points from two draws, a hot, heady August afternoon saw the youth team parade the European Fairs Cup around the ground and then the first team go on to demolish a star-studded Manchester United 4–0. Writing in the Arsenal *Matchday Programme* for that opening game, chairman Dennis Hill-Wood wrote that the club was looking to win either the 'Championship of the League and/or the FA Cup', adding that these two competitions were surely the hardest in the world in which to be victorious.

Spirits were high and whilst there was real belief that a League Championship could be won, nothing could have been further from anyone's thoughts – at the club or in the stands – than that a League Championship and FA Cup Double was waiting a little over eight months down the line. Hill-Wood's use of 'and' in his address was perhaps bad editing and what he was suggesting was that the club would like to win both of them soon – and so they did. It just happened to be in the same season.

Just over 30 years after those jottings, Highbury would be celebrating the club's third Double – something that at the start of the 1970–71 season had only been performed once in the modern era – ironically by Tottenham Hotspur – and would become a regular target for Arsenal, along with their first home opponents that day, Manchester United. Arsenal clinched two of the Championship titles of those three Doubles on the grounds of those two teams. How fate conspires!

The 1970–71 Double was achieved using just sixteen players for the League campaign and thirteen in the FA Cup, with three of those players competing in the fifty-one games required for the Double: Armstrong, McLintock and Wilson. The 1997–98 and 2001–02 Double teams used 26 and 19, and 25 and 24 players respectively, with no single player competing in all the games of the Premiership and FA Cup – 49 in all. The increase in players used for the FA Cup games clearly proved its decreasing lack of appeal in the competition hierarchy. Of course, in 1970–71, the team was taking pride in their eventually unsuccessful defence of the European Fairs Cup, whilst in the latter two the toils of the Champions League were taking their own special toll.

The table below compares the League-playing record of all three teams. Only the 1970–71 team remained unbeaten at Highbury and amazingly Bob Wilson, the Arsenal keeper of that era, conceded just six of the twenty-nine goals put past him at home that season. The 1970–71 side, having played four more games, suffered six losses in total – the same as the 1997–98 team – whilst the 2001–02 team suffered just three defeats in total. Amazingly, all three of these were at Highbury, where the defence leaked an astonishing twenty-five goals. All three Double teams went through their League campaigns in very different circumstances. Had three points for a win been in place in 1970–71, Frank McLintock's side would have put ninety-four on the board, albeit from four extra games.

The Double Teams' Playing Records

	P	HOME W D L F A	AWAY W D L F A	TOTAL W D L F A	Pts
1970–71	42	18 3 0 41 6	11 4 6 30 23	29 7 6 71 29	65
1997–98	38	15 2 2 43 10	8 7 4 25 23	23 9 6 68 33	78
2001–02	38	12 4 3 42 25	14 5 0 37 11	26 9 3 79 36	87

THE FIRST DOUBLE: 1970–71

Highbury was the key to the success of the League Championship – no doubt about it whatsoever. Only three of the twenty-one visiting sides that season went away with even a single point and none of those in the 1971 half of the season. Leeds United secured a goal-less draw and pushed Arsenal all the way; indeed the Elland Road side led the League table by a substantial margin at one stage and seemed certain to take the title themselves. Crystal Palace secured the only score draw in north London, but had gone into the game having secured a sensational 2–0 win at Highbury in the League Cup just a few days beforehand – and this in the days when top clubs contested the competition with their full sides. Southampton took their point from Highbury on Boxing Day but only because of one of the greatest displays ever by a visiting goalkeeper. Eric Martin produced an incredible display of acrobatics on a snow-covered, freezing surface and homed in on the orange ball in use that afternoon time after time. In the second half especially, as the home side attacked the North Bank, the Scot went head-to-head with Gunners' centre-forward John Radford, who, on another day, might have had five.

The six goals conceded by Arsenal at Highbury were the work of four teams. Remarkably, one of those was West Bromwich Albion, against whom Arsenal rattled past six goals. Ipswich Town played their part in a 3–2 thriller, whilst Wolverhampton Wanderers and Crystal Palace took one goal each.

Bertie Mee, the manager who steered Arsenal to that first Double, had no pedigree for his job – he had been promoted from within the club after the departure of Billy Wright, Mee having been the club's physio for a number of years previously. But what Mee did bring was discipline, something that had been lacking in earlier years. Dave Sexton took the coaching reins early on but moved to Chelsea, and so Mee looked within and promoted the Arsenal second-team coach at that time, Don Howe. It proved to be an inspired move, as Howe's love for the club and enthusiasm to succeed rubbed off on those around him. The result was that in tandem Mee and Howe steered Arsenal to success in the European Fairs Cup in

1969–70 and the monkey of 17 years was lifted at the end of a season that instilled esteem and belief.

Equally important that season was that Mee and Howe made a decision to switch Frank McLintock from midfield – where his age was starting to show – into a central defensive position alongside Peter Simpson. Never mind he was well under six foot, his reading of the game and his ability to control it in a verbal sense was inspired and he deservedly won the FWA Footballer of the Year award at the end of his greatest season.

Looking back at the results from the 1970–71 season, there are clearly four distinct phases.

Slow Starting (15 August – 1 September)
Two points from two away games didn't have the press shouting from the rooftops, but if anything did come from those games it was an injury to Charlie George. Having him sidelined with a broken foot for a while forced Bertie Mee's hand in blooding Ray Kennedy. The young striker had made his mark with the away goal against Anderlecht in the previous season's Fairs Cup triumph and he immediately struck up a partnership with John Radford that looked formidable. They consequently hit 34 of Arsenal's 71 League goals that season – indeed, Kennedy ended up as Arsenal's top League scorer.

The first Highbury game was against Manchester United and in the baking sunshine Arsenal romped to an emphatic 4–0 home win. Radford scored a versatile hat-trick and George Graham added the fourth as Arsenal dominated the airwaves. The game is also remembered for Bob Wilson's wonder save at the feet of George Best.

Huddersfield were the next visitors to Highbury – amazingly their first in the League since the 1955–56 season – and it took Kennedy's first goal of the season to break the deadlock. A late defeat at Stamford Bridge a few days after was a further setback and another point was dropped when Leeds United left Highbury with a goal-less draw. Arsenal had to play almost an hour of the game with ten men after Eddie Kelly had been sent off for kicking out at Billy Bremner. Leeds had won their opening five games and were already established at the top of the table and so it was the first point any team had taken from them.

DOUBLES GALORE

Arsenal completed the first phase of the season having taken seven points from the possible twelve in the six games – five points dropped and in sixth place behind Leeds, Manchester City, Chelsea, Liverpool and Derby County.

The Winning Streak (5 September – 9 January)

Arsenal's title challenge and their scaling of the League table were kick-started by a home win over local rivals Tottenham Hotspur. Two first-half goals from George Armstrong were the start of an eighteen-match run that would bring fourteen wins and three draws – just three points dropped from the twenty-eight on offer. The run, as such, also included one emphatic defeat. There was an advantage in that ten of the seventeen games were at Highbury, but then so were two of the three draws. Radford and Kennedy scored for the first time together in a League game to secure the points at Burnley. The next two Saturdays in late September provided an incredible contrast. On the 19th, West Bromwich Albion were the Highbury visitors and Arsenal went in 2–0 ahead at the interval. After the restart two further goals made it 4–0 before West Bromwich Albion pulled one back for what was the first League goal conceded at Highbury to that point. Arsenal added two more and West Bromwich Albion doubled their tally to leave the final score at 6–2. It was the first time Arsenal had scored six in a League match at Highbury since 6 November 1965 when Sheffield United were beaten by the same score.

A week later Arsenal travelled to Stoke, having moved into the next round of the Fairs Cup following a 2–0 win over Lazio. What transpired at the Victoria Ground shook the side to the core as City ran out 5–0 winners. McLintock often said afterwards that it 'was a wake-up call' as Arsenal dropped to fourth in the table. Arsenal's next four games at Highbury produced ten goals with none conceded. Nottingham Forest and Everton were dispatched 4–0 apiece and Derby 2–0. Ray Kennedy helped himself to his first club hat-trick against Forest and scored in five of seven games. A 1–1 draw at Newcastle was followed by a 3–1 win at Coventry to complete the away fixtures in the sequence. The home run came to an end when Crystal Palace earned a

1–1 draw at Highbury and became only the second side to take a point there.

George Armstrong scored the only goal at Portman Road as Arsenal got back to their winning ways with a victory over Ipswich Town. Goals from Graham and Radford secured the points at home in a 2–0 win over Liverpool, and they were on the score sheet again when Wolves were the visitors a couple of weeks later. Sandwiched either side was a 2–0 win at Manchester City and an even better return to the north-west with a 3–1 victory at Old Trafford! On Boxing Day, Highbury staged the Eric Martin wonder show and the New Year was celebrated with a 2–0 home win over West Ham United.

Confidence Lost (16 January – 27 February)
Arsenal's fantastic winning run had left them in second place just three points behind leaders Leeds United and with a game in hand; however, things were about to take a turn for the worse and Arsenal lost three of their next five League matches. The defeats were all away from Fortress Highbury, and two came in quick succession, with losses at Huddersfield (0–1) and Liverpool (0–2) – the game at Anfield being only the fifth time Arsenal had failed to score in the League. Scrappy Highbury wins over Manchester City (1–0) and Ipswich Town (3–2) did little to ease the jitters which were compounded by a defeat at the hands of Derby County at the Baseball Ground. This run left Arsenal seven points adrift of Leeds United, who were already being hailed champions elect by the dailies.

The Grand Finale (2 March – 8 May)
The run-in to the end of the season was about to start, taking the club through the difficult Easter period, the final three games on the fixture list reading Leeds United (away), Stoke City (home) and Tottenham Hotspur (away). Arsenal would need to produce something of exceptional quality to have the journos re-writing their back pages. The defeat at Derby was the first of three successive away games facing Arsenal – and the reversal of the club's fortunes at the Baseball Ground had been their third away defeat in succession.

The Black Country was the Gunners' next destination, home to a

Wolves side that had troubled Arsenal at Highbury earlier in the season. As it was, Arsenal produced arguably their best display of the season to win 3–0 and re-establish much-needed confidence. The win was the first of nine on the bounce in which only one goal was conceded. Two great goals by Graham and Sammels sealed a win at Crystal Palace. Arsenal could now look forward to three successive home games in the League as Blackpool (1–0), Chelsea (2–0) and Coventry (1–0) were beaten, with Kennedy scoring three of the five goals. Chelsea's visit drew 62,087 into the stadium – the biggest Highbury attendance of the season.

Southampton became the first side to score against Arsenal in six games, but could not avoid defeat at The Dell. Next, a trip to the Midlands saw a 3–0 win over Nottingham Forest. On 17 April Newcastle United's visit to Highbury produced a game tingling with tension at Highbury. At the start of play Arsenal were just two points behind Leeds with two games in hand. The atmosphere was incredible and it took a wonder strike from Charlie George – one that many supporters described as the greatest goal they had ever seen – 20 minutes from time, to secure the points. Whilst the strike by the local lad was brilliant, it was the sheer relief experienced by the Highbury crowd that was probably the reason for that description. With Leeds losing controversially at home to West Bromwich Albion on the same afternoon, Arsenal were top of the League! A Charlie George penalty midway through the first half at Highbury won two more points from Burnley and the crowds started to near the 50,000 mark as Arsenal consolidated their position.

* * *

During this period Arsenal had also marched to the FA Cup final, having been drawn away in every round, although replays against Portsmouth and Leicester City brought FA Cup action to Highbury. Charlie George was to prove key throughout the Cup run, scoring in the replay with Portsmouth, hitting two great goals at Maine Road to ease the side past Manchester City 2–1 and in the replay with Leicester after a 0–0 draw at Filbert Street, his late headed winner at the North Bank separating the teams in a sixth-round battle every bit as tense as the encounter with Newcastle.

Despite that 0–5 loss in the League at Stoke, Arsenal were hot favourites to win at Hillsborough and go through to the FA Cup final; however, a freak rebounded clearance off Dennis Smith and a bad back pass from Charlie George that put John Ritchie through saw Stoke leading 2–0. The unlikely hero for Arsenal on that day was Peter Storey; his flying volley from outside the area reduced the deficit and then, with almost the final play of the game, a Frank McLintock header was handled on the line and up stepped Storey to equalise past Gordon Banks. The replay at Villa Park never looked in doubt and goals by Graham and Kennedy secured a place in the final.

* * *

In the League two away games in three days saw Arsenal pegged back as points were dropped. A 2–2 draw at West Bromwich Albion, in which the visitors came from behind only to be denied a win through a last-minute equaliser, was the prelude to the showdown trip to Elland Road. Arsenal arrived for the blockbuster encounter with 61 points from 39 matches; Leeds had 60 points from 40 matches – a draw would at least put Arsenal firmly back in the title driving seat.

Chances were few and far between as the game drew to a goal-less draw. Then, in the dying moments, Jackie Charlton steered the ball past Wilson to give the home side a vital win and dent the Arsenal Championship hopes. Typically, controversy surrounded the goal – Charlton looked offside but replays showed that left-back Bob McNab had played him on. Leeds United were now a point clear at the top with a game to play, but Arsenal had their game in hand. Two wins would capture the title regardless of what Don Revie's side did. At Highbury, substitute Eddie Kelly scored a second-half winner against Stoke City as 55,011 attended Highbury for the last home game of the season. Leeds United had completed their final game with a May Day win over Nottingham Forest.

One final game remained for Arsenal. A win would ensure the

Championship by a point. A 0–0 draw would give the Championship to Arsenal on goal average. Any score draw would give the Championship to Leeds United on goal average. This last game was at White Hart Lane – home of local rivals Tottenham Hotspur and, as we know, the only team to have done the Double at that point in the twentieth century. It was, of course, the stuff of comic books and Arsenal's Roy Race proved to be Ray Kennedy, who nodded in the winner two minutes from time after George Armstrong had crossed following Pat Jennings's parry of Radford's shot. Arsenal were champions for a record eighth time and had done it by a point.

Five days later the Double was completed. The game against Liverpool should have been out of sight long before the 90 minutes ended; Ray Kennedy, especially, should have had a simple tap-in hat-trick. Then, as extra-time got under way, Wilson let in Heighway's shot at his near post. Kelly slipped a soft equaliser and midway through the second period Charlie George again delivered the winner in an FA Cup tie, his thunderous shot from the edge of the area rasping past Ray Clemence after he had exchanged a one-two with John Radford.

THE SECOND DOUBLE: 1997–98

The second Double pretty much came out of the proverbial blue. Arsène 'Who?' Wenger had guided the club to third place in the Premiership in his first part-season in charge, but not very far in the cup competitions. Having taken the reins with the 1996–97 season already under way, Wenger used that year for planning and it should not be overlooked as it had a major bearing on the success that was to follow. New techniques, new diets and new outlooks suddenly transformed an ageing defence at the end of its usefulness into something every bit as good as in previous years and with a new sense of purpose. A significant signing at Wenger's request, even before he arrived, was that of another unknown, a French Under-21 international languishing in the Milan reserves – Patrick Vieira.

The close season had also seen new talent arrive. Following an injury, the electric pace of Marc Overmars had been in question by many;

Wenger showed faith in the Dutchman and his £5 million outlay was repaid by a player anxious to prove the Arsenal manager right and the rest of the footballing world wrong. Other arrivals were that of Emmanuel Petit and his fellow countryman Gilles Grimandi, plus young potential in the form of Nicolas Anelka and Alex Manninger was added to the squad. All would have a significant impact when added to the defensive five of Seaman, Dixon, Winterburn, Bould and Adams, the midfield elegance of Bergkamp and the raw energy of Vieira. Up front Ian Wright remained as prolific as ever and would break the club's goal-scoring record during the course of the season. By the time the big kick-off came along in August 1997, the whole club was raring to go. What followed, though, was better than any could have believed.

The Arsenal of 1997–98 were not quite as dominant at Highbury as the team of 1970–71. Of the six defeats suffered in the Premiership two came at home, but with fifteen wins and just two draws it was certainly the backbone of the season. Away form was indifferent at times – just eight wins and a defence that leaked too many goals in reality. Although the final table of the season shows the margin of victory over second placed Manchester United as being just a single point, the truth was that Arsenal had sewn up the title with two games to spare, relaxing in the final two games of the season with an FA Cup final with Newcastle United looming.

As with the first Double, the season of the second Double can be divided into distinct stages: this time there were three of them.

Solid Start (9 August – 4 October)
Arsenal started their season on a run of 12 games undefeated with a mixture of wins and draws. An opening-day draw at Leeds United was followed by two wins. Coventry City were the season's first home visitors and Ian Wright followed up his Elland Road goal with a brace against the Sky Blues. The atmosphere was intense as Wright moved to within a goal of Cliff Bastin's long-standing scoring record. There were mixed feelings that night – the Highbury crowd desperately wanted Wrighty to take the record but they also wanted it to evaporate before their eyes on their home ground – with away trips to Southampton and Leicester next up, it looked

as if it might unfold elsewhere. But on those trips it was Bergkamp who reigned supreme, scoring twice in a 2–2 draw at The Dell and then scoring the most brilliant of hat-tricks in a 3–3 draw at Filbert Street. Bergkamp's goals took first, second and third place in the *Match of the Day* 'Goal of the Month' competition – the first time that had ever happened.

Spurs at Highbury were seen as the ideal targets for Wright to notch up the goal he needed but a goal-less draw left Arsenal in fifth place, four points off the top of the table. After a week of international action in which Wright had broken his international scoring drought against Moldova, Bolton Wanderers were next up at Highbury where the home crowd were doing everything they could to support the Arsenal striker's destiny. The visitors threatened to spoil the party when Alan Thompson's diving header put them in front, but Bergkamp was still imperious and when he slipped the ball through a static Wanderers' defence, there was only one outcome. Bastin's record of 178 goals had been equalled and shortly thereafter broken as Bergkamp's shot was saved and the scraps fell to Wright, who banished the ball into the netting and took the record for himself. He then confirmed it in typical style as he completed his hat-trick – but he was always going to keep the match ball anyway! After the game, the crowds gathered outside in Avenell Road and Ian Wright responded by throwing his kit into the throng as memorable souvenirs. The undershirt – marked with '179 Just Done It' – was torn to shreds.

A 3–2 win at Chelsea was sealed by a last-minute net buster from Winterburn and followed up by an emphatic Highbury win over West Ham United. A 2–2 draw at Everton took Arsenal to the top of the table where the position was consolidated with the 5–0 thrashing of Barnsley.

Nose Dive (18 October – 13 December)
After the first ten games Arsenal had accrued six wins and four draws, giving them a tally of twenty-two points from a possible thirty and twenty-seven goals scored with ten conceded. Positioned at the top of the table things were looking good – the only disappointment being an exit from the UEFA Cup at the feet of PAOK Salonika. Two goal-less draws – one at Palace and the other at home to Villa – were points lost with average performances, but in retrospect they also marked the beginning of a slide

that would look to damage Premiership-title hopes beyond repair. Matters were not helped by a succession of injuries and form loss that disrupted the core of the side. As it was, Tony Adams's long-term problems earned him a month in the south of France, resting and having treatment. Although it didn't look like it at the time, his return in the New Year would be significant.

A trip to Pride Park, the new home of Derby County, emphasised the problems in defence and more specifically in front of the defence, as the team crashed 0–3. Given that the next game at Highbury was against Manchester United, it wasn't the best of preparations and the arrival of the champions in north London also saw Petit and Bergkamp suspended for the game. But it was their replacements – Anelka and Platt – who would have a say in the encounter. First Anelka fired Arsenal into the lead and then Vieira whipped in a curving shot that Peter Schmeichel could only flail at. United responded and drew the game level, and a third draw in a row looked likely until David Platt rose above all and sundry to head home the winner.

The victory over United was a false dawn and indeed the three points were the only ones secured by the team that November, the next two games also ending in defeat, away at Sheffield Wednesday and home to Liverpool. Arsenal moved into December having dropped from top to fifth place, with plenty of talk about the overseas players in the side not being up to scratch and the defence showing its age (once again). A 1–0 win at Newcastle went some way to answering the critics, but a 1–3 defeat at Highbury to Blackburn Rovers just nine days before Christmas was the low point and in many respects the watershed. Arsenal simply surrendered to the visitors and players' heads were not so much hanging down as dragging on the grass below them.

Eight games, two wins, two draws and four defeats had provided eight points from a possible twenty-four in Arsenal's slide down the Premiership table; the side had also been outscored five goals to eleven. Nobody leaving Highbury that day after witnessing the Blackburn defeat would have believed that Arsenal were about to set off on a run that would see them win fifteen and draw three of their next eighteen games, and then clinch the Premiership with two games to spare.

Lift-Off (26 December – 20 May)

Goal-less at half-time, Arsenal's visit to Wimbledon was abandoned there and then when the Selhurst Park floodlights failed and a scraped 2–1 win over Leicester was followed by a draw at Tottenham. Although it didn't look like it at the time, the rot had been halted. Nevertheless Arsenal were 12 points behind leaders Manchester United and in sixth place. In the FA Cup, a goal-less draw meant a trip to Port Vale for a replay, which was only won on penalty kicks. Sandwiched between, Arsenal's win at Upton Park in the League Cup to move past West Ham United into the quarter-finals of the competition, the key moment being Seaman's penalty save from former Arsenal player John Hartson. Premiership action resumed with a trip to Coventry and in a bad-tempered 2–2 draw, Vieira was red-carded and Seaman suffered a finger injury that would sideline him for weeks.

A return to Highbury was a welcome break from being on the road and three home Premiership games in succession brought three wins. Alex Manninger was between the posts for the injured Seaman and took his opportunity well, seeding belief that the England keeper's successor had been found. Arsenal were also boosted by the return of Tony Adams, whose absence from the Arsenal defence due to a series of niggling (and ultimately career-ending) injuries was one of the reasons for the pre-Christmas slump. The Arsenal skipper celebrated his return with a headed opening goal in a 3–0 win over Southampton. Derby wins over Chelsea and Crystal Palace made it maximum home points. The Premiership games against the London sides were mixed in and around two cup encounters with both teams as well. Chelsea were beaten 2–1 at Highbury in the semi-final of the League Cup and only a wonder save from the Chelsea keeper prevented Bergkamp from wrapping up the tie. And it proved decisive, as the Blues won the return leg – in which Vieira was sent off again – and were through to the final. Arsenal then faced Crystal Palace in an FA Cup replay which was won at Selhurst Park 2–1 after a goal-less draw at Highbury.

Arsenal's opponents in the quarter-final of the Cup were West Ham United whom, as seemed so common during this season, they also faced in the Premiership at that time. The first encounter in the League was one of three games Arsenal had in hand over leaders Manchester United and it ended goal-less in east London. United were now 11 points ahead and the Gunners' fixture backlog got worse when the FA Cup tie ended 1–1 at Highbury, Bergkamp's goal earning the replay. Before another trip to east London, Arsenal faced two away games. First, in the replay of the abandoned game, Wimbledon were beaten 1–0 and then Arsenal travelled north to Manchester United in a game they simply had to win. Arsenal looked supremely confident with Overmars a constant threat and it was no surprise when he slipped Arsenal into a second-half lead that proved good enough to win the game. As United had dropped points prior to the encounter, Arsenal with their three games in hand would be clear at the top provided they converted the nine points.

A penalty shoot-out was required to settle the FA Cup tie at West Ham, where Arsenal had played an hour of normal time and extra-time without Bergkamp who was sent off for elbowing an opposition player. The Gunners prevailed from the spot for a second time in the competition where their luck seemed decidedly 'in'. Arsenal recorded a fourth consecutive 1–0 Premiership win to take the points at Bolton.

It was Christopher Wreh who found the net early on to settle the FA Cup semi-final as Wolverhampton were dispatched. The win teed up a final against Newcastle United, Arsenal's next Premiership opponents. Newcastle arrived at Highbury for a game that was much more than a rehearsal for the Wembley Cup final. Arsenal were on a roll and needed to continue to pump up the pressure on a fading Manchester United. A couple of goals from Anelka and a twenty-yard pile-driver from Vieira secured the points as Manninger conceded his first goal in nine Premiership games.

Easter loomed large and the Holiday Monday trip to Blackburn proved an ironic turnaround. When Rovers had visited Highbury in mid-December, Arsenal had hit their lowest point. At Ewood Park for the return, Arsenal were sublime and produced one of their best displays of the season in front of the TV cameras. The only real threat to the Gunners came from the late snow blizzards that threatened an abandonment as Arsenal romped to a 4–1 victory.

Wimbledon were blitzed 5–0 at Highbury and the Arsenal fans

celebrated in delight as the Gunners went top of the League when Manchester United could only draw at home to Newcastle. The crowd were also celebrating Petit's first goal for the club – right in front of the North Stand – as Arsenal's forward line set about a move that left the blond Frenchman with a tap-in which he gleefully thumped into the net with all his might. Points were still needed for the title, but nothing could stop the Arsenal momentum and the players knew it too.

It took Petit one more game to double his tally of goals – and to secure Arsenal another victory, avenging the slide-starting 0–3 defeat at Derby earlier in the season. The three points meant that Arsenal needed just one win from their three remaining games. The first of those was Arsenal's last at Highbury for the season. Everton were the visitors but before the Merseysiders' arrival in north London, Dennis Bergkamp had been named Player of the Year by his fellow professionals. The Dutchman had, at his worst, been merely brilliant and was mostly superb throughout a sensational season that provided him with 19 goals in 39 games.

The Toffees arrived at Highbury in a sticky situation. Relegation-threatened Everton had a defensive-looking line-up and Highbury was a noisy theatre as Arsenal looked to secure the title in front of their own crowd. The fans were on their seats inside six minutes when Adams pressured Slaven Bilic from a corner and forced the defender to head into his own goal. The stadium erupted. As the half-hour mark approached, it was another Marc, this time Overmars, who accelerated beyond the static back line and slipped the ball past Southall to double the lead. Overmars produced a similar act in the second half to make it 3–0, and then Adams and Bould combined in superb fashion to send the Arsenal skipper through and the ball crashing into the net. Four goals without reply had Highbury erupting as it hadn't for 28 years; since a European night in 1970.

Arsenal had two more games to complete the season and, with players rested for the impending FA Cup final, shipped five goals without reply in games at Liverpool and Aston Villa. David Seaman returned in goal for the final game at Villa Park and walked out in the number 1 shirt at Wembley four days later against Newcastle United. In a mediocre game, Alan Shearer went close for the Tynesiders midway through the first half before Overmars raced on to Petit's chip over the Newcastle defence and slipped the ball between Shay Given's legs to put Arsenal ahead. Anelka, who had missed two great opportunities earlier, sealed the Arsenal victory by galloping on to Parlour's pass to drive the ball into the far corner of the net.

THE THIRD DOUBLE: 2001–02

Two years passed before Arsenal reclaimed the Premiership title – two runners-up spots were little consolation for a team that had achieved so much. The 1998–99 season at least went as far as the final round of games with Arsenal pushing Manchester United all the way to the end of the season, but eventually losing out by a single point. The Gunners were denied an FA Cup final spot by the same opponents a few weeks before. The 1999–2000 season proved even more of a disappointment. In the Premier League Manchester United again won the Championship, but this time Arsenal were 18 points off the pace and also failed to produce any form in any of the cup competitions. Arsène Wenger was already building the team for a new season, though. Spanish clubs snapped up some of Arsenal's better-performing stars: Anelka went to Real Madrid for a fortune, whilst Marc Overmars and Emmanuel Petit travelled to Barcelona. Across those two seasons Wenger rebuilt the core of the team. In came Henry, Silvinho, Wiltord, Kanu, Lauren, Pires and Edu amongst others; however, perhaps the biggest news was the signing of Sol Campbell from arch rivals Tottenham Hotspur on a free transfer.

This time around, it was the club's away record that was the outstanding component of its third Double. Of the nineteen games played, fourteen were won and five drawn, and, impressively, none were lost. At Highbury, Arsenal won twelve, drew four and lost three games. Their tally of 87 points was the best of the three Double teams. Equally, the 79 goals they scored showed the side as an emerging attacking force; 37 goals came away from home and just 11 conceded. What was more impressive was the way that they ended the season, clinching the Premiership title in real Roy of the Rovers style.

DOUBLES GALORE

This season was divided into two distinct phases: the first phase in the period up to Christmas and the second running to the end of the season. It was in this first phase that Arsenal would suffer their three home defeats.

Phase One (18 August – 18 December)

A 4–0 win at Middlesbrough on the opening day of the season was an impressive start to the campaign, although Dennis Bergkamp's two late goals gave extra gloss to a flattering scoreline. The opening game at Highbury a few days later was to prove a frustrating encounter as Leeds United inflicted a 2–1 defeat on the Gunners. The result typified the early-season inconsistencies Arsenal experienced, Leicester City then being dispatched for four without reply in the next Highbury encounter. A 1–1 draw at Chelsea was followed by a 3–1 win in west London over Fulham, whilst back at Highbury for the next game Bolton went back to the north-west with a point. Successive wins at Derby and Southampton were followed by four games without a win. Typical of Arsenal's form at the time was the enthralling 3–3 draw against Blackburn at Highbury in which Rovers snatched a point with a last-minute equaliser. Things got much worse three weeks later when Charlton became the second team to win at Highbury that season – it was the south London side's first win at Highbury for 46 years!

Arsenal then faced two games in succession against their toughest rivals. The visit to Tottenham was given more flavour by Sol Campbell's return to White Hart Lane for the first time. A superb drive by Robert Pires gave Arsenal the lead, only for Tottenham to secure a draw in the dying moments. Perennial rivals Manchester United were next to Highbury where Arsenal used their third goalkeeper of the season, Stuart Taylor making his Premiership debut replacing the injured Richard Wright, who had replaced the injured Seaman. Visitors to Highbury that day will remember the game for United goalkeeper Fabien Barthez's performance which left the home fans chanting his name in glee. Cries of 'Give it to Barthez' and 'Barthez is a Gooner' echoed around north London that winter afternoon as a game of great passion was played out. Arsenal won 3–1. Successive wins at Ipswich and then at home to Aston

Villa moved Arsenal into second place in the table. A 1–1 draw at West Ham United raised the curtain on a tough sequence of games for the Gunners.

Arsenal's last game at Highbury before Christmas was against Newcastle United. The home team went into the game knowing a win would take them to the top of the table and this looked all the more likely after Pires opened the scoring after 20 minutes. However Newcastle equalised and grew in confidence, and were then awarded a penalty which Shearer converted. With Arsenal in all-out attack mode in search of an equaliser, Robert increased Newcastle's lead to give them all three points. Although the Arsenal fans didn't know it at the time, this defeat mirrored that of Blackburn Rovers' win at Highbury in the previous Double season, when the scoreline was also 1–3. It was a turning point that had the action of strengthening the team's resolve and, coupled with the forthcoming return of a number of players who had been out injured, it would be the last time Arsenal would taste defeat in the Premiership that season.

Phase Two (23 December – 11 May)
The skill and determination inherent in the Arsenal side was clearly visible at Anfield two days before Christmas. Reduced to ten men after van Bronckhorst had been sent off for a second bookable offence, Arsenal responded brilliantly to win 2–1. On the surface it was a gutsy win, but in reality it was underpinned by the intelligence of Arsenal's football. That victory marked the start of an incredible twenty-one-match run to the end of the season without defeat, during which time Arsenal would drop just six points from three drawn games.

Chelsea provided the Boxing Day opposition for the first of three home games in succession. Sol Campbell opened his Arsenal scoring account against the London rivals whilst another defender, Ashley Cole, scored and ensured three points against Middlesbrough a few days later. Arsenal had their return encounter with Liverpool in the middle of January, but with eleven men this time could only muster a 1–1 draw. The result saw Manchester United top of the Premiership table by a single point. Arsenal now faced three away games in their bid to maintain the pressure on United.

DOUBLES GALORE

A draw at Leeds was followed by a win at Leicester but the Gunners dropped vital points in a disappointing 1–1 home draw with Southampton. The result dropped Arsenal further down the table where just three points separated the four teams at the top – Manchester United, Newcastle United, Liverpool and Arsenal.

With these other teams picking up wins regularly, Arsenal would need something special to take the title. Thirteen wins on the trot were just that. The sequence started at Everton, but it took a rather lucky goal from Wiltord to ensure all the points. Two goals by Henry helped Arsenal to a 4–1 win over Fulham at Highbury but saw the French striker suffer a rare injury that put him out of the trip to Newcastle in the next fixture. He was replaced in the attack by Bergkamp, who responded in typical fashion by supplying the goal of the season yet again. Bergkamp's goal at St James's Park, a flick around the defender and a side foot into the goal, just like his hat-trick during the second Double season, was one of the highlights of a tremendous year and emphasised his importance to the team. In their next ten games Arsenal would concede just two goals as they set about demolishing their opponents in the first thirty minutes of every game – only Aston Villa and Tottenham Hotspur would break an impressive-looking Arsenal rearguard.

During this period Arsenal were also making impressive progress in the FA Cup, where they again came up against two of the teams they were challenging for the title at that time. Watford, Liverpool and Gillingham were beaten to take Arsenal to the two sixth-round games with Newcastle United; a 1–1 draw on Tyneside was followed by a 3–0 lunchtime win at Highbury. Back in the Premiership a 3–0 win at Charlton was sandwiched between victories over Sunderland and Tottenham.

With just five Premiership games left, the title race was now between Arsenal and Manchester United, with the Gunners still having to travel to Old Trafford in what was looking increasingly like a title decider. Ironically, Arsenal had an earlier appointment at Old Trafford first for an FA Cup semi-final encounter with Middlesbrough. Arsenal prevailed in a dour game, the only goal of the 90 minutes coming early off the knee of a Middlesbrough defender.

Ipswich Town and West Ham United visited Highbury in the space of four days and both suffered 2–0 defeats. The game against West Ham United was effectively Arsenal's long-running game in hand over Manchester United and sent the Gunners clear at the top. Arsenal then travelled back to the north-west of England and a potentially tricky game at Bolton. Almost predictably, it was Ljungberg who opened the scoring. The Swede had scored in Arsenal's previous four games – this one making it six goals in all. Wiltord added a second and another 2–0 victory meant that Arsenal now had their destiny in their own hands: they were just one win in their remaining two games away from the title.

Arsenal knew they could now clinch the Double in the space of five short days. Cardiff's Millennium Stadium was the setting for the FA Cup final against Claudio Ranieri's talented Chelsea team, whom Arsenal seemed to encounter in the Cup consistently. A classic encounter was expected, but like most finals the first half proved to be a disappointment, although there were chances for both sides to take the lead. The Arsenal goal – when it came – was from an unexpected source and at a time when Chelsea were enjoying their best period of the game. Adams and Wiltord combined to present Ray Parlour with the ball just inside the Chelsea half. The Arsenal midfield player, whose only other goal that season had been earlier in the competition against Gillingham, was still some 40 yards from goal; looking up, he simply burst through the square Chelsea rearguard and at the end of his run curled a 25-yard shot over and beyond the diving Carlo Cudicini. Thanks to Sky Sports Fans Zone commentary, the phrase 'Don't worry, it's only Ray Parlour' will be forever remembered uttered, as it was, by the Chelsea commentator as the Arsenal midfielder broke through. Ten minutes later Ljungberg continued his impressive scoring streak, netting a not-too-dissimilar-but-probably-more-impressive goal to secure a 2–0 win and Arsenal's first trophy in four years.

On 8 May a small but significant part of Highbury relocated to one corner of Old Trafford. Home-made banners proclaiming 'Champions Section' were unfurled; Arsenal needed one win from their final two games to secure the title and their second Double under Wenger. What better place to do it than Old Trafford! Comparisons with 1971 and 1989 were obvious, although then Arsenal had a strict definition of what they had to do. That night any sort of victory would do, and there was the safety net of the final home game against Everton to come.

The match proved to be a slow-starting, dogged affair, but Arsenal appeared for the second half in a much more determined and confident mood. This was typified by the manner in which Edu was spraying his passes around the pitch and opening up the spaces. Arsenal deservedly took the lead after 57 minutes when Ljungberg ran on to a through ball only to see his shot parried by Barthez; the rebound fell straight to the incoming Wiltord who had the simple task of guiding the ball into the far corner of the net. One-nil to the Arsenal! The champions elect provided Henry with chances to extend their lead and in the final ten minutes Highbury's 'Champions Section' was in full voice, as the home fans streamed from the stadium.

The last home game of the season was back in north London and Islington was in party mood. The club also looked to provide several fringe players, such as Stuart Taylor, with the tenth game they needed to qualify for a Premier League Championship medal. Perhaps not surprisingly, Arsenal's defence succumbed to the carnival atmosphere as Everton became the first side to score three goals at Highbury since the Newcastle United turning point. Arsenal, however, scored four, with Henry, who scored twice, Bergkamp and Jeffers doing the damage. The win set a new sequence of successive Premiership victories to a record-breaking 13 games.

THE DOUBLE PLAYERS

Comparisons between extraordinary teams are always inevitable and whilst it is easier to relate between the second and third Double sides, not least because many of the players were the same, comparing the first and second Double sides requires bridging a gap of 26 years, and different footballing eras. Players in the first Double team were on a basic weekly salary of between £50 and £100; a bonus of £4 for a win and £2 for a draw were the added incentives! Winning the FA Cup final was worth around £700 to each player, whilst others received a loyalty bonus. Winning the

Double in 1971 gave the longest-serving players a total of around £17,500, salary and bonuses included. Even in modern-day terms this represents around just £200,000 – less than a month's salary for many of the third Double team's players!

The two managers were worlds apart too. Bertie Mee was a manager in the true sense of the word. The former Arsenal physio left all practical and coaching matters to Don Howe, himself concentrating on instilling pride and discipline back into a club that had been lacking it for many years. Wenger, on the other hand, was manager and coach, and also brought ideas and philosophies into the Marble Halls that would have been laughed out of sight in Mee's era.

The differences in the backroom staff at Highbury are also amazing. The 1970–71 Double side was supported by just half a dozen people – Mee and Howe, plus George Wright (physio), Steve Burtenshaw (reserve-team coach), Tony Donnelly (kit) and Gordon Clark (chief scout). The later Doubles had almost 20 supporting staff, including Wenger, Pat Rice (assistant manager), Bora Primorac (assistant coach), Eddie Niedzwiecki (reserve-team coach), Bob Wilson (goalkeeping coach), Gary Lewin and Colin Lewin (physios), Tony Colbert (fitness coach), Steve Rowley (chief scout), Joel Harris and Craig Gant (masseurs), Vic Ackers and Paul Ackers (kit), Paul Johnson (travel manager), Dr Yan Rougier (diet and health), Phillipe Boxiel (osteopath), Tiburce Darrou (rehabilitation), and Dave Elliot (motivational speaker).

Arguments will continue over which was the best of the Double teams and whilst they are subjective, it is clear each of the teams had their own individual characteristics and players. All three Double teams were brimming with talent and determination – they were just packaged differently in each. Which of these teams was the greatest modern-day Arsenal side of all? Probably none of them – that honour undoubtedly went to the Untouchables.

THIRTEEN

Managers Change

The role of the Arsenal manager changed quite drastically in the post-Second World War era. As the game grew bigger, the responsibilities changed and the role of administrator became a more demanding one. With an increasing fixture list and a desire to succeed, the ability of one person to undertake the administration of the club and the stadium as a whole, and also manage and oversee the coaching of the team, along with scouting and recruiting players, was severely tested. The powers that be at Highbury had already identified this and had employed the services of Bob Wall to undertake the administrative and secretarial tasks of the club and stadium after the death of Tom Whittaker. Ken Friar would later take on a similar role and become a Highbury legend himself. This left the ensuing managers free to carry on with the sole task of looking after on-field affairs for almost the next half-century. With this responsibility gone, the post-war managers had little or no say in developments at Highbury, although, in truth, apart from two new roofs for the North Bank and other small alterations, there was little to oversee other than an increasing amount of running repairs, and that responsibility was overseen by the establishment of a stadium management department. As we have seen, the arrival of David Dein kick-started a final phase in Highbury's development, and for the first time since Chapman, the board's subsequent appointment of Arsène Wenger placed someone in charge with the capacity to not just manage change but metamorphose the club both on and off the field.

The second half of the twentieth century, then, saw Highbury managers measured by the success of their teams on the field of play and the size of the crowds that their football produced.

CONTINUING SUCCESS

Tom Whittaker was both an Allison and Chapman man: he was Arsenal through and through, devoting the majority of his life to his only professional club. He was the first manager of Arsenal to have played for the club as a professional footballer, having been spotted playing for the army in 1919. It was on a tour of Australia in 1925 that he suffered a cracked knee socket, which effectively terminated his playing days; however, Whittaker was an intelligent man and, determined to stay in football, studied physiotherapy (something that long-term club physio Gary Lewin would do to great effect many years later), which enabled him to remain at Highbury first as assistant trainer (1926) and then later as chief trainer (1927).

After Herbert Chapman's death in 1934, Joe Shaw and Tom Whittaker took over the running of the team under Allison's paternal guidance. After the Second World War, Whittaker returned as Allison's assistant manager. When his boss had to retire through ill health in 1947, the Arsenal board wasted no time in appointing him as manager of Arsenal.

Whittaker employed Leslie Compton as the archetypal 'stopper' centre-half, and Joe Mercer led the team brilliantly, used shrewdly as a purely defensive half-back to save wear and tear on his ageing knees, whilst Ronnie Rooke was a significant signing and blossomed in the autumn of his career to become the League's leading marksman. Arsenal romped home with the League title in Whittaker's first season.

Then in 1950 came another FA Cup triumph, as Whittaker's Arsenal beat Liverpool 2–0, pre-war striker Ray Lewis scoring both goals. The honours continued as the League was won again in 1952–53. Thus in seventeen playing seasons since 1930, Arsenal had won the League seven times and the FA Cup three times in five appearances.

However the champions were growing older and Arsenal simply could not maintain their own high standards. Whittaker found it extremely difficult to come to terms with the team's inability to rise above the mediocre. Eventually he was taken ill, suffering from nervous exhaustion, and in October 1956 he died of a heart attack at the age of 58. Like his mentor Chapman before him, he had literally given his life to his beloved Arsenal.

THE BARREN YEARS

Given Arsenal's position at the time, both pre- and post-war, it would have been absurd to have suggested at the time of Whittaker's death that the 1953 title would have been the last one at Highbury for some 18 years, but that is exactly how it panned out, as the club went into a decline that would see poor crowds and flirtation with relegation.

After Whittaker's death Arsenal continued the highly successful 'promote from within' strategy and elevated assistant manager Jack Crayston, also a former Arsenal player, into the role. Crayston had been one of George Allison's signings, coming from Bradford Park Avenue in May 1934. This appointment also marked the first time the role of Arsenal manager did not encompass the post of secretary, these duties being delegated to Bob Wall, which left Crayston free to concentrate on the team.

In his first season he steered the side to a credible fifth place in the League and the sixth round of the FA Cup; however, 1957–58 was not a good season, with 19 defeats, hardly what the Highbury faithful had come to expect. Twelfth place was a poor return and a third-round FA Cup defeat at the hands of humble Northampton Town (1–3 away) was almost a 'Walsall' level disaster. Although the traditional 'Arsenal style' persisted, the defence was not Arsenal quality and without the unanimous backing of the board and after 24 years of service to the club, Crayston tendered his resignation after less than two years in the job.

After his resignation, Arsenal again looked to a former player, but this time not to someone who was currently on the Highbury staff. George Swindin had been a first-class goalkeeper, regarded by many experts as the best uncapped keeper in the League. He joined Arsenal in 1936 and after his debut he rarely lost his place until 1953 when Jack Kelsey took over. Swindin won League Championship medals either side of the war and two FA Cup medals in the 1950s (one winner, one loser).

On his arrival as manager, Swindin had a clear-out, with no fewer than 17 players being disposed of during his first season in charge. His signings included the abrasive Preston wing-half Tommy Docherty; Jackie Henderson, Wolves's energetic forward; and a young Irish full-back, Bill McCullough, was signed from Portadown.

A revitalised side finished in third place, although a fifth-round FA Cup defeat at Sheffield United was disappointing. In his second season Mel Charles, brother of the great John, was signed, but this was offset when Docherty broke his ankle. His presence on the team was badly missed as Arsenal slipped to 13th place whilst suffering another embarrassing ejection from the FA Cup, Rotherham United surprisingly triumphing after two replays.

In 1960–61 Swindin masterminded what was at the time the most sensational transfer in League history, as George Eastham arrived from Newcastle United for £47,500 following a long, bitter wrangle with his old club. The Magpies were preventing Eastham from playing, but refusing to allow him to sign for another club. The whole question of working conditions came into the spotlight – at the time players were limited to a mere £20 a week, regardless of their standing in the game, with no freedom to move at the end of their playing contracts. Later Eastham, along with Professional Footballers' Association (PFA) chairman Jimmy Hill, would fight a famous High Court case, which resulted in players being granted freedom to both negotiate their own salary as well as enjoy freedom of contract.

Despite Eastham's brilliance, Arsenal could do no better than eleventh and tenth place in Swindin's third and fourth seasons. Arsenal simply could not break free from mid-table mediocrity, made all the worse by Tottenham's sudden emergence as the team of the moment winning the then so-called 'impossible' League–FA Cup Double in 1961. All this combined to increase the pressure and it was no surprise that Swindin resigned at the end of the 1961–62 season. But things would not get any better for the club or the fans.

It was clearly a sign of Arsenal's desperation after ten seasons of under-achievement that they completely broke with tradition when selecting George Swindin's successor. Not only did they not promote from within, or at least choose an Arsenal 'old boy', they chose a man with no managerial skills whatsoever: yet Billy Wright's playing credentials were second to none – he was football's golden boy with an amazing record. Captain of Wolverhampton Wanderers for most of his career, a one-club man with almost 500 League appearances to his name as a combative, yet utterly fair defender, he had led Wolves to three League Championships and one FA Cup success as they overhauled Manchester United as England's leading club. Not only that, he could boast 105 England caps, 90 as captain with an unbeatable run of 70 consecutive internationals at one stage.

Billy Wright made an immediate impression, unrealistically raising Arsenal's expectations as he signed England centre-forward Joe Baker from Torino for £70,000. Baker was an immediate success scoring 29 goals in the League, with colleague Geoff Strong proving an ideal partner with 18. Yet Arsenal's defence was scarcely the traditional immovable object, with 77 conceded, meaning a modest seventh place in 1962–63. Arsenal slipped to eighth in 1963–64, finishing the season with a humiliating 0–5 thrashing at Anfield as Liverpool stormed to their sixth Championship. The season had seen Arsenal's first venture into Europe in the Inter Cities Fairs Cup, an early exit doing nothing to appease the supporters' dismay as Tottenham had become England's first European winners the previous season.

The 1964–65 season saw a further dip in Arsenal's fortunes as the club slipped into the bottom half of the League, finishing 13th, and another FA Cup humiliation when Peterborough United beat them 2–1 at London Road in the fourth round.

Astonishingly, Arsenal, in a bid to rid themselves of the Herbert Chapman 'millstone', decided to abandon the famous red shirts with their distinctive white sleeves introduced by the great man. Now Arsenal turned out in all red, redolent of their Nottingham Forest connections in the Woolwich 'Reds' days. To their credit, the club quickly saw the error of their ways and to their supporters' glee soon re-adopted the original strip. However, the famous shirts could not alone bring about an upswing in the team's fortunes as Arsenal finished 14th – their worst position since 1930.

The second half of the 1965–66 season was an unremitting disaster – of twenty League matches played only three were won – and supporters started to stay away. A mere 4,554 turned up at Highbury to witness a third-consecutive 3–0 defeat, surely the worst sequence for many years. When the news of Billy Wright's dismissal came, it scarcely caused a ripple.

THE REVIVAL

After the euphoria of England winning the 1966 World Cup, the press turned its attention back to domestic matters – high on the list was who would be Arsenal's next manager. To say that Bertie Mee would have been the last person anyone thought of is not an exaggeration, since it is doubtful he ever appeared on anyone's shortlist – or longlist, for that matter.

Bertie Mee's football history bears striking resemblances to that of Tom Whittaker. Hailing from the Nottingham area, Mee found his playing career (with Derby County and Mansfield Town) cut short by a serious injury, after which he studied physiotherapy. He had been Arsenal's physiotherapist since August 1960, before which (like Whittaker) he had been a sergeant in the army for several years. Mee installed a strict code of discipline within the club and then guided it back to the very summit of English football, and in doing so provided Highbury with arguably its greatest-ever moment.

His first and possibly his most important signing was Dave Sexton as coach, who soon won the respect of all the players with his quiet coaching expertise, thus enhancing the manager's reputation amongst the players as a man who knew his stuff. Unlike an outsider, there was no need for Mee to work at earning the respect of the players since they already had a high opinion of him. Similarly, Mee already had the most intimate understanding of each of his playing staff – who needed encouraging, who needed bullying, who needed a kick up the pants.

His first season in 1966–67 was one of consolidation, with seventh place in the League a reasonable start. By this time Arsenal had entered the League Cup for the first time and in the 1967–68 season reached the final at Wembley. Hopes for the club's first trophy in 15 seasons were dashed by Leeds United's 1–0 win. The following season saw the League Cup final reached again, this time with Third Division Swindon Town as opposition. Again, there was disappointment when, with most of the Arsenal playing staff suffering with influenza, Arsenal went down 3–1 to two sensational Don Rogers' goals in extra-time.

Despite the massive disappointment, this was at least progress, with fourth place in the League attained and the structure of a useful side starting to take shape, with greatness just around the corner. After a modest 12th place in 1969–70, Arsenal ended a 17-year drought with the European Fairs Cup victory in 1970–71. Suddenly everything clicked. Out of the youth team had emerged Pat Rice, Eddie Kelly, Ray Kennedy and Charlie George to supplement Simpson and Radford, and one of Mee's first signings in charge – George Graham. Don Howe had been promoted to replace Sexton as coach and immediately there was an even greater rapport within the team.

The story of that first Double season in 1970–71 is recalled elsewhere in these pages as the League Trophy and FA Cup were lifted in the space of five glorious May days. So Arsenal, and Bertie Mee in particular, had done what Herbert Chapman and his famous side of the 1930s could not do – win the League–FA Cup Double. The Highbury faithful were beside themselves with joy. After 18 years without a domestic trophy of any sort, they had won the two greatest trophies available in the English game, in a single, magnificent season.

Strangely, no more trophies followed during Bertie Mee's Highbury reign. The runners-up Double was achieved the following season, as Arsenal finished behind Liverpool and Leeds in League and Cup. Despite Mee's superb efforts in taking Arsenal to the pinnacle of achievement there was now a despairing feeling amongst the support that the team had been one-season wonders rather than laying the seeds for a period of domination. In retrospect, perhaps Mee had tried to rebuild the side too quickly after his Double triumph.

In 1974–75 the dread of relegation suddenly emerged as Arsenal finished 16th and then the following year in 17th place, despite the signing of World Cup hero Alan Ball. Ball's arrival spurred local lad Charlie George to ask for a transfer and when he signed for Derby County, Arsenal's world seemed to be falling apart. At the end of 1975–76 Mee announced his retirement from management. He died on 22 October 2001 at the age of 82.

CUP FIGHTERS

After Bertie Mee's resignation Arsenal once more went down the tried-and-trusted road of appointing a former player to manage the team. This time Terry Neill, club captain between 1959 and 1970, was appointed, a strong intelligent man with management experience at Hull City while still a player, and then at Tottenham Hotspur, whom he left to move to Highbury. He had also been chairman of the PFA for a spell and played for Northern Ireland 44 times, being captain on many occasions.

One of his first tasks was to prise England centre-forward Malcolm Macdonald away from Newcastle United (where he was something of a cult hero in the famous No. 9 jersey) for the then massive fee of £333,333. The news was sensational, encouraging Arsenal supporters to believe they were on the way back to glory. Although 1976–77 saw Arsenal rise to eighth position, with Macdonald scoring 25 League goals, there had been a hope that, with the side containing David O'Leary, Liam Brady, Frank Stapleton and Alan Hudson alongside the big signing, a more determined assault on the title could have been mounted. Neill also brought the colossal Willie Young to Highbury, another who moved across the Seven Sisters Road from White Hart Lane. Young was far from accepted on his arrival but went on to become one of the club's biggest cult heroes.

One of Neill's problems was that several of the older members of the Arsenal side had played at the same time as him and this led to some friction. The 1977–78 season saw Arsenal rise to fifth and reach the FA Cup final, where unfancied Ipswich looked fitter on the day, deservedly winning 1–0. This would be the first of three consecutive FA Cup finals for Arsenal, with Manchester United famously beaten in the 'Five-Minute Final', then a disappointing defeat as a Trevor Brooking header gave Second Division West Ham a surprise win. In the same season there was further disappointment for Arsenal as they lost the final of the European Cup Winners' Cup against Valencia in Brussels, with the agony of a penalty shoot-out after a disappointing 0–0 draw – four finals and just one win.

So into the '80s with finishes of third, fifth and tenth not exactly setting the football world on fire, and with just one FA Cup win to show in the ten years following the Double. A League Cup defeat in November 1983 by, of all clubs, Walsall, proved the last straw, the Gunners' ancient nemesis pulling off a 2–1 win at Highbury, the much-expected axe falling before Christmas.

It was a rarity indeed for Arsenal to sack a manager mid-season and they replaced him with their experienced coach, Don Howe, in an effort to make a seamless transition. Howe returned to Highbury with an intimate knowledge of the club gained from his playing and previous coaching spell. He signed Paul Mariner to form an all-England strike partnership with Tony Woodcock, supplemented by the mercurial Charlie Nicholas. Yet in 1984–85 Arsenal still struggled for goals: just 61 in the League. It spoke volumes that workhorse Brian Talbot was joint leading scorer with ten goals. Arsenal suffered yet another FA Cup humiliation, this time to York City 0–1 at Bootham Crescent. The League Cup was little better, Oxford United progressing at the Gunners' expense. No European competitions again and the crowd were already becoming restless as Arsenal's old problem of a lack of consistent goal-scoring resurfaced.

Season 1985–86 would get worse with a derisory 49 goals in the League, the defence alone achieving a respectable seventh place. New names appeared on the teamsheet, Tony Adams and Martin Keown beginning what would be long Arsenal careers. But now it was not unusual to see home gates dropping below 20,000, unheard of for over 50 years. In fifteen years since the Double only one trophy had been won – the FA Cup in 1979; this was just not good enough. Don Howe's record was nothing to be ashamed of, but in March 1986 he asked to be released from his contract. Steve Burtenshaw saw the season out as caretaker.

Howe often said that during his various 'stints' at the club there were times he stayed when he should have gone, and times he went when he should have stayed. In reality it might be said that when he accepted the manager's role it was a time when he probably should have 'left' – but this should never take away from his phenomenal service and the backroom success he put on show at Highbury. Howe is and will remain an Arsenal legend.

GRAHAM'S RED ARMY

Before the start of the 1986–87 season Arsenal announced that George Graham, the Millwall manager and, more importantly, a former player for the club and a member of the Double team, was to take charge at Highbury. Graham's record at The Den had earned many plaudits and his appointment was met with universal approval. Always a confident and most elegant player – hence his nickname at the club: 'Stroller' – Graham strode into the Marble Halls determined to exorcise the ghosts of the glorious past which had intimidated a string of managers over the years.

Graham decided to give the existing players a chance rather than plunge impetuously into the transfer market. Players like Tony Adams, David O'Leary, Steve Williams and Niall Quinn suddenly blossomed under Graham's coaching and management talents, which included the sergeant-major-type approach he had been subjected to by his Arsenal boss, Bertie Mee, which had been at odds with his high-life social standing during his playing days.

An unbeaten League run of 22 matches from September (a club record at the time) put Arsenal in with a shout of the League, although both Merseyside clubs, as usual, were in the frame. One of the highlights of the season was the club's centenary celebration on 27 December 1986, with a whole host of former stars invited to the home match with the great club, not inappropriately, sitting at the top of the League. In the end, Everton pipped Liverpool for the title, with Arsenal a creditable fourth. There was the consolation of winning the League Cup for the first time in the club's history – their first major trophy since 1979 and only their second since the Double year of 1971. To make the occasion extra sweet, mighty Liverpool were the beaten finalists.

The 1987–88 season was one of consolidation. Alan Smith, Leicester City's prolific striker, was now on the staff in a season that contained a sequence of ten consecutive League wins, which was part of a fourteen-match winning sequence (including League Cup matches), setting a new club record. More shrewd signings included two full-backs, Lee Dixon from Stoke and Nigel Winterburn from Wimbledon, who would play a big part in Arsenal's future during the next ten years or so. Arsenal again reached the League Cup final only to lose, surprisingly, to Luton Town – a game where Arsenal truly snatched defeat from the jaws of victory.

But this shock reverse was simply the prelude to a glorious 1988–89 season which saw the League title wonderfully and sensationally won with a last-day, last-minute, last-gasp winner at Anfield, snatching the title from Liverpool's unbelieving grasp. George Graham, in winning the League title for Arsenal, had joined a short list of men who had won League medals as players and managers, a list headed by Ted Drake, Arsenal's record-breaking centre-forward of the 1930s. Drake, in fact, was the first person to achieve the feat, securing his managerial success at Chelsea, whom he guided to the League title in 1955, just three years after joining them as manager.

After fourth place in 1989–90, the League title was lifted again in 1990–91, this time in true Arsenal fashion, with just a single League defeat all season, a new record for a 38-match season. To satisfy the purists, just 18 goals were conceded, with David Seaman now firmly established as the country's top goalkeeper.

A fourth-place finish in 1991–92 was followed by an even more disappointing tenth place in the first Premier League season, all the more so given that the club should have become much more competitive with the signing of Ian Wright, the Crystal Palace striker, who was destined to be the Gunners' all-time top goal-scorer for a period. Yet the consolation of winning both domestic cups – both, coincidentally, against Sheffield Wednesday – tended to obscure Arsenal's patchy League form in a season which saw 16 League defeats. Importantly, it gave Arsenal a place in the Cup Winners' Cup, which would be lifted in Copenhagen a year later as Alan Smith's early goal proved enough to beat Serie A side Parma. Thus George Graham won his sixth major trophy in eight seasons with Arsenal, crowning him as Arsenal's most successful manager of all time.

Everything in the garden seemed rosy, both for Arsenal and for George Graham, the 'dream team' seemingly on the verge of more great deeds. Then, during the 1994–95 season, rumours began to surface about dubious dealings with certain football agents who were used to broker deals with overseas players. Suddenly, it seemed that George Graham might be involved, with a huge amount of money unaccounted for following transfer deals. It seemed that Graham had declared an unsolicited gift of £425,000 from an agent to the Inland Revenue. Graham apparently paid the money back to Arsenal, but the damage was done and he offered to terminate his contract at the end of the season. Then the dramatic news broke on 21 February 1995 that Graham had been dismissed.

SHORT TERM

Stewart Houston took over the team until the end of the season, which finished dramatically with Arsenal again in the Cup Winners' Cup final, this time facing Real Zaragoza in Paris. With the scores level at 1–1 in the final minute of extra-time, ex-Tottenham player Nayim launched a 50-yard bomb at Seaman's goal, scoring incredibly in what seemed like slow motion. The dejected Arsenal side summed up a very disappointing season. George Graham's position as one of Arsenal's great managers, possibly now third in line after Wenger and Chapman, cannot be airbrushed out of history regardless of the unsavoury end to his reign at Highbury.

Stewart Houston was passed over for the job on a full-time basis when, early in June 1995, Arsenal announced that the Bolton manager, Bruce Rioch, would be their next helmsman, Arsenal opting again for an 'outsider' and one of the game's brightest new managers.

MANAGERS CHANGE

Rioch's Highbury reign started with a signing that would fundamentally change the Arsenal playing style at Highbury. It would not be an understatement to say that the signing also changed the club forever. The arrival of a young Dutchman would proliferate shirts in the years ahead with one of two things on them: '10 God' or '10 Ice Man'. Dennis Bergkamp arrived from Internazionale for £7.5 million; he was joined by the then England captain David Platt from Sampdoria for £4.75 million. Whether Rioch was actually instrumental in these signatures is a point of debate. In the excellent *Rebels For the Cause*, Jon Spurring outlines the increasingly prominent role of David Dein as key activist in their arrivals. (At this point in time the Arsenal board had opted for Rioch, having turned down Dein's preference for one Arsène Wenger . . .)

Fifth place in the League was an improvement, although an early FA Cup exit to Second Division Sheffield United was a major disappointment. A semi-final appearance in the League Cup promised a consolation trophy, but Aston Villa sneaked home on the away-goals rule to deny Arsenal even a crumb of comfort. However the style of football was also in transition as Rioch ousted the direct ways of George Graham and started to implement a passing game that fully utilised his significant signings' skill sets. The tone for football at Highbury had changed.

Rioch had done little wrong – indeed, by any criteria he had enjoyed a very successful first season on and off the pitch – however, behind the mahogany doors of the east wing first floor the Arsenal board were being persuaded by Dein a year on that Wenger really was the man to take the club into the twenty-first century. Dein was to get his way and, with Wenger accepting an offer, just before the start of 1996–97 season came the news that Rioch had been sacked, his Highbury reign having lasted a mere 61 weeks, the shortest in Arsenal's history. It would be 22 August before the board admitted what everyone really already knew: that French coach Arsène Wenger, then managing Grampus Eight in Japan, had agreed to join the Highbury club.

THE ENTERTAINERS . . .

The appointment of Frenchman Arsène Wenger took English football totally by surprise – even if it had been the worst-kept secret of the time. Although the domestic game now had many overseas star players, it was still felt that home-grown managers were the best bet. There was no record of any Continental manager having any success in England, especially in the League. Little was known of this bespectacled man – although it was rumoured that he could speak five languages fluently – yet on the Continent he had a considerable reputation as a coach: players like Glenn Hoddle, who had played under him in France, testified to his considerable expertise. Others also pointed to how he had unearthed world-class talent – the likes of Liberian George Weah, who would go on to be a World Footballer of the Year, a case in point.

Born in Dusenheim, France, on 22 October 1949, he had grown up supporting his local side, Racing Strasbourg, for whom he would eventually play. In a career stretching from 1969 to 1980 he played professionally in the lower French leagues for Mutzig, Vaunban and Mulhouse. He made a few waves during his time at Mulhouse, once scoring four goals in a division two league encounter. In a move to the first division, he made his debut for Racing Strasbourg at the age of 29 in a *libero* role, but played just a handful of games at the top.

After pursuing an academic career he was tempted back to football in 1984 as coach of AS Nancy Lorraine, where he suffered relegation three years later. Despite this, Nancy offered him a five-year contract and a total free run of the club – already seeing the greater abilities that he would later use to rebuild Arsenal in every sense. Wenger also had offers from Paris St Germain and Monaco. In 1987 he opted for the potential and lifestyle of the principality and success quickly followed for Monaco when the French championship – *Le Championat* – was won in 1988; then, in 1989, they reached the French cup final, the cup finally being won in 1991, followed by a European final in 1992, Wenger's side, including George Weah, losing 0–2 to Werder Bremen in the Cup Winners' Cup. During his time at the club, Monaco never finished outside the top three – and there was one championship and two runner-up positions. This was achieved against the background of the corruption and big-money spending of l'Olympique de Marseille.

Next Wenger took up an appointment to manage Nagoya Grampus Eight in Japan's J League, where more trophies followed. But then Arsenal came calling, asking Wenger to take up his position immediately in August 1996. He had unfinished business in Japan, however, which he insisted on seeing through.

So, as the 1996–97 season got under way, assistant Pat Rice took over the reins, but despite his 'caretaker' tag there was little doubt who was in charge. As early as 14 August (two days after Rioch's sacking) two Frenchmen, Patrick Vieira and Gilles Grimandi, signed for Arsenal. A third Frenchman, Remi Garde, was to arrive soon after, as the Gallic influence took hold inside Highbury.

Arsène Wenger officially took up his duties on 22 September 1996, quickly confirming Pat Rice as his number two and bringing Boro Primorac, his compatriot from Monaco and Grampus Eight, with him as first-team coach. So-called experts expected Wenger to dispose of his back four 'dinosaurs', but contrary to expectations they all took on a new lease of life as the French manager introduced his theories on playing and lifestyle, and, above all, diet. Among the players Tony Adams – who said on Wenger's arrival: 'What does this Frenchman know about football?' – was one of many stalwarts not just to have his playing career extended beyond even optimistic expectations but to forge a bond that was more than evident in the celebrations that would follow a season later.

That first season Arsenal finished level with Newcastle and Liverpool and seven points behind Manchester United, who retained their title, but three goals' difference denied Arsenal a European Cup place, which went to Newcastle. The season 1997–98 was one which defied even the most optimistic follower's expectations and, as documented elsewhere in this book, took Arsenal to an incredible Double – and with both fans and the media taking 'The Professor', as he had been dubbed, to their hearts. It was the start of a sequence of success that would, in many respects, emulate his time at Monaco – this time Arsenal never finished outside the top three; indeed outside the top two, if you omit that first season when Wenger took control already some way into the season.

FIELD OF DREAMS

Behind the scenes the relationship between Wenger and Dein continued to strengthen and the two shared their dreams for the ultimate footballing side with facilities to match. With a growing commitment to the club, Wenger and Dein knew that to attract the very best players they needed not necessarily the best wages, but certainly the best facilities. Taking a 'build it and they will come' attitude, the two set about creating their own 'Field of Dreams'. Wenger took it all on his shoulders, dedicating himself to helping oversee the completion of a new state-of-the-art training facility at London Colney and then taking an active role in promoting the construction of the new stadium just across the road. With new facilities and the development of a new stadium on the go, the pressure was also on to create a team that would be able to fill the new space.

However, despite the many highs that were to follow under Wenger, the one thing the team under his control at Highbury never managed to do was to retain and win back-to-back titles. Indeed, the three successive Championships Arsenal won in the early '30s were the only back-to-back success the club has ever achieved at Highbury – an amazing and ultimately disappointing fact. No one Arsenal manager has been involved in such title successes – Herbert Chapman died midway through the second of the three successive Championship seasons!

Continual 'failure' in Europe was another bugbear – in this respect, failure to win the Champions League. Indeed, the team has not passed the quarter-final stage at any point to get within touching distance of a final. Much has been said and written about it, but European champions down the years, with little exception, are normally categorised by their great defensive prowess, rather than their attacking excellence. There lies the quandary, given Wenger's philosophies for open attacking football. And although in the final few years at Highbury a more conservative approach was often sought, the inability to maintain a clean sheet was often the final downfall.

Expectations for 1998–99 were high but for three successive seasons Arsenal had to settle for the runners-up spot behind Manchester United as the two clubs developed a bitter rivalry. In that first season United also won an extra-time FA Cup semi-final between the two sides at Villa Park, which will always be remembered for a last-minute penalty miss by Bergkamp and a sensational extra-time winner by Ryan Giggs. The reward for failure in the Champions League in 1999–2000 was ironically a UEFA Cup place and Arsenal reached the final with Galatasaray of Turkey waiting in Copenhagen. It proved to be Arsenal's poorest match of the tournament, although French striker Thierry Henry was proving a brilliant replacement for the departed Nicolas Anelka. A goal-less draw produced the almost inevitable penalty shoot-out, but Arsenal simply did not have their shooting boots on that night, giving the Turks their first European trophy.

The FA Cup looked to be the salvation for the 1999–2000 season, as, with just minutes remaining, Arsenal led Liverpool by Ljungberg's goal in a game that should have been dead and buried. But spurned chances did indeed come back to haunt the wasteful Gunners, with two late strikes by Michael Owen meaning a defeat that hardly looked possible.

The 2001–02 season brought success in abundance when a second Wenger Double was secured with gas left in the tank. Liverpool were prised from their grip on the Cup in the fourth round and United left behind in the Gunners' wake in the Premiership. But a year later it was a familiar story in the Premiership, second to United – this time by five points – although a 1–0 win over Southampton ensured the FA Cup remained in the trophy cabinet for another year. The 2003–04 season proved to be the greatest in the club's history as the Untouchables were born and eschewed all Wenger's philosophies.

With Dein's and Wenger's vision of the stadium beginning to show its form behind the West Stand, Arsenal started their penultimate season at Highbury full of the form and confidence that continued to extend their undefeated record and entice them to the top of the table. The run was pushed to 49 games without defeat and if the half-century was to be achieved it would have had to have been secured at the home of their greatest rivals: Old Trafford was brimming with expectation. United won 2–0.

Often a great side is best judged by how well it deals with defeat, and in this respect Arsenal could be seen to be lacking. The side went on to take just six points from a possible eighteen, but it could have been worse.

In the end the team got their act back together but it was much too late: Chelsea had already established an uncatchable lead and the defence of the title had again failed. Defeat in the first knockout phase of the Champions League coincided with probably the worst run of injuries since Wenger had come to Highbury. When they took their toll, it was thanks to the younger talent Wenger was now blooding and relying on that the team stayed on course, overtaking United and clinching second place – and an automatic Champions League spot – and beating them on penalties in the FA Cup final, which ensured at least one pot of silverware was on display in the Marble Halls during the final season at Highbury.

FINAL IRONY

The rebuilding tone continued unabated during 2005–06, in which Arsenal experienced their worse Premiership season under Wenger – suffering 11 defeats over the course of the campaign, as many in total as they had encountered in the previous three season put together – and a final fourth position in the Premier League, Arsenal's lowest placing for a decade (the Gunners had not ended a Premiership campaign outside the top three since the 1995–96 season, when they were fifth with 63 points). No one was in any doubt as to the reason for the 'demise': it was the departure of Patrick Vieira, who had returned to Italy and the black-and-white stripes of Juventus for a reported £12 million. After years of speculation about a move to Real Madrid, it was ironic that after pledging himself to the team for the rest of his career it was the club who decided to cash in on him by accepting the offer from Turin.

Late in the season, Wenger admitted himself that the departure of 'the man from Senegal' had created a void that was more disruptive than he had anticipated. It was not helped either by the fact that during the season the team was plagued with long-term injuries to many senior players, including the likes of Sol Campbell, Ashley Cole and Lauren. Wenger's decision had even the more ardent Arsenal fans questioning the sanity of their manager well into the New Year, as the side dropped to League positions that at one point made even a UEFA Cup qualification place in serious doubt. However, as the season unfolded, the emerging players with big shoes to fill did so and, all of a sudden, Arsenal's season started to turn around, being transformed in such a way no one could have imagined. What the manager had seen, others started to as well.

One player to emerge was Arsenal's only major signing for the start of the season —Aleksander Hleb. The Belarusian started slowly but in the final stretch his energy and dribbling skills were a feature of the Arsenal right, where he combined with an even more impressive Emmanuel Eboue, whose marauding runs from his right-back position lifted supporters from their seats with regularity. Philippe Senderos and Mathieu Flamini filled in for the absent Campbell and Cole to such an extent that only injuries late in the season denied them places in the Champions League final. Flamini in particular moved from right-midfield to left-back as through it was his natural position. And then there was Cesc Fabregas, whose influence on the Arsenal midfield grew from game to game, belying his 18 years of age.

Arsenal made use of the mid-season transfer window, with the notable signing of Theo Walcott from Southampton, who was heralded as a future great of the game – reflected in the £5 million down payment made in a deal that could ultimately be worth £12 million – and who, at the age of 17, was named as part of the England 2006 World Cup squad despite not having played a single game for the Arsenal first team.

Ironically, it was the continual changing of the team that helped it find a formula that would take the club into a first-ever Champions League final and bring it within 13 minutes of an unlikely triumph over Barcelona. A scintillating aggregate win over Real Madrid was the catalyst that sparked the team into life. A defence that could not defend in Europe suddenly set a record of ten games without conceding a goal. And, as always in these things, fate conspired to bring Vieira back to Highbury and pit him against his replacement, Fabregas. The young Spaniard won the battle and scored one of the goals that put paid to the Old Lady of Turin in the quarter-finals.

The Champions League final had promised so much between two teams of similar attacking ilk but was ultimately destroyed by goalkeeper Jens Lehmann's 18th-minute red card for a foul on Samuel Eto'o, and left

Arsenal with a monumental task. In typical fashion, the Highbury side for one last time took the lead when Campbell rose to head home Henry's free-kick late in the first half. Having given everything, fatigue finally took its toll and late on two goals in five minutes for Barca meant there was no way back.

Just ten days earlier, Highbury had witnessed its final day and the end of a season, as well as an era, that had had its lows but also many highs. Home form was good, with the 7–0 win over Middlesbrough the highlight of the Premiership season, although away form was dismal. It was this that undermined the season, starting with an early reversal at Chelsea on 21 August 2005 – a defeat that ended Arsenal's record of consecutive unbeaten matches in London derbies that ran for 35 games after losing 4–2 at home to Charlton.

It was a season in which Thierry Henry cemented his place as the club's greatest goal-scorer. First he became Arsenal's all-time top scorer when he notched his second goal in Prague against Sparta, thereby taking him past Ian Wright's record of 185 goals for the club. He then passed Cliff Bastin's record of 150 league goals for the club with a January strike in the 2–3 home defeat by West Ham. Then, just a few days later, a goal at Birmingham made him the first Arsenal striker to score 200 goals for the club. A move that, in the Football Writers' Association view, meant he had became an all-time great, and was voted FWA Footballer of the Year for a record third time.

Henry ended the second half of the season with his future at the club still to be resolved, but within days of the Champions League final committed himself to the Gunners for a further four years – siting the loyalty of club supporters as one of the main reasons for wanting to end his career as a Gooner. David Dein later said the Arsenal Board had rejected two £50 million offers from Spain that would have made him the world's most expensive player.

As Highbury as a stadium was finally decommissioned, Arsenal finished their 93 years without a trophy, but with the promise of many more to come, and with the Emirates Stadium beckoning and waiting to accommodate silverware won on its own pitch, playing the game the Wenger way – under Arsenal's and Highbury's greatest ever manager.

FOURTEEN

The Untouchables

In historical terms the arrival of Arsène Wenger at Highbury was every bit as significant to the team and to the future of Highbury as the arrival of Henry Norris on Woolwich Arsenal's Plumstead doorstep some 70 years earlier. Whilst Norris had taken a bankrupt, ailing club and provided drive, leadership and a new home, along with laying the foundations for the Team of the '30s, Wenger created the greatest footballing side ever to grace Highbury – and perhaps English football – at the same time orchestrating a move to new facilities and a financial foundation to lead them into the heart of the twenty-first century as one of the top clubs in the world.

However, despite the constraints imposed by a perceived lack of cash in the transfer market, Wenger continued to unearth exceptional talent at supermarket-style prices. Not every player acquired on the cheap has surfaced at the top but those who made it often did so with world-class style. Curiously, when Arsenal were probably at their most challenged financially, struggling with funding for their new stadium, they produced arguably Arsenal's best-ever side, certainly one of the best footballing sides ever, and one that rewrote the record books.

* * *

The 2002–03 season was one when Arsenal lost their way on the pitch. As the team looked set to clinch their first back-to-back Championship success since the days of Herbert Chapman, the season simply fell apart at its very seams. In the final dozen games or so Arsenal uncharacteristically dropped points. The 2–2 home-draw showdown with Manchester United was significant not because Arsenal had twice led, but for the sending off of Sol Campbell, the bedrock of the Arsenal defence. A four-game suspension followed after an appeal at a time when the side was clearly tired and lacking players through injury. Campbell requested that Solskjaer confirm one way or the other whether the Gunner's arm actually made contact with him, and his refusal to do so made a mockery of the view that players stand together under the PFA banner. Perhaps the silence spoke louder than any potential answer.

The uncertainty and doubts were never more apparent than at the Reebok Stadium and a 2–2 draw with Bolton. Arsenal had led 2–0 and a win that afternoon would probably have ensured their retention of the Championship, but the visitors lost control of a game that was won and the hosts restored parity. Ultimately, another FA Cup success, this time at the expense of Southampton, ensured silverware, but it could and really should have easily been the first-ever back-to-back Double.

During that season a comment early on by Arsène Wenger was taken out of context and widely promoted as suggesting that Arsenal could complete the Premiership season undefeated. This had been consistently thrown back in the club's face, especially as games were lost and the Championship slipped away. Indeed, Arsenal's impressive away record, which had seen them undefeated outside of Highbury during the 2001–02 season, was ended by the then Evertonian Wayne Rooney in the last minute of the game on Merseyside in mid-October.

THE RUN STARTS

The visit of Leeds United to Highbury in early May 2003 confirmed Arsenal had lost the title as the visitors won by the odd goal in five. With the pressure off, Arsenal completed their final two league games of the Premiership, scoring an amazing ten goals and conceding just one at the home win over Southampton – just days before the FA Cup final with both teams resting players – and an impressive 4–0 win at Sunderland. Unbeknown at that time, the 6–1 win over Southampton signalled the start of the most amazing unbeaten run in English league, and indeed world football.

The close season saw some changes but Arsenal's French three – Henry, Pires and Vieira – all signed new contracts, as did the evergreen Dennis Bergkamp. The most significant change came in goal when David Seaman ended his 13-year association with Arsenal by moving to Manchester City. Wenger signed Jens Lehmann from Borussia Dortmund, a German with Champions League experience. That apart, the first-team squad had a very familiar look about it; although when it took to the field, Wenger had opted to start Kolo Toure in the centre of defence alongside Sol Campbell – a pairing that would provide a formidable partnership in the games that lay ahead.

The season started with a 2–1 win over Everton, Henry's penalty following Stubbs's handball placed right down the middle as former Double-winning Arsenal keeper Richard Wright dived to his left. The points were secured when Pires tapped home from close range after shots from Henry and Vieira were parried. A 4–0 win at Middlesbrough demonstrated the team's ability on the counter-attack on both flanks. Indeed, Arsenal were already three goals ahead as early as the 22nd minute, as Henry, Gilberto and Wiltord all found the back of the net. Wiltord added a second later in the game, but the performance was more an interesting sampler of what was to follow during the season. This Arsenal side simply started most games at full pace with the sole aim of virtually securing the points as early as possible, thus allowing a certain degree of coasting and energy-saving for much of the rest of the match. This would become a particular feature of play in the final weeks of the season at a point when the Premiership title had already been won and the momentum to avoid defeat, at the very least, was maintained in the lead-up to Euro 2004. It was typical of the maturity the side was showing and revealed a ruthless streak that had not been overly apparent during the previous season.

Next up at Highbury were David O'Leary's Aston Villa side whose resolute defence was finally breached by a second-half header by Sol Campbell following a corner. Henry added an opportunist second in injury time. The 100 per cent start to the season was maintained in Manchester with a 2–1 win over City, despite Lauren scoring an embarrassing own goal early on. This encounter saw the Arsenal attack facing David Seaman for the first time since his Highbury departure and unfortunately for the former Arsenal legend, he was badly at fault for the winning goal. Wiltord swept in a second-half equaliser but then Seaman failed to collect a ball played into the heart of his goal area and Ljungberg was on hand to sweep the ball over him into the far corner. Four played and a maximum twelve points gathered in the process – it was Arsenal's best start to a season in fifty-six years!

Highbury was to provide the foundation stone on the way to this title success. Fifteen wins and four draws and the outscoring of the opposition by almost four goals to one was an impressive record. Arsenal's nineteen road trips produced eleven wins and eight draws whilst the goals ratio of almost three to one proved that attack was always the main consideration. One of the four sides to take a point away from Highbury that season was Portsmouth (indeed Pompey would be only one of two sides Arsenal failed to beat in the Premiership during the season). They took the lead in north London and Arsenal needed a twice-taken Henry penalty to restore parity. Fulham, Manchester United and Birmingham City would be the three other sides to depart from Arsenal Stadium with a Premiership point.

A 3–0 home defeat by Internazionale in the Champions League was not the best preparation for a trip to Old Trafford. The Wenger–Ferguson mind games were in full swing and it was important psychologically for the team to ensure they did not lose, especially given the way that United had wrested the title from Arsenal in the dying stages of the previous season. Adversity has always produced resolve for Highbury teams down the years and this time it was no different. The Gunners produced a typically solid performance in a game that finished goal-less but will forever be remembered for the final few moments. First Vieira was shown the red card for what could best be described as a soft foul on Ruud van

Nistelrooy, then, with what was almost the last kick of the game, United were awarded a penalty, which van Nistelrooy thumped against the bar. When the ball was cleared the two sets of players were involved in a mêlée of handbags as the game ended – the outcome of which was that several Arsenal players were suspended: Lauren, Keown, Ashley Cole and Parlour. It was as close as Arsenal came to losing a game during that momentous season.

Arsenal secured a four-point lead at the head of the Premiership after defeating Newcastle United 3–2 at Highbury, Henry scoring the winner, with a penalty in the final minutes of the game. Arsenal had twice taken the lead as Henry continued his record of having scored in every Premiership home game to that point. Vieira limped out of the Newcastle game with an injury that would keep him sidelined for a month, and the armband was handed to Ray Parlour, who responded by guiding Arsenal through the month of October, which included one of the club's greatest performances of all time.

A creditable goal-less draw against Locomotiv in Moscow was followed by an equally arduous trip to Anfield. Arsenal found themselves a goal down early on and were largely outplayed in the first half and perhaps lucky to still be in reach of the home side. The second half provided a stark contrast to the first with Arsenal dominant. Edu headed an equaliser off the heel of a Liverpool defender and then a spectacular curling effort by Pires from outside the area – that was in from the moment he hit it – secured what at half-time had looked an unlikely victory.

West London rivals Chelsea, who had literally spent hundreds of millions of pounds on developing their side, thanks to Russian influence, fell behind at Highbury inside five minutes as Edu struck a free-kick, but the visitors equalised before the interval when Hernan Crespo hit a corker from 25 yards. In the final 15 minutes, Arsenal pounded the Chelsea goal but following a succession of great saves, keeper Cudicini fumbled Pires's cross and Henry was on hand to slip the ball home for the winner and leave Arsenal clear at the top of the table.

Arsenal took their Premiership form to Kyiv and were unlucky to lose 2–1 to Dynamo. The result left them floundering at the base of their mini-league with just one point from three games – making it eight games in European competition without a win. That would soon change. A 1–1 draw at Charlton was followed by a 4–1 victory at Leeds which was largely orchestrated by Henry who brought his Premiership goals tally for the season to nine. For the return game with Kyiv, the Highbury crowd were rewarded for their patience in the 88th minute, with the sight of left-back Ashley Cole sneaking up at the far corner of the six-yard box to dive and head home a winner to reinvigorate Arsenal's Champions League quest. Back in the Premiership Tottenham were beaten 2–1 and a 3–0 victory at Birmingham was the perfect preparation for the midweek trip to Milan.

SAN SIRO NAP

The Italian city was very cold and very wet as Arsenal took to the field at the San Siro, knowing a draw was the very least they could accept if they were to progress in the competition. What took place was an Arsenal performance that matched in almost every way the one Highbury supporters witnessed when Spartak Moscow were the visitors 22 years earlier. Arsenal destroyed Internazionale with slick counter-attack passing that left no one prouder that night than stand-in skipper Ray Parlour. 'Five–One in the San Siro' was the chant as Arsenal became the first English team to beat Inter in Milan since Birmingham City during the 1960–61 season.

The euphoria of the win was tempered at the weekend as London-rivals Fulham became only the second side to take a Premiership point from Highbury, this largely due to the outstanding display in goal by Edwin Van der Sar. A 1–1 draw at Leicester City was followed by a comfortable 2–0 over Lokomotiv Moscow at Highbury as Arsenal secured the points that left them top of their Champions League group, a feat that hardly looked likely even a few weeks before.

In the Carling Cup, Wenger had taken the opportunity to provide experience for the younger players in the squad. This included a debut for Francesco Fabregas, who became the youngest player to represent Arsenal at a senior level when he took to the field against Rotherham aged 16 years and 177 days. Following a 1–1 draw at Highbury Arsenal won 9–8 on penalty kicks. In the next round Arsenal disposed of a near full-strength Wolverhampton Wanderers side 5–1, this time Fabregas doubled his entry in the record books as Arsenal's youngest-ever senior goal-scorer. A 2–0 win at West Bromwich saw the young Arsenal side advance to the semi-final stage where they would face Middlesbrough.

Back in the Premiership, the Leicester blip aside, Arsenal went through December undefeated. Blackburn Rovers made their traditional trip to Highbury, which has often been a good hunting ground for them in the lead-up to Christmas, but were sent back up the M6 point-less, courtesy of Dennis Bergkamp's goal. Arsenal followed them back up the motorway a week later, taking the M61 to Bolton, and returned south with a point, thanks to Pires's goal. It was an important fixture and the result a real morale booster in terms of putting the previous season's collapse at the Reebok behind them. Wolverhampton Wanderers were the Boxing Day visitors, and Henry got back on the goal trail in the 3–0 win. Pires was the only scorer in the game at St Mary's as Southampton completed Arsenal's December opponents list. On completion of the year's fixtures Arsenal lay in second place, a point behind Manchester United. Despite not having lost a game, six draws had accounted for twelve lost points.

Two goals were shared at Everton as 2004 got under way but a 4–1 win at home to Middlesbrough got Arsenal back to winning ways. The Boro encounter marked the first of four games between the two clubs in a little under four weeks. A 2–0 win at Aston Villa moved Arsenal into top spot and two points clear of Manchester United, who had dropped points.

January saw the start of the FA Cup and the opponents in the third and fourth rounds mirrored early Premiership opposition. A trip to Leeds United resulted in a repeat of the 4–1 win there in the Premier League. Leeds had taken the lead early on after a Lehmann error, but Arsenal never looked in serious trouble as goals from Henry, Edu, Pires and Toure took them through. Middlesbrough arrived at Highbury for the fourth-round game and were soundly beaten 4–1 just as they had been in the Premier League two weeks earlier. The highlight of this tussle, though, was an exquisite goal by substitute David Bentley, who produced an inch-perfect chip over Boro keeper Mark Schwarzer for a goal reminiscent of Bergkamp at his very best.

The FA Cup game was sandwiched between two Carling Cup semi-final encounters between the sides. Middlesbrough had previously won the first-leg semi-final game at Highbury by a single goal against what was pretty much a reserve XI, although not without experience. The second leg went Boro's way and the Teesside club went through to the Cardiff final 3–1 on aggregate.

The Premiership win over Middlesbrough marked the start of a run of nine successive victories in the League which resumed at the start of February with a visit from Manchester City, before which legend David Seaman (who had by this time retired) was given a special presentation by the club. Arsenal had uncharacteristically made a big-money transfer-window signing at this stage, acquiring the signature and undoubted talents of José Antonio Reyes from Spanish club Sevilla. The 20-year-old forward was touted as one of Spain's hottest talents.

Reyes made his debut at Middlesbrough in the second-leg tie (unfortunately scoring an own goal) and came on as a late substitute in the 2–1 win over Manchester City. Victories over Villa, Wolves and Southampton all came in the space of just ten days, Henry scoring four out of Arsenal's seven goals in the fixtures, including a quickly taken free-kick against Aston Villa that was hotly contested. The pick of the bunch, though, was the winner against Manchester City driven in high across the face of the goal with the ball hardly moving in the process. Against Southampton, the Highbury faithful were all assembled to see Henry score his 100th Premiership goal – the first of his brace that afternoon. The game against Wolverhampton saw Arsenal set a new club record of 24 games unbeaten in the top division, a record that would continue to be beaten on an almost weekly basis for some time to come.

MORE OF THE SAME

The FA Cup draw once again conspired to pit Arsenal against opposition they were facing in the Premier League at that time, the fifth-round draw this time matching them against title rivals Chelsea in the first of two games in four days between the two sides. The FA Cup encounter at Highbury saw the Blues take the lead. In attack Arsenal were missing Henry, so Reyes got his starting chance alongside Bergkamp. The young striker took his opportunity early in the second half, receiving the ball from Edu and accelerating past his marker before thundering a brilliant 25-yard drive into the top-left corner of the Chelsea net for what was a breathtaking equaliser. Seven minutes later, Reyes ghosted on to a through ball from Vieira and cleverly slipped the ball into the far corner of the net to secure Arsenal a sixth-round spot. Arsenal had ended Chelsea's FA Cup dreams for the fourth season in a row!

The Premiership encounter produced the same result, Arsenal winning 2–1 this time. Vieira and Edu scored the all-important goals at Stamford Bridge after Chelsea had taken the lead once again, this time after just twenty-seven seconds! Arsenal now led the Premier League by nine points with sixty-four points from twenty-seven games.

A 2–1 win over Charlton Athletic at Highbury was notable because it, and the win at Chelsea, came either side of a trip to northern Spain for a Champions League game. A 3–2 win at Celta Vigo – Arsenal's first-ever win in Spain – was an excellent result, featuring a second strike from Edu who curled the ball home from the edge of the area, as the tournament entered the straight two-leg knockout phase. A 2–0 win at Highbury two weeks later saw Henry score his first Champions League goals in north London for over two years and saw Arsenal through to the quarter-final stage. The Champions League draw had seen them paired with Monaco and Porto (who would later face each other in the final) in the two rehearsals. When the draw proper was made in front of the TV cameras, they followed Chelsea out of the bowl.

The FA Cup run continued in early March as Arsenal headed to a wet south coast and the quarter-final tie against Portsmouth. The resultant 5–1 win for Arsenal was indicative of the superb passing game the side played that day and it drew comparisons with the earlier performance in Milan. Henry's side-foot pass into the net for the fourth goal, from well outside the area, was simply indicative of the quality and surety of their play. At the end of the game the Pompey fans gave the visitors a standing ovation, which matched their good-humoured chants of 'You're not very good' and 'We'll win 6–5' during the game. A 2–0 win at Blackburn Rovers and a 2–1 home win over Bolton Wanderers consolidated Arsenal's position at the top of the Premiership table, but as March went into its final week Arsenal faced a testing schedule that would determine whether the newspaper talk of a Treble was founded. Twenty-nine games played and seventy-three points secured meant that Arsenal had equalled the best-ever start to a League season. Nine points below them in the table, in second place, were their next opponents.

CUP WOES

Arsenal travelled to Stamford Bridge for the first leg of the Champions League quarter-final with Chelsea. The home side had not beaten the Gunners in their previous 16 games but there was a sense that the visitors were showing signs of fatigue from the heavy fixture schedule. Chelsea took the lead when Eidur Gudjohnsen took advantage of a parried clearance by Lehmann, playing the ball into the back of an empty net. Arsenal started to look dangerous and a cross from the left by Ashley Cole was met perfectly by the deep-running Pires who timed his run perfectly to head the ball home for a very untypical Arsenal goal, but an equaliser nonetheless! Henry might have won the game late on, but a 1–1 draw and the advantage of an away goal put Arsenal in the driving seat.

In the Premiership Manchester United travelled to Highbury trailing by 12 points. Henry produced a typical piece of skill to hit an unswerving shot from almost 25 yards out for the first goal of the game in the second half, but United equalised in the closing minutes of the game to share the points. Despite not having won, Arsenal had set a new League record of 30 successive games unbeaten in a season.

Almost instantly they found themselves facing Manchester United again – this time at Villa Park for the FA Cup semi-final, fate once again drawing them against opposition they were facing in the Premiership at that time. Mindful of the return with Chelsea, Wenger opted to leave Henry on the bench. The game should have been secured inside the first few minutes as Edu hit the bar and Bergkamp drove wide with the goal at his mercy, and those misses were punished, United scoring the only goal of the game on the half-hour, and despite second-half substitutions, which saw Henry and Reyes on the pitch, Arsenal could not find the equaliser. It was their first FA Cup defeat in 19 successive ties and also the fourth time in succession the side had reached the semi-final stage.

So, having reached, and lost, in two cup semi-finals already, Arsenal faced Chelsea just three days later at Highbury in a bid to make it three semi-finals for the season, and also mark new ground because the club had never made it that far in the number one European competition before. The crowd that assembled at Highbury for the second leg were full of anticipation and witnessed a well-marshalled Chelsea defence keep Arsenal's fast attack at bay – that is until the last minute of the first half when Lauren's cross from the right was headed on by Henry and fell to Reyes who gave Arsenal the lead from five yards. Arsenal had dominated the first half and could well have had the tie sealed by then, but as Chelsea came out of their shell in the second period, Arsenal looked to tire as an extensive schedule of games took its toll. On the offensive, the visitors equalised within six minutes of the restart when Frank Lampard drove home a rebound after Lehmann could only parry Claude Makelele's drive. With 87 minutes showing on the scoreboard and extra-time looming, Wayne Bridge found himself free on the right side of the area to strike home Chelsea's winner.

In the space of four days Arsenal's Treble dream had evaporated. The cup encounters with Manchester United and Chelsea showed how narrow the margin is between victory and defeat at the top levels, as both of these games could easily have gone the other way. To quote the old cliché, Arsenal could now concentrate on the League, and were immediately faced with a visit to Highbury by Liverpool on the first day of the Easter holidays, and it was to prove a very Good Friday. The visitors twice took the lead and the home side had to dig deep to turn the game around and deliver a really gutsy performance in which Henry was the star, delivering a hat-trick of goals, the second of which was a simply sensational solo effort: picking the ball up alongside his defensive teammates on the halfway line, and two-stepping a waltz through the Liverpool midfield and then defence, before slipping the ball home. It was a game that Arsenal had to win, coming off the back of such disappointments, and clearly demonstrated the character and spirit of the squad on a day when the title was secured mentally, if not mathematically.

A goal-less draw at Newcastle was followed by Leeds United's arrival in north London and a game in which Thierry Henry scored four goals – the first Arsenal player to do this since December 1991 when Ian Wright hit four past Everton. Henry's fourth goal, Arsenal's fifth of the day, was his 150th for Arsenal, and his 38th of an incredible season. Arsenal's unbeaten Premier League run now stood at thirty-three games with just five games of the season remaining.

TITLE MEMORIES

The first of those five games was at White Hart Lane, and Arsenal arrived at the home of their north London rivals knowing that a single point would be good enough to confirm them as champions. News echoed around the Arsenal fans inside the ground of Chelsea's defeat at Newcastle in an early fixture and they now trailed by nine points with just three games to play. Recollections of Arsenal capturing the 1971 League title at Tottenham were quick to surface, although this encounter did not have the divisive factor of the earlier encounter.

After just three minutes of play Tottenham won a corner; the ball was cleared by the Arsenal defence and found Henry, who ran fifty yards into the opposition half before feeding Bergkamp on the left. The Dutchman sprinted forward and squared the ball into the Spurs penalty area where Vieira arrived late, stretching out a gangly leg to slide the ball into the back of the net. A classic counter-attack and 1–0 to the Arsenal! In the minutes before half-time Pires tapped home his 19th goal of the season, having been the fulcrum of a multi-passing Arsenal move and arriving late in the area to complete the pivot. The destiny of the Premiership title looked assured; however, Spurs pulled one back on the hour and then equalised in the fourth minute of added time. Lehmann fouled Robbie Keane and the home side were awarded a penalty, which they converted. Almost immediately the full-time whistle went, and with Spurs celebrating their draw – 'as though they had won the World Cup', Henry said after the game – the Arsenal players released their own emotions and headed towards the Champions Section once again to celebrate. It was the 13th Championship and what Arsenal fans were quick to note was that Arsenal had now won more Championships at White Hart Lane than Tottenham themselves! Later that evening Henry was crowned PFA Footballer of the Year for the second successive season and would complete a unique back-to-back double a few weeks later when he collected the Football Writers' Association award again too.

The clear target now was to remain undefeated and thus add substance to Wenger's misquote at the start of the previous season. With Euro 2004 fast approaching, and many of the players involved in the tournament, the remaining games were often played at half-pace by the Gunners, doing just enough to get through. A familiar sight was the late appearance of Martin Keown as a substitute as he looked to make the ten appearances that would assure him of a medal in his final season at the club.

A goal-less draw at home to Birmingham City was perhaps an anti-climax for the celebrating fans assembled at Highbury for the first time since the point at Tottenham. A 1–1 draw at Portsmouth four days later saw an Arsenal performance that was perhaps too complacent for anyone's liking, especially as the home side missed an excellent opportunity to win the game late on, which was denied by Lehmann. A 1–0 win at Fulham left Arsenal with one fixture left to play, at Highbury against already relegated Leicester City.

It was party time at Highbury on 15 May 2004. Leicester City, with nothing to lose and some pride at stake, packed the midfield and left a lone striker up front, frustrating Arsenal at every opportunity. The game needed a goal and it came from a different script, as ex-Arsenal player Paul Dickov – somehow ignoring his lack of height – headed home a long cross. Arsenal used half-time to regroup and came out in the second half showing greater urgency. It paid off almost immediately when Ashley Cole was tripped in the box and Henry struck home the resultant penalty. The goal was Henry's 30th in the Premiership as he became the first Arsenal player to score 30 League goals in a season since Ronnie Rooke's 33 goals 56 years previously as part of the 1947–48 title-winning side.

With Arsenal now dominating play and passing the ball around the edges of the Leicester City penalty area, Vieira ran into space and was picked out perfectly by Bergkamp's through ball, which the Arsenal captain took in his stride, calmly sidestepping the keeper before slipping the ball into the net for the winner.

At the final whistle, Arsenal had become the first team since Preston North End in 1888–89 to complete a season unbeaten in the top division. In the inaugural year of the Football League, Preston had played just 22 games; Arsenal had done it over 38 games and in a very different footballing era. Played 38, won 26, drawn 12, lost 0.

THE FORTY-NINERS

The plaudits Arsenal received with headlines such as 'Gunbeatable', 'Immortal' and 'Invincible' were well deserved, not just for the feat in itself but for the style and flair of the football Arsenal produced that season. In that respect alone this team, the Untouchables, were the best side ever to grace Highbury. The fans who gathered at Highbury during the 2003–04 season saw a team that was almost permanently on a high. The goals were always of the highest quality – every goal a 'special moment' in a team that made light work of the spectacular and who simply didn't do 'ordinary'. There was never a tap-in. The truth was that the spectacular was simply a matter of combining the easy things in quick succession. It was simply brilliant football and brilliantly simple football that left every goal and near miss (of which there were many) having to be described by reference to the Oxford English Book of Superlatives. The 2003–04 Arsenal side had produced one of the greatest achievements since English football began. The BBC pundit and ex-Liverpool and Scotland player Alan Hansen described that Arsenal side as 'arguably the finest attacking side this country has ever seen . . . the most devastating team in British history'.

Although Arsenal had completed the 2003–04 League season undefeated, the unbeaten run extended to forty games, given the two wins at the end of the 2002–03 season, so as the 2004–05 season approached there was talk about how long they could maintain their invincibility. Six straight wins at the onset took Arsenal to the top of the table: the quality of the football remained top-notch and the goals flowed freely, 19 in all to that point. An opening day away win at Everton was followed by successive home games against Middlesbrough (5–3) and Blackburn Rovers (4–1). Arsenal repeated their three-goal winning away form with a 4–1 win at Norwich and a 3–0 win at Fulham. The first hiccup came when Bolton Wanderers took a point from Highbury in a 2–2 draw, but a win at Manchester City and successive home wins over Charlton and Aston Villa extended the sequence to 49 games undefeated in the Premiership.

Sunday, 24 October had been earmarked as Arsenal's first big test of the season: a trip to Old Trafford and Manchester United. Despite playing well, the incredible run came to an end and, as might have been expected in a game involving Manchester United, did so in controversial fashion. Wayne Rooney tripped over thin air and was awarded a penalty, which this time van Nistelrooy converted. Arsenal sought an equaliser but a late Rooney goal ensured Arsenal's record run was halted a game short of the half-century mark.

The game ended acrimoniously not least because the Arsenal players felt they had been cheated by Rooney's flop; however, whilst that will remain a debatable point, the truth is that perhaps the famous Arsenal luck had expired. This is not to suggest in any way that the incredible run was in any way lucky, unless one's definition of luck is brilliance, that is. But what is interesting is that, in the run, Arsenal never suffered at the hands of a fluke result or because something out of the ordinary occurred – over a period of 49 games you would expect that to happen. After all, without upsets and fluke occurrences, football would become predictable; it is the unpredictability that makes it such a wonderful game. There were occasions during the run when Arsenal came close to losing their Premiership invincibility: twice to newly promoted Portsmouth and the early game at Old Trafford, and perhaps also the game against Liverpool following the FA Cup and Champions League exits. These were perhaps the key points of that season and that run.

Unbelievable, Unbeatable, Untouchable.

FIFTEEN

Landmark Games

There have been literally thousands of matches staged at Highbury down the years – everything from schoolboy games and trials through to Premiership, Champions League and internationals. Virtually all of them will make a special memory for someone who played in them or who witnessed them from the terraces. From an Arsenal point of view, some are landmark games, not perhaps because they were the best games ever played, but because they contained within their 90 minutes a record or action of some significance. The following, listed in chronological order, is a selection of some of these landmark games – not a definitive list by any stretch, but certainly some moments of Highbury history to be remembered at the very least.

FIRST HIGHBURY GAME

6 September 1913: Woolwich Arsenal 2 Leicester Fosse 1
The headline of the *Islington Daily Gazette & North London Tribune* on 8 September 1913 said it all: 'Woolwich's Winning Ways – Change of Luck Follows Change of Ground. Well Won Woolwich'. So much for the short snappy headline but this was the first game at what the press initially

referred to as Gillespie Road Stadium, but what fans were already calling Highbury. There were no turnstiles in those days but receipts of £308 on the afternoon indicate around 20,000 fans turned up to watch the Second Division encounter with Leicester Fosse. The Reds won 2–1 and in doing so recorded Arsenal's first opening-day win since victory over Notts County in 1907. The match report, written by Candid Critic, suggests that the crowd was 'wonderfully enthusiastic' and that the fine weather meant that a lack of cover because of the unfinished grandstand didn't matter at all. That said, those in attendance witnessed many who had climbed into its open body and sat on planks of wood strung between scaffolding. It also related that those who went to Gillespie Road thinking they would have to rough it a bit in unfinished surroundings were 'surprised and delighted' to find they were able to watch the game from the terraces in comparative comfort. That first Highbury pitch was prepared by the stadium's first groundsman, Alex Rae.

The North London Excelsior Band provided a special march for the opening of the ground. It was entitled 'Arsenal' and the conductor, Mr John Pursglove, was also the composer. The band played 'The Conquering Hero' when Woolwich Arsenal took to the field.

Leicester Fosse had the honour of scoring the first senior goal at Highbury when Benfield drove home Douglas's cross unchallenged. But the home side went in all-square at the interval when Tom Winship's corner was headed home by George Jobey. The second half saw Woolwich secure their historic win when McWhirter was adjudged to have handled and Archibald Devine drove home the resultant penalty. Arsenal finished the game with ten men though, when Jobey had to retire injured ten minutes from time. The forward was at first thought to be suffering from broken ribs after a challenge by Clay, but it later transpired it was simply bruising. Interestingly, he was attended to by Dr Brenber – brother of the Fosse goalkeeper that afternoon!

FIRST 'ARSENAL' GAME

4 April 1914: Arsenal 1 Bristol City 1

The Football League sanctioned the changing of the club's name from 'Woolwich Arsenal' to simply 'Arsenal' prior to this near end-of-season encounter with Bristol City; however, the club had affectionately been known as 'The Arsenal' by locals, fans and media for most of the season, so, in reality, the name change was reflecting what was simply an accepted term of endearment at the time.

The game report was also centred largely on the fact that the Corinthian H.G. Yates was unable to turn out for the team due to an injury sustained in the London League match against Fulham earlier in the week. Bristol took the lead five minutes into the game. A Brown drive from fully 25 yards beat Joe Lievesley in the Arsenal goal. The Reds, though, were back on level terms seven minutes later when Tom Winship raced on to Joe Shaw's cross and drove home. Arsenal were denied a winner when Winship looked to have scored but the goal was disallowed; the 12,000-strong crowd were aggrieved and forced the game to be stopped as the police were called to put a stop to the 'tumult' on the Highbury Hill bank.

The point saw Arsenal maintain their second place in the table on forty-two points, ahead of Bradford on goal average, but nine points behind Notts County. The table reflected the official name change for the first time.

FIRST IN THE FIRST DIVISION

30 August 1919: Arsenal 0 Newcastle United 1

Arsenal played Newcastle United in their first-ever First Division League game at Highbury after their board of directors, led by Sir Henry Norris, had sensationally lobbied their way into the top flight at the expense of Tottenham Hotspur after a vote following the end of the Second World War.

Around 55,000 were in Highbury when the gates were shut well before kick-off, leaving thousands locked outside in the surrounding streets. There was still plenty of space inside the ground but the admitted spectators were stubborn and a lack of stewarding failed to get them better distributed. Frustration in the streets at not being able to see the return of League football after several years of absence resulted in a number of arrests and one prosecution during the week that followed. The game ended in a one-goal victory for Newcastle, Henderson scoring midway through the first half, as the Magpies' experience became apparent. That said, Arsenal were unlucky not to take their first point of the season.

Just a week beforehand, over 10,000 fans had turned up to witness a trial match between the Reds and the Blues. The Reds team was effectively the starting Arsenal XI for the Newcastle encounter. The Reds won at a canter 5–0 and remarks were made in the local reports of the improvements to the ground for the start of the season.

RECORD LEAGUE WIN

28 January 1931: Arsenal 9 Grimsby Town 1
This is Arsenal's biggest League win at Highbury and although the nine goals scored would be matched a year later, the margin of victory – eight goals – remains the biggest. The score was not misleading, as Arsenal were much quicker and more creative on the day. David Jack and Alex James were in devastating form and were able to display their wide repertoire of skills and trickery whilst Joe Hulme was unstoppable on the wing.

Grimsby held out for ten minutes before Jack Lambert scored twice – the second being a header – after Hulme had supplied pinpoint crosses for both strikes. There was certainly no indication of what was to come when Grimsby reduced the deficit, Prior finding the net through Preedy's legs from an acute angle. Cliff Bastin worked an opening, enabling Jack to restore Arsenal's two-goal advantage before the 'Boy' Clifford added one himself to send Arsenal in 4–1 to the good at the interval.

With the breeze in Arsenal's favour in the second half, Read scooped out a shot by Bastin only to see the ball fall to Hulme, who was on hand to score. Jack made it 6–1 after Hulme's shot was initially parried.

Lambert completed his own hat-trick after Hulme and Bastin had interchanged passes. Jack then did likewise, thanks to passes from Hulme, and made no mistake with either. The win put Arsenal on top of the table on goal difference, but with three games in hand. Sadly, and strangely, only 15,571 were there to witness this historic result.

FIRST CHAMPIONSHIP TROPHY PRESENTATION

2 May 1931: Arsenal 5 Bolton Wanderers 0

Arsenal had already won their first-ever League Championship prior to this game at Highbury as the crowd flocked to north London to see the official presentation to Herbert Chapman's side. Before the game started the club announced that it 'welcomed' fans onto the pitch at the end of the game to see the presentation in front of the old wooden East Stand.

Three minutes before time a phantom whistle sounded from the crowd and, thinking the game was over, the crowd stormed onto the pitch to celebrate. It took several minutes for the match and club officials to get the crowd to realise the mistake (there was no loudspeaker system at this stage – just megaphones) and clear the field of the celebrating supporters and play the final seconds. When the final whistle did sound, the crowd were quickly onto the pitch again and the likes of Cliff Bastin soon found himself shoulder high. League chairman Mr McKenna presented the trophy and a bugle sounded from within the crowd as both chairman and manager made speeches. Insistent calls of 'We want Parker' finally brought the captain and his team back to the grandstand to 'rousing cheers and great applause', it is reported.

Alex James was the artist of the day, making the initial two goals: the first for Jack on 14 minutes and then Lambert on 28 minutes. He then initiated the move that led to Lambert scoring again after Bastin centred. Three up at the interval, James hit a cannon to make it 4–0 and Jack added the fifth, but only a missed penalty by Blackmore maintained Arsenal's clean sheet.

Arsenal won the encounter easily with a 'delightful display' on a day when Tottenham failed to gain promotion from the Second Division. The

Islington Gazette suggested that 'All good north London sportsmen sympathise with Tottenham Hotspur at just failing to gain promotion . . .' That would be right, then.

BIGGEST FA CUP WIN

9 January 1932: Arsenal 11 Darwen 1
A preview of this FA Cup tie in the local Darwen paper put it thus:

> Darwen has many claims to fame. It was the first town in the provinces to house the notorious Gandhi; was the cockpit of the General Election; and now Darwen has its eye on the spoils of the great Soccer Knockout. What Darwen is thinking: Can these boys from Lancashire Mills and workshops put out the £40,000 Highbury battery! Goliath fell! Rome fell! It may be that the great Arsenal fall!

Someone was clearly getting a bit carried away in the lead-up to the game as Arsenal recorded their biggest win at Highbury in the FA Cup. Cliff Bastin scored four of the goals and his match tally remains a Highbury record for a player in the competition. Darwen, from the Lancashire Combination, fielded a side that cost £25 to assemble compared to the £45,000 of talent of Arsenal.

Around 500 travelling supporters watched Arsenal score five in the opening twenty-five minutes and move eight goals ahead by the interval. The biggest cheer from the 37,486 crowd, though, came when Dale scored Darwen's consolation 12 minutes from the end. Darwen brought their own mascot, 'Young Proos', son of the Darwen trainer, who cavorted on the pitch with the Arsenal Duck prior to the game.

Arsenal swept into a 3–0 lead inside 15 minutes and afterwards it was pure pantomime as only Rowlands in the Darwen goal and Quigley, the captain and inside-left, showed any pretensions to class. Moss, in the Arsenal goal, didn't touch the ball until a half-hour into the game. Bastin helped himself to a first-half hat-trick – along with Jack – and added a fourth in the second half to give him the record.

MOST GOALS IN A LEAGUE GAME BY A SINGLE PLAYER

24 December 1932: Arsenal 9 Sheffield United 2

Arsenal matched their highest-ever goals tally at Highbury by scoring nine in this Christmas Eve encounter; however, this game saw Jack Lambert score five of the home goals, which remains the most by a player in a single League game at Highbury.

Lambert's unique record came at a bad time from the reporting point of view: five games in ten days across the holiday period left the news coverage of his remarkable feat lost to the ether. Lambert, though, was in the twilight of his Arsenal career and the five he shot past Sheffield were a significant portion of the fourteen goals from twelve appearances for the season. Although he started the 1933–34 season at Highbury, by October he had been sold to Fulham for £2,500. His demise was as sudden as his rise to prominence. In the 1930–31 season he had come into his own by scoring 38 League goals – including seven hat-tricks (five of which were scored away from Highbury) – to set a new Arsenal record. In 1931–32 he had netted 22 in 36 games.

Lambert returned to Highbury in 1938 to join the team's A side before being killed in a road accident in Enfield two years later.

ARSENAL WEAR WHITE SLEEVES FOR FIRST TIME

4 March 1933: Arsenal 0 Liverpool 1

Arsenal's new colours had a disappointing baptism: 'The shirts are red, except the sleeves and collar, which are white,' reported the *Islington Gazette*. Simple, really! The club had previously played in a dark-red, almost maroon, colour. The report went on to comment: 'Arsenal's new shirts created quite a commotion. They look rather nice and are certainly unusual and distinctive.' The report of the day also focused on the over-elaborate style of play by Arsenal, who 'use 27 passes when three would suffice'.

This result came on the back of an eight-goal thrashing of Blackburn the previous week, and certainly the finishing, or rather the shooting, of the Arsenal forwards was distinctive, for the wrong reasons, as Riley in the Liverpool goal led a charmed life. The only goal of the game came via Hodgson's head, which rose to meet Taylor's cross. Arsenal should have had several goals in reply as they camped in the visitor's half. Arsenal remained top of the table despite the defeat as they marched on to retain the Championship.

BIGGEST ATTENDANCE AT HIGHBURY – 73,295

9 March 1935: Arsenal 0 Sunderland 0

The newspaper headline was simple enough: '71,000 at the Stadium'. Final counting of gate receipts placed the attendance some 2,000 more than the initial estimated figure. The crowd that packed into Highbury that afternoon accounted for more than a third of the total First Division attendance that afternoon: 237,000; nearly half of the Second Division attendances: 149,000; was almost equal to the whole of the Southern Section: 73,000; and more than the total of the eleven Northern Section games: 58,000. Over £6,000 was taken in gate receipts.

This was a top-of-the-table clash and the attendance reflected it. The goalless draw left Arsenal top on 43 points with Sunderland and Manchester City close behind and only separated on goal average with 41 points apiece. According to reports the game was 'exceedingly fast' and the tackling so swift that players did not have time to think. The best scoring chance fell to Arsenal with Bobby Davidson shooting over the bar. A postscript to the match in the *Islington Gazette* relating to the band that afternoon detailed that the conductor for the day, Horatio Nicholls, had gone down with influenza prior to the game and was unable to conduct his two pieces. 'I thought I ought to let you know as some might have wondered what had happened,' he commented.

FIRST BRAZILIAN CLUB SIDE TO PLAY IN ENGLAND

20 February 1954: Arsenal 7 Portuguesa de Desportos (São Paulo) 1

This game marked the first time a Brazilian club side played a game in England and it is one they would probably want to forget. Arsenal produced a sizzling display of attacking football to win 7–1. Cliff Holton scored five of Arsenal's goals, three of them from headers, to please the crowd of 44,491 who got full value for money. Portuguesa had finished fourth in the Brazilian league prior to this encounter and had been champions the previous season. Their side included two current internationals in Barbosa and Violani.

Perhaps not surprisingly, given the scoreline, reports from the game indicate that the Brazilians were committed to attack and especially late in the second half, when they trailed heavily, reports suggest they 'ripped the Arsenal defence to bits time and time again'. Obviously without scoring, though. The *Islington Gazette* reported: 'Portuguesa had an interesting style: they were fast and clever ball players, but their defensive play was inclined to be rather loose. Their centre-half occupied the role of a sixth forward.' Reading the report while reflecting on the scoreline brings a smile to the face.

Jack Kelsey in the Arsenal goal was outstanding and the home side could well have scored more goals. It was end-to-end stuff with the difference between the teams being the respective keepers' abilities. Padua, in the visitor's goal, was only remarkable for the large '1' on his shirt – it was the first time the reporter at the game had seen players with numbered shirts!

Arsenal's aerial power shocked the visitors and the opening four goals all came from headers. Holton opened the rout by heading home Logie's cross, Walsh did likewise from Roper's centre and shortly before the interval Logie again supplied Holton. Almost immediately after the restart Roper provided the cross for Holton to complete his hat-trick. A typical Brazilian free-kick left the home crowd gasping and warmly applauding Ortega, whose dead-ball effort curled into the net. Padua couldn't hold Dickson's shot and Holton was on hand to sweep home Arsenal's fifth before the scorer laid on a pass for Doug Lishman to extend the Gunners' lead. With Portuguesa on the attack, Holton completed the rout by racing on to Logie's through-ball totally unchallenged.

THE PHANTOM FINAL WHISTLE GOAL

17 December 1955: Arsenal 4 Blackpool 1

It was an unusually big crowd at Highbury – 45,086 – given that Christmas was just around the corner. No other First Division match on the final Saturday before the holidays attracted over 30,000, but Stanley Matthews was in town! Blackpool travelled south to the capital sitting top of the table; Arsenal were a lowly 16th and were expected to struggle against arguably the best side Blackpool had ever produced.

The Gunners played with verve and were comfortably leading the game by a scoreline that had hardly been predicted. Reports suggest Vic Groves opened the scoring with 'a goal worthy of the greatest' taking a Clapton pass in his stride and hitting a left-foot drive 'that almost tore a hole in the net'. Mike Tiddy made the next for Holton as Arsenal went in two goals to the good at half-time. In the second half Groves laid one on for Tapscott, and Bloomfield walked the ball into the net late on to give the home side a 4–0 lead and with it two well-deserved and much-needed points. The home side had completely outplayed the League leaders.

With the game deep into time added on and only seconds remaining, Dennis Evans, the Arsenal full-back, was in possession of the ball just outside his own penalty area. A long blast on the whistle sounded and players turned to leave the pitch. As Arsenal goalkeeper Con Sullivan picked up his cap from inside the goal, Evans celebrated the 'victory' by thumping the ball into the back of the Arsenal net. Unfortunately, the sound had not come from the whistle in possession of referee Mr F.B. Coultas, but from within the crowd, so Evans had effectively scored an own goal that is reflected as such in the record books.

The owner of the 'Phantom Final Whistle' that day was never ultimately identified; however, some spectators recalled noticing a railway guard at the game who blew a whistle at that point, then was followed angrily out of the ground. Appeals were subsequently made in the

Matchday Programme for fans to refrain from bringing whistles to the game. The *Islington Gazette* summed up the afternoon, reporting: 'This was a sad end to a match that had thrilled and shown us a revitalised Arsenal with all eleven men in top form.'

THE GREATEST GAME EVER?

1 February 1958: Arsenal 4 Manchester United 5

Was this the greatest game ever played at Highbury? Those who witnessed it would say yes. The answer remains subjective. What cannot be contested is that this was a historic game because of what was to follow on from it. It was the last League game played by Manchester United before the aeroplane disaster at Munich's Reim airport on 6 February in which twenty-three lost their lives, including eight players, eight journalists and seven others on the flight.

Known then as the Busby Babes, United had sprinted into a 3–0 half-time lead. The great Duncan Edwards opened the scoring with a drive from the edge of the area and then only a wonder save by Harry Gregg prevented Vic Groves levelling the score. But United went straight back up the field and Bobby Charlton extended the visitor's lead. Shortly before half-time Tommy Taylor scored the third and the game looked all over bar the shouting.

However Arsenal produced a stunning comeback, stunning not in the least because the scores were levelled within 2 minutes 30 seconds of the restart thanks to an effort from Herd and two from Bloomfield. The home supporters in the 63,578 crowd were in raptures but then had to watch United open up their lead with goals by Dennis Viollet and Taylor again. Derek Tapscott added a fourth for Arsenal to complete the nine-goal thriller.

Of the eleven United players in the starting line-up that day five were killed – Eddie Coleman, Mark Jones, Duncan Edwards, Roger Bryne and Tommy Taylor, who scored two of the five goals. United returned to Highbury shortly after the disaster to re-play an FA Cup semi-final against Fulham. In typical fashion the Busby Babes won 5–3 in a thriller.

EIGHT-GOAL THRILLER

15 October 1963: Arsenal 4 Tottenham Hotspur 4

Some 4,000 fans were locked out ten minutes before the start of this classic encounter. The gate of 67,986 was Highbury's best for ten years and the second highest since 1934 – both those games were against Spurs as well. The result was a reflection on the game but a lesser team might have given up as Arsenal trailed 2–4 with only five minutes of play remaining, and with the home support starting to ebb away. Those fantastic final five minutes were amongst the most thrilling in the club's League history.

The action started much earlier, though. In the second minute Jimmy Greaves flicked Spurs into the lead from a Danny Blanchflower free-kick, then Bobby Smith rocketed home the second for Spurs to give the visitors a two-goal lead inside the first quarter of an hour. Things looked decidedly bleak for Arsenal.

George Eastham pulled one back from the penalty spot only to see Dave Mackey restore Spurs's two-goal advantage straight from the restart. Eastham was on the score sheet again, driving home his shot before Smith added another to make it 4–2 at the interval.

In the second half Arsenal threw everything at Tottenham but the visitor's defence looked to be holding out. The tension of the game was such that fans were fainting in the capacity crowd and at one stage Jimmy Greaves was helping them.

Then, with 85 minutes showing at the Clock End, Joe Baker escaped the shackles of his marker, Maurice Norman, and blasted the ball into the back of the net. Highbury erupted and got even louder when Geoff Strong rose above everyone to head home the equaliser from a late, late corner. Spurs took the restart and the final whistle went. Lucky Arsenal? Unforgettable, certainly!

MOST GOALS BY AN OPPOSITION PLAYER

14 March 1964: Arsenal 2 Chelsea 4

Bobby Tambling destroyed Arsenal and gave League debutant Peter Simpson a torrid time at Highbury. Tambling celebrated his return to the

Chelsea team by scoring all four goals – a record for an opponent at Highbury in a League game. The drenched pitch was not ideal, as Arsenal manager Billy Wright looked at the pairing of Simpson and Terry Neill for the first time.

Tambling opened the scoring after seven minutes but Neill sought some sort of revenge when equalising three minutes later. Joe Baker then wasted a great chance to put Arsenal into the lead. Fourteen minutes into the second half Tambling added a second, and then two goals in as many minutes (68, 69) helped the Chelsea player complete the rout. Baker reduced the deficit on 77 minutes but the game had already been won by Chelsea, and Tambling in particular.

ARSENAL WIN THE EUROPEAN FAIRS CUP

28 April 1970: Arsenal 3 Anderlecht 0

This was the night Highbury erupted. These were the most amazing scenes ever at Highbury as Arsenal won the European Fairs Cup to end a frustrating spell of 17 years without a trophy. The celebrations continued for 25 minutes after the game as fans and players alike celebrated on what was Highbury's greatest night.

Having lost 1–3 in Brussels in the first leg Arsenal needed at least a 2–0 win to secure the trophy on the away-goals rule. The Belgian side were destroyed by the Man of the Match, George Armstrong, who never stopped running and continued to create chances for the team.

The first goal was important and it came on 25 minutes when, following a cleared corner, Eddie Kelly took a pass from McLintock, transferred the ball from his left to his right foot and then hit a long-range effort high into the net. The visitors remained dangerous and when Nordahl's shot hit the post it was a timely warning. With less than 20 minutes remaining and time ticking away, Graham slipped the ball wide on the left to the advancing McNab who crossed the ball deep into the penalty area. Racing in with arms spread either side of him, John Radford met the ball high above the defence and powered it down into the net. Radford then set off on his trademark air-punching run as he and Charlie George led the celebrations in front of the North Bank.

Almost from the restart, with the stadium still buzzing, Arsenal won the ball in midfield; Charlie George held it deep on the left before delivering the pass of the night. Sweeping the ball 50 yards or so across the pitch, he found Jon Sammels racing forward on the right, taking the ball and drilling it past Trappeniers. Three-nil, two goals in a minute and the Belgian side didn't know what had hit them as the Highbury faithful willed the big clock round to 9.15 p.m.

The final whistle sparked unprecedented scenes of joy as supporters released years of pent-up frustration. Sadly for one supporter it was simply too much: 52-year-old Harry Tilbury collapsed and died of a heart attack during the game.

THE GREATEST SAVE

22 August 1970: Arsenal 4 Manchester United 0

It was the second weekend of the season and after two points from two away fixtures Arsenal welcomed Manchester United for the opening day of the season at Highbury. Little did the 54,117 who packed into a sun-drenched stadium that afternoon know that the parading of the European Fairs Cup prior to the game would be superseded 12 months later with the League Championship and FA Cup trophies.

The Arsenal side were a mixture of experience and youth and the 4–0 rout was typical of the performances that would become commonplace in the opening phase of the season. A superb defence – just six goals would be conceded at home across the course of the League season – was complemented by a razor-sharp attack, where the emphasis was on directness. This was the original Arsenal back five, brilliantly marshalled by Frank McLintock and with a much underrated Bob Wilson. The Arsenal goalkeeper made most saves look easy and could never be accused of showboating. He was regarded as fearless and his headlong dives at advancing forwards' feet were his trademark – and not a few times did they leave him injured and out of games.

Arsenal took the lead when Radford drove home after Armstrong and Kelly had combined, and the Arsenal number 9 was soon on hand to double the score, this time from Kennedy's cross. Arsenal scored twice more in the second half, Kennedy heading down for Radford to complete his hat-trick and Graham added the fourth with a looping header from Armstrong's cross.

Things might have been different though, but for a moment of typical Wilson brilliance. Having just fallen a goal behind, United were presented with the perfect opportunity to equalise. George Best – in top form and vying with Pele for the accolade of world's best footballer – found himself clean through the Arsenal offside trap with just Wilson to beat. Close control kept the ball within the Irishman's body as he advanced. The green shirt of Wilson crept forward near the edge of the area and, with a shimmy, Best waltzed the ball to the right before slipping it into the net. Except that the ball was not at Best's feet any more but in the clutces of a beaming Wilson. The Arsenal keeper dived to his left to pluck the ball from within. Even 30 years later Best was still rankled by the save, and in his autobiography Wilson rates it as arguably his best. Anyone who witnessed it that hot August afternoon has no doubt.

ARSENAL WIN THE CHAMPIONSHIP

6 May 1991: Arsenal 3 Manchester United 1
Arsenal secured their second title in two years with Alan Smith scoring a hat-trick against United in the process. It was a Championship that came despite the club having suffered two blows during the course of the season. First there was the deduction of two points following a player brawl at Old Trafford when the two teams had met earlier in the season. Then there was the continuing absence of skipper Tony Adams, who had been found guilty of drink-driving related offences. At that point the Gunners had been some eight points behind Liverpool in the table and so a big effort was required, as well as a further honing of the famous siege mentality that manager George Graham had grown at the club for them to come out on top.

Smith's hat-trick propelled Arsenal to their tenth title and put the team into the European Cup – the first English entrant since the five-year ban imposed on English clubs by UEFA following the Heysel disaster. Arsenal led 2–0 at the interval, the League's top scorer netting in the 18th and 40th minutes. He completed his hat-trick from the penalty spot 12 minutes into the second half. Steve Bruce scored United's consolation goal five minutes from full-time, firing home from the penalty spot after David Seaman was adjudged to have tripped Mark Robbins. That United goal prevented Seaman making it a quarter of a century of clean sheets in the League season.

Arsenal set a record at that time, which they would maintain in their final game against Coventry City, going the most number of games in a season undefeated, a run that stretched back to the previous February when they lost 2–1 at Chelsea.

LAST GAME IN FRONT OF THE NORTH BANK

2 May 1992: Arsenal 5 Southampton 1
An Ian Wright hat-trick was the highlight of Arsenal's thumping of Southampton in what was the last game to be played at Highbury before the North Bank was demolished to make way for the new all-seater North Stand. Entrance to the terracing that afternoon was made all-ticket as around 13,000 packed onto the famous steps – many seats in the stands were empty as season-ticket holders left their relative comfort to be a part of Arsenal history.

The Saints had kept the game tight in the first half but Kevin Campbell broke the deadlock 21 minutes into the second half. Less than ten minutes later Wright made it 2–0 and Alan Smith made sure of victory, netting five minutes from time. With time running out on the clock and the North Bank, two goals in the final two minutes as Wrighty completed his hat-trick gave the Arsenal fans something else to remember on a sad afternoon for frequenters of the Laundry End.

FIRST GAME IN FRONT OF THE NEW NORTH STAND

14 August 1993: Arsenal 0 Coventry City 3

Just days before the opening game of the season in front of the new North Bank Stand, an army of extra workers were called on by contractors Norwest Holst to complete the installation of seats in the lower tier of the stand. Noise restrictions had meant that work could not continue after 6 p.m. in the evening and on the opening day there were still three sections that did not have seats installed.

Players were commenting on how weird it had been playing in a three-sided stadium during the previous season and striker Ian Wright had added, 'Hopefully the new stand will make for a better atmosphere.' Well, the opening game in front of the new stand didn't have quite the atmosphere the fans wanted as visitors Coventry City spoilt the party. In truth, it was a dismal Arsenal performance and, having taken the lead in the first half, the Sky Blues' win never looked in doubt. It was the large frame of Mick Quinn who did the damage as he helped himself to a hat-trick – the last visiting player to do so at Highbury. Just 26,237 were there to witness both events.

ARSENAL REACH CUP-WINNERS' CUP FINAL

12 April 1994: Arsenal 1 Paris St Germain 0

This result put Arsenal on the verge of their first European success for 24 years with a 2–1 aggregate win. The all-important goal came as early as the sixth minute, with Kevin Campbell's glancing header from Lee Dixon's cross providing the dream start. But Paris St Germain were always dangerous on the counter-attack and Ricardo and David Ginola both wasted good opportunities to equalise and cancel out Arsenal's away goal.

There was heartbreak for Ian Wright, though, who picked up a needless booking for a pointless lunge on Alain Roche which would rule him out of the Copenhagen final against Parma. Ironically, Wright had scored in every round of the campaign, but was not able to set a record as his teammates went on to lift the Cup-Winners' Cup.

WRIGHT BREAKS BASTIN'S RECORD

13 September 1997: Arsenal 4 Bolton Wanderers 1

Ian Wright shot himself into the Arsenal and Highbury record books with a hat-trick that took him in front of Cliff Bastin as Arsenal's all-time top scorer at the time. Newspaper headlines of 'Top Gun' were perhaps predictable for the player who had always worn his Arsenal heart on his Arsenal sleeve since his £2.5 million signing from Crystal Palace in 1991. Bastin's record of 178 goals had stood untouched for 50 Highbury years and would only subsequently be challenged by Thierry Henry.

Wright had become an instant hit with the Highbury faithful, scoring on his debut in a 1–1 draw at Leicester and following this up with a hat-trick three days later in his League debut against Southampton. The fact he would take the record with another hat-trick was typical and no more than was expected of him by the fans.

Going into the game, Wright was so confident of breaking Bastin's record that he had a Nike T-shirt on under his Arsenal shirt emblazoned with '179 Just Done It'. However it was Bolton who opened the scoring when Thompson netted – the first goal Arsenal had conceded at Highbury so far that season. However the faithful didn't have to wait long. Bergkamp slipped the ball through the back line and Wright raced across the goal, firing across Brannigan for the equaliser – Arsenal's on the day and Wright's with the record. The now joint-top scorer got carried away and flashed his vest to the crowd prematurely; however, it became real when he scored his second and 179th after 25 minutes and sent the stadium roaring. It is doubtful he ever had an easier conversion. Bergkamp's surging run took him into the area and his shot was saved; the rebound rolled goalwards and Wright was on hand to drive home from all of a yard, then Parlour's shot was deflected to pretty much ensure the points by the interval.

Wright changed his boots at half-time to wear a special commemorative gold pair and used them to complete his hat-trick of goals in spectacular fashion. David Platt lofted the ball over the Bolton defence for Wright to nonchalantly produce a side-foot volley from just inside the area to complete his hat-trick. Manager Arsène Wenger did the right thing and took the new record holder off before the end so he could receive the ovation he so richly deserved: Ian Wright, Wright, Wright!

HIGHBURY'S FAVOURITE GOAL

3 May 1998: Arsenal 4 Everton 0

Steve Williams picked up the ball just inside his own half. Looking up, he saw the run from deep by Tony Woodcock. Quick as a flash he lifted the ball over the defensive players in front and hit the space between the high back line and the edge of the penalty area. Woodcock's turn of pace saw him free and onside. Running on to the high bounce, he chested the ball down and from the edge of the penalty area took the ball on the half volley and drilled it past the advancing Neville Southall. Goal!

Replace Tony Adams for Tony Woodcock, Steve Bould for Steve Williams, Thomas Myhre for Southall and you have the players that actually took part in the move described above. But you may not have believed me if I had used those names from the start. Ask any long-time Arsenal supporter to name their favourite Highbury goal and this one will be in their list.

Arsenal were on their way to their first Double under Arsène Wenger. With three games to go, they needed just one win to take the title. The visit of Everton to Highbury marked the last home fixture of the season, so this was the day, if Arsenal were to celebrate in front of their fans. As the final moments of the game ticked by, Arsenal were leading 3–0 and the party was well under way. The stands rocked and the players' smiles couldn't be contained any more. Then David Platt made a decisive tackle on the halfway line and fed the ball to Bould. Adams saw his chance and charged forward . . .

Images of Adams with arms spread wide in front of the North Bank, lapping up the adulation in the simplest of styles, adorned the back pages the next day. Whilst Martin Tyler's high-octave commentary of that moment in its own way defines the season. Forget about some people being on the pitch because they think it's all over – this is the ultimate commentary line for the Highbury faithful: 'Would you belieeeve IT! That . . . sums it all up!' It certainly did.

THE UNTOUCHABLES – ARSENAL GO UNBEATEN

15 May 2004: Arsenal 2 Leicester City 1
The final game of the 2003–04 season was the last hurdle for Arsenal to overcome in their quest to become the first team to go through a League season unbeaten since Preston achieved the feat in 1888–89. One hundred and fifteen years earlier on a sunny afternoon in north London Preston produced their invincible season in just 22 matches and in the inaugural Football League competition that contained not one club south of the Midlands.

Just as Leicester City were the first-ever opponents at Highbury, they now stood between Arsenal and a unique place in history. City also had themselves to play for – already relegated back to the division in which that first-ever encounter had taken place, their own pride was at stake. The immensity of what the Arsenal players could be about to achieve weighed heavily on their shoulders. With the League already secured several weeks beforehand, by their own admission the Arsenal players were largely going through the motions, doing enough to keep the record intact but also 'saving' themselves for the rigours of the 2004 European Championship to be held in Portugal the following month.

Highbury was in party mood well before kick-off, but City were industrious and it was not a great shock when they took the lead midway through the first half. Ironically, it was former Arsenal man Paul Dickov who did the damage, getting his small frame high and heading past Lehmann at the far post. In some respects it was just what the game needed and Arsenal emerged to a second half filled with urgency, in their play and in the home support. Through the season, Wenger's side had shown stunning ability with the priceless element of a seemingly unbreakable team spirit. More than ever, the latter came into play for the second half and within a minute of the restart the scores were level, after Ashley Cole was fouled by Sinclair – the creator of Dickov's goal – inside the penalty box and Henry evened the scores from the ensuing penalty kick.

Arsenal were now in all-out attack mode, seizing the initiative, and the record swept to within touching distance after 66 minutes when Bergkamp unlocked Leicester's defence with a typical moment of brilliance to slide Vieira through and in. The Arsenal skipper skipped around Ian Walker in the Leicester goal and was running to the North Bank in celebration even before the ball had crossed the line.

From that point on, the result was never in doubt and as the final whistle went, the Gunners took their place in history and a set of letters and figures would tell the story for all-time to come: played 38, won 26, drawn 12, lost 0.

THE ALL-FOREIGN GUNNERS

14 February 2005: Arsenal 5 Crystal Palace 1

Trailing Chelsea by fourteen points and Manchester United by five, this was a game that Arsenal just had to win, at the very least to keep the pressure on United for the second automatic Champions League place. But the news that dominated the airwaves from this game was not about another five-star performance from the Gunners, but the fact that Wenger's side for the game did not contain one national English player – this was the first foreign sixteen-man squad in English football history – mainly because Ashley Cole was ill and Sol Campbell was out injured.

The squad featured six Frenchmen, three Spaniards, two Dutchmen, one Cameroonian, one German, one Brazilian and one player each from the Ivory Coast and Switzerland. The Arsenal manager came under fire from the English media but defended his decision: 'I didn't know about that until I was told about it. I don't look at the passport of people; I look at their quality and their attitude.'

Arsenal demolished Crystal Palace with a scintillating display of football that was typical of the Untouchable season. Three goals in seven first-half minutes put paid to Crystal Palace's defensive wall of players. Bergkamp, who was outstanding on the night, slotted in from close range; Reyes crashed in a 20-yard bullet and Thierry Henry bagged a supreme solo strike before the break, playing a one-two from a corner on the left, cutting inside and unleashing a stunning shot for the third on his 200th Premiership appearance. Vieira rounded Gabor Kiraly for the fourth, but Johnson pulled one back from the penalty spot following a trip by Vieira before Bergkamp set up Henry for another fine finish from the edge of the area. Swedish national Sven-Göran Eriksson, the England team manager, was amongst the crowd!

Chelsea fielded the first complete overseas starting XI line-up in English football at Southampton on Boxing Day 1999; however, there were four English players on the bench – Jody Morris, Jon Harley, John Terry and Mark Nichoor that game. The Arsenal sixteen that evening featured: Lehmann (Germany), Lauren (Cameroon), Toure (Ivory Coast), Cygan (France), Clichy (France), Pires (France), Vieira (France), Edu (Brazil), Reyes (Spain), Bergkamp (Netherlands), Henry (France). Subs: Fabregas (Spain), 80, for Pires; Flamini (France), 61, for Edu; Van Persie (Netherlands), 79, for Bergkamp. Subs not used: Senderos (Switzerland), Almunia (Spain).

BIGGEST PREMIERSHIP WIN

12 May 2005: Arsenal 7 Everton 0

This was the game in which Arsenal played in white-sleeved shirts at Highbury for the last time, the club reverting to the original redcurrant shirts for the final season. The side celebrated with its biggest-ever win in the Premiership with a display of attacking football that was as good as they had ever produced. It was also an evening when Dennis Bergkamp rolled back the years and produced a typically brilliant display just days after his 36th birthday as he headed into his final year in the professional game. 'One more year' chanted those privileged to be at Highbury that night.

The performance should be put in perspective as well – this was an Everton side which had qualified for the Champions League by finishing fourth in the Premiership. David Moyes, their manager, was also awarded the accolade of Manager of the Year. Arsenal were simply awesome. They shredded Everton's defence to pieces. The rout began after seven minutes of play when José Antonio Reyes won the ball, fed Bergkamp, who rolled a pass between two defenders for Van Persie to stroke the ball past Richard Wright. Four minutes later Arsenal doubled their lead. Bergkamp again released Reyes behind the lines and his cross was met by Pires who followed up his own blocked shot to head home. Edu, Van Persie and Bergkamp combined in a sweeping one-touch passing move which left Vieira clear to execute a delightful chip over Wright for number three.

Three minutes after the interval, substitute Henry's lay-off rebounded into the path of Pires, who had no problem making it 4–0. The fifth came from the penalty spot, Henry having chipped the ball on to Carsley's arm. Edu, playing his last game at Highbury, was handed the ball and converted, much to everyone's delight. The biggest cheers, though, came for the sixth: Bergkamp closed down Weir's clearance, expertly controlled, and drilled the ball home from ten yards. Just reward for a sublime display. The massacre was completed when Reyes laid back Henry's cross for Flamini to hit the magnificent seventh.

START OF LAST SEASON AND THE RETURN OF REDCURRANT SHIRTS

14 August 2005: Arsenal 2 Newcastle United 0
The final season at Highbury arrived as Arsenal kicked it off with a 2–0 win over the Geordies. To mark the significance of the season, the club decided to change from the traditional red-and-white shirts to plain redcurrant-coloured ones – the same shade the club had played in when they moved to Islington in 1913. Highbury itself was not to be left out and so cut into the pitch on all four sides was: 'Highbury – 1913–2006'.

In the end, Arsenal comfortably won the game – the first competitive fixture without Patrick Vieira, who had departed for Juventus after nine trophy-rich years in north London – although the goals did not arrive until late on. The first came from Thierry Henry, who converted a penalty.

kick that was awarded after Freddie Ljungberg had been fouled. The second was scored by Robin van Persie, who slipped the ball home from a tight angle to finish a flowing move that had started in the far corner of the other end of the pitch. Arsenal had, in fact, utilised an all-red shirt in place of the more traditional 'Arsenal' style for a few games during the managerial reign of Billy Wright; however, the outcry against it was so forceful that the club reverted to white sleeves.

BASTIN'S RECORD EQUALLED

14 January 2006: Arsenal 7 Middlesbrough 0

It was another scintillating Arsenal performance – one that matched their 7–0 win over Everton just seven months earlier. A hat-trick from Thierry Henry brought his all-time Arsenal League goal tally to 150 and, in doing so, equalling the record that had stood as Cliff Bastin's own for 67 years.

Henry opened the scoring with a superb volley after 20 minutes of play, connecting perfectly with Ljungberg's cross to send the ball into the corner of the net. Two minutes later, Senderos doubled the lead, heading home Reyes's corner. Henry notched his second on the half-hour, sprinting clear of the Boro defence and reaching Reyes's inch-perfect through-ball, then side-footing the ball home past the out-rushing Boro goalkeeper. In added time, Pires sent a delicate chip over the luckless Bradley Jones to make it four at the interval.

Arsenal's fifth goal came just before the hour, when Gilberto rose high above the visitors' defence to head in Henry's free-kick. Henry completed the hat-trick the home fans were willing him to score – in the process notching his landmark 150th league goal – when he was put clean through by another superb pass from Reyes.

In the dying minutes of the game, Aleksander Hleb couldn't miss from close range to notch his first goal for the club and complete a memorable day for the Gunners, as they equalled their biggest Premiership win.

Henry would make Bastins' record his very own a few weeks later, scoring in a 2–3 home defeat to West Ham United, and would extend his tally further in the remaining matches at Highbury, cementing his position at the ground as the club's greatest ever scorer.

UNIVERSAL PRAISE AGAINST THE GALATICOS

8 March 2006: Arsenal 0 Real Madrid 0

There have been passionate nights before at Highbury, probably none greater than the one in 1970 when Arsenal came from two goals down to win the Inter-City Fairs Cup – Highbury's Greatest Night – but in sheer footballing terms this was a masterpiece and probably the most entertaining stalemate ever played at the stadium; certainly the game caught the imagination of the viewing public both at Highbury and around the world!

The scene for the game had been set two weeks earlier when, against all the supposed odds, Arsenal had travelled to the Bernabéu for the first time in a competitive game and secured a 1–0 win with a superb display and a typically magnificent solo effort by Henry.

Arsenal could have sat back for the return at Highbury but that is not the Wenger way. Real had to attack and so they did. What a captivated Highbury audience witnessed was a feast of attacking football that culminated with Real Madrid's galacticos on their knees and Arsenal's burgeoning team of youth and passion in the quarter-finals of the Champions League.

From back to front, Arsenal were in mesmerising form, every player delivering a formidable display – in fact, it is hard to single out individuals, because they all shone. But some shone more than others.

The defiance starting with Lehmann in goal – his fingertip save off the floor from Raul's own rebound off the far post will not be forgotten. Neither will the performances of Kolo Toure, Emmanuel Eboue, Cesc Fabregas, Aleksander Hleb and particularly Jose Antonio Reyes in midfield. The Spaniard blotted his copy book, though, crashing a glorious chance against the bar when it was easier to have scored.

Real included all their stars – Ronaldo, Raul, Carlos Roberto, Zidane and a first-club return to England for David Beckham – but their aging legs could never quite get the better of the young Gunners. It was breathless stuff; end-to-end entertainment of the highest order.

THE FINAL ENCOUNTER

7 May 2006: Arsenal 4 Wigan Athletic 2
The game had everything.

The emotion one would expect as the stadium staged its grand finale. A hat-trick from Theirry Henry, the fans paying tribute to their record goal-scorer, and with it a win that secured fourth place in the Premiership table, a position that allowed access to the Champions League or at least the qualifying stages for it – made all the sweeter because it came at the expense of local rivals Tottenham Hotspur, who had occupied the position for much of the season.

A record Highbury Premiership attendance of 38,359. The stadium looked magnificent as each and every supporter was handed out a T-shirt proclaiming, 'I was there.' When seated, Highbury was striped red and white from head to toe – unfortunately, the redcurrant of the team remained as the only blemish to Arsenal colours.

A swash of blue in the corner of the South Stand ensured Wigan came to the party wearing their T-shirts, as the newest of Premier League sides played their part in making this a captivating game, their direct, hard-running style in stark contrast to the carnival football that Arsène Wenger's team produced in typical swashbuckling fashion.

The first hour the game seesawed. Robert Pires scored the first goal at the second attempt, Mike Pollitt in the visitors' goal having smothered his initial effort after Gilberto had headed on Cesc Fabregas's ball into the area. But with the back-slapping just subsiding in the stands, Wigan equalised when an unmarked Paul Scharner connected with David Thompson's free-kick at the near post to prod home an equaliser. Wigan were awarded another free-kick some 35 yards out and, with Lehman organising his defence, Thompson drove the ball for the same near post in speculative fashion and was rewarded for his cheek with what was to be the last goal at Highbury by a visiting player: 2–1 to Wigan.

With ten minutes of the half remaining, Aleksander Hleb won the ball and from his short pass Pires was able to thread the ball through the square Wigan defence and Henry slipped the ball past Pollitt to send the sides in level at the interval.

Back on terms and having regrouped for the second half, Arsenal were more emphatic. However, they were gifted the lead when Thompson this time hit a wayward pass back to Pollitt, which Henry intercepted and waltzed around the Wigan keeper before gleefully thrashing the ball home from close range.

Andreas Johansson was introduced to freshen the visitors' attack, but he remained on the pitch less than a minute as his first and last action was to pull Fredrik Ljungberg back inside the six-yard box following a free-kick. A red card and penalty was the result and Henry completed his hat-trick from the spot, sinking to his knees to plant a kiss on the Highbury turf. It was to be Arsenal's 2,010th, and last, Highbury win.

As the stadium rocked, Bergkamp appeared. As he trod into the Highbury theatre for the final time, the news arrived that Tottenham were losing at West Ham. The noise at the Library simply rose to a level it had arguably never experienced before. As the final whistle sounded, the stately Old Home of Football bowed gracefully in favour of a new era for Arsenal Football Club.

SIXTEEN

Highbury Futures

After 92 years, the 2005–06 season marked the final one at Highbury, the Home of Football. Attachments are inevitable and a central issue to the whole redevelopment of this special corner of the universe has been just what will happen to the stadium structure when the club leaves.

The national Listing of the East Stand and local Listing of the West Stand went some way to securing the future of the structure itself. It is an irony that the pressures of space which finally required Arsenal to relocate from Highbury were also the same pressures that would allow the club to fund part of that very move, using the prime market value of that very same land in N5. Highbury, it was negotiated, would be developed into a number of residential units and the pitch would remain as lawns within the development. The Home of Football would survive, in structure at least.

Rather than sell the land directly to a developer, the club opted to undertake the project itself, most likely in conjunction with a partner. Whilst the cost of funding this would have to be taken into consideration and borne at a time when the stadium itself was eating heavily into the money being loaned for its development, the benefits would be that the club could thereby maximise their profit on the sale of the units.

The redevelopment of Highbury was to form part of a major

regeneration package affecting the immediate surrounding area, in addition to the obvious relocation to Ashburton Grove. As well as housing, there was the development of land for light industry and community uses. To facilitate this, architects Allies and Morrison were appointed by Arsenal Football Club to develop proposals for the conversion of Arsenal Stadium and adjoining land at Highbury for residential use, initially based on a number of constraints set by Islington Council, which included the proviso that 25 per cent of the new housing would fall within the category of 'affordable housing'. This is slightly less than the 31 per cent stipulated by the Greater London Council (GLC) and a major requirement set by Mayor Ken Livingston – a huge supporter of the redevelopment in the Islington area.

The scheme is based upon the retention and conversion of the existing Grade II Listed East Stand, the West Stand – also of historic significance – and the existing pitch area located between the two stands. The East and West stands are to be converted into residential accommodation – their façades will be cleared of the turnstile blocks and ticket offices and returned to the stunning, straight-lined simplicity originally designed by Claude Ferrier and his partner, William Binnie. On the other side of each stand, the one facing the pitch area, a lightweight glass screen will be constructed, allowing a minimum of 180 flats to be built inside.

The imposing entrance to the Marble Halls, complete with art deco staircases picked out with Arsenal motifs, will remain. So, too, will the players' tunnel and the approach to the directors' box. Other glimpses of the pitch will be afforded within the flats themselves by the glass frontage and the use of transparent stairwells throughout.

Although differing in size, the flats will stick to a basic design of having the bedrooms at the back where the club offices and the dressing-rooms currently are, while the living areas will be situated in the parts occupied by the seats. All of them will be split-level developments, retaining the sense of the banking of the stands. Meanwhile, the corner flats will be cut back to incorporate the structure's striking side-glass panelling.

As part of a £60 million project, the North and South stands are to be demolished and new residential blocks have been proposed in their place. The format of these has changed drastically since the original designs were approved and released to the world and a new scheme released towards the end of Highbury's penultimate season is more focused on one- and two-bedroom units and much less on affordable housing, and is certainly outside the requirements of both the GLC and Islington Council. It would seem likely the club will get its way in this respect, further maximising its revenue.

These new North and South buildings are similar in height to the existing stands, yet are significantly smaller in mass than the structures they replace. The developments here will also include a community health centre, doctors' surgery and some low-level business units.

The sense of enclosure in the existing space is retained and as with the proposed conversion of the East and West stands, the dominant aspect for residential units within these blocks will be towards the 'pitch'. The pitch will be reinstated after construction and landscaping has been completed and car parking situated in an undercroft below the area of the pitch. It is not only a matter of the pitch itself, but also of respecting the memories of those fans whose ashes have been scattered there down the years.

The architects approached award-winning landscape gardener Christopher Bradley-Hole and commissioned him to design and integrate the central pitch area. The result was an area sectioned off into squares, the grid of garden reflecting the straight lines of the stands. The perimeter of the pitch would be preserved but reformed to make a series of spaces in an abstract composition of terraces, hedges, lawns and plants intermingled with water walls and screens.

Towards the north of the site a light vehicle/pedestrian route will form a permeable link from Avenell Road through to Gillespie Road, adjacent to Arsenal Station. Mews housing, single aspect in form and three storeys high, is to be located along the northern boundary leading to a courtyard area flanked to the west by residential units and to the north by light industrial accommodation.

The issue of the ashes of supporters scattered in the stadium, especially on the pitch, has been a concern, and so in their memory it was decided that the areas of turf where the ashes were buried will be lifted and re-laid alongside the new pitch at Ashburton Grove. In addition, a permanent memorial will be erected at Highbury, following discussions with the relatives of those whose ashes were scattered there.

A DETAILED LOOK

On 10 December 2001 Islington Council granted planning permission for Arsenal's application for the redevelopment of Arsenal Stadium based on revisions to the Stage 1 report first published on 10 October 2001. The main changes between the two reports were a reduction in the amount of intermediate residential accommodation and the number of live work units to be provided; clarification of the number of affordable homes to be provided; a reduction in the total number of car parking spaces; an increase in the financial contribution towards public transport; and an increase in the amount of commercial floor space.

Central to the redevelopment was, of course, the Listed nature of the East and West stands and the need for Listed Building Consent to allow redevelopment to go ahead. Without this, progress would be stopped dead in its tracks. This was granted provided that the redevelopment scheme would protect the character and appearance of the East Stand and that the setting of the Listed building could be protected during the development and proposed future conditions. Internally, it was required that the loss of internal fabric was kept to a minimum, typically the removal and relocation of items of note. Approval from English Heritage was required to alter the structure of the East Stand and this was provided after a number of consultations and the exchange of letters in late 2001. The main conditions were that the conversion of the Listed stand maintained its existing style; the new north and south apartment blocks would be designed and built in such a way as to protect the Listed buildings; and the existing original features in the East Stand would be retained. In addition, the landscaping of the pitch area and around the new developments would not be overly fussy and its segregation kept to a minimum.

Beyond this, the main concern lay in the roof lines of the north block, which were seen as being derogatory to those of the East Stand. Sport

England were approached as a matter of obligation, as it is a requirement that they are approached as part of 'Planning Authority' whenever the loss of a playing field (which the Highbury pitch is defined as) takes place.

Both Islington Council and the GLC dictated that the redevelopment had to include facilities for the nearby community and that local people should have a say in what form these should take.

Again, central to the housing issue in the original Stage 1 report was that inclusion of 31 per cent of affordable housing on the site, which also includes subsidised accommodation. As can be seen in the descriptions of the proposed works to each of the current stands, much, if not all, of this is located outside of the prime 'pitch view' units.

The inclusion of the health centre was a requirement of the Camden and Islington Health Authority and was enlarged from the original proposals to reach the 1,000-metre-square size requirements.

As part of protecting the local community, the Conservation Advisory Panel were consulted on a number of occasions in relation to their concerns. The panel is composed of a number of local laypeople who meet on a rota basis to consider the effect of development proposals on the appearance and character of the conservation areas and Listed buildings of Islington. The people who form the panel are not elected representatives and the panel itself has an advisory status only within the development process, however many of the issues they raised influenced the final design.

Some of the recommendations the panel made over the course of three meetings which were taken on board included the preservation and re-use of the boardroom and trophy cabinet – which was also a condition imposed by English Heritage. Both of these are being relocated to Ashburton Grove. There was also a concern that the new north and south blocks were too dominant. The design was then revised so that its number of storeys was reduced from the centre to the sides, thus provided a stepped-down look.

The descriptions that follow outline the proposed developments in each of the stands, including details relating to the number of flats (apartments) and houses that the architects intend to create in each of these. It should be borne in mind that these numbers are likely to change prior to and during the redevelopment stages. One aspect that could halt redevelopment is, of course, the unearthing of an archaeological site; however, the Archaeology Service were consulted previously and assessed that the possibility of interesting remains being found is low.

THE EAST STAND

As part of the redevelopment of the East Stand a new basement will be excavated – around 18,000 cubic metres in all to be dug out and removed from the site. The excavated basement area will be used as office and light industrial areas (around 360 metres square) and the remaining space of around 1,000 metres square is to be fitted out as a private gym/health club.

The main entrance – the Marble Halls – will be retained with all the existing detailing, including the bust of Herbert Chapman. This will serve as the entrance to the proposed apartments, eighty-seven in total situated over six floors. These are due to include thirty-two one-bedroom units, fifty-one two-bedroom units and four three-bedroom units. None of these dwellings are in the 'affordable housing' category and are therefore expected to offer premium retail returns, given they are also within the Grade II category of Listed buildings.

From the outside the East Stand will look largely as it did in the final season, albeit with a new coat of paint. The only alterations will be the demolition of the stair tower at the south end of the stand and the replacement along the ground floor of wooden gates with windows. These changes are designed to reproduce the style of the original. There are also some minor changes to fenestration at top-floor level. The glazed walls at both ends of the stand will be retained in their entirety. A glazed wall is proposed on the pitch-side elevation of the building.

The current roof profile will be unchanged and it is hoped that most of the roof structure can be retained. It is probable that the existing roof trusses, cantilevers at least, can be re-used. To facilitate the interior redevelopment, much of the inside of the East Stand, including the tiered seating, changing-rooms, offices, board room (proposed to be relocated to the new stadium) and press and function rooms would need to be removed.

THE WEST STAND

As with the East Stand, the existing six-storey building will be retained along with its basement. At the rear of the stand there is a single-story extension that backs on to gardens in Highbury Hill. This will be demolished and will be converted into a garden. Opaque-glass windows will be fitted in the rear of the stand (that faces on to Highbury Hill) to facilitate privacy, as they look on to the back of the Highbury Hill residences. The pitch-side elevation of the West Stand will be completed with a glazed wall, in a similar fashion to the East Stand.

Internally, the conversion will be fitted with ninety-four apartments comprising forty one-bedroom, forty-eight two-bedroom and six three-bedroom units. As with the East Stand, it is not proposed that any of these units will be categorised as affordable living.

Running directly from the north end of the West Stand and at the rear of Highbury Hill will be a nursery with residential units up to the junction with Gillespie Road. The nursery is to be constructed across the ground and first floors at the southern end of the accommodation, with nine residential units at the northern end. The size of the nursery would indicate enough places for around 70 children.

The Highbury Hill entrance to the West Stand – consuming numbers 133 to 139, currently residential – will be refurbished and retained as eleven flats, comprising eight one-bedroom and three two-bedroom units. This block is designated as affordable housing. Two properties owned by the club on Highbury Hill will also be redeveloped – number 189 is to be redeveloped as two four-bedroom houses and number 191 Highbury Hill into a single four-bedroom house.

NORTH AND SOUTH STANDS

After just 15 years or so of life, the North Stand will be demolished and in its place will rise a new structure. The original approved design provided for two rows of buildings, one directly facing on to the pitch and the other behind and parallel to it with a mews area in between the two. These were to be six- or seven-storey blocks with semi-basement and full-basement levels. Some of the rear block was designated as affordable housing.

Revised plans produced in February 2005 (but not approved at that point) provided for something different. The pitch-side structure remains, and is confirmed at seven storeys, but the rear structure has been pushed back towards Gillespie Road and three cross-structures have been added running north to south. Thus, the effect is of a square figure of eight with the open areas within creating two courtyard areas. An additional four-storey building is included on the front to Avenell Road and this provides an additional courtyard behind it, although this is not totally enclosed.

The existing South Stand will also be demolished. The original plans called for two buildings running the width of the site separated by a series of seven three-bedroom townhouses, each with a small garden to the front. The revised February proposals employed a format similar to that of the north end, but deeper and higher in construction.

The February 2005 proposals significantly increased the number of units available for sale at both ends of the site. This is facilitated by decreasing the size and number of bedrooms in the available units and also by making more effective use of the space available. The contentious issue will be the requirements for affordable housing units. Financially, the club will wish to keep this to an absolute minimum to maximise its profit from the sale of the units. Any affordable housing will be sold at a more conservative cost to a local Housing Association and made available for rent. Clearly, the positioning of designated affordable housing also could have an effect on the sale of private housing close to it, thus potentially reducing the market sale value of those units.

THE PITCH AREA

The pitch area will be replaced at the end of the conversion process and it will lie around 50 centimetres higher than it did as a playing surface. It will sit on about one metre of earth and gravel (to provide drainage), which itself will be supported by the roof of the car park it covers. A number of glass chimneys will populate the pitch, which will provide some natural ventilation to the enclosure below but will also act as water features.

A memorial garden is proposed on the south-east corner of the gardens and this may contain the ashes of supporters which were scattered under the original playing field. The gardens themselves will enclose an area of around 200 metres square. Beyond this, the gardens will consist of a series of squares and rectangles at the centre of which will be a 629-metre-square open space. The square and rectangular area will be marked out in a series of enclosures created by hedges and glass towers.

In addition a children's park of around 75 metres square has been proposed, furnished with swings and slides. There was also a plan put forward to include a small all-weather playing surface of around 110 metres square. However, neither of these spaces is to be accessible and open to the public – the children's playground would be for the use of the new nursery and the all-weather surface for residents and local schools.

Public access itself is proposed only as a general through-route, but it will not be as a public right of way around the pitch and the redevelopment. Underneath the pitch area an excavated basement space would extend under the East Stand and north and south blocks, and this will provide some 473 car parking spaces, 527 bicycle spaces and 152 enclosed storage units.

HIGHBURY SQUARE

In the first half of 2005 Arsenal sought planning permission from the GLC for what was now officially called 'Highbury Square' – with a final apartment count of 711 in the overall development. The club also created a website requesting that those interested in purchasing a property register their interests. This indicated that prices will start from £230,000 for studio apartments, rising to about £1.5 million for a three-bedroom penthouse. The development is expected to be complete in 2010.

Afterword

May 2005 – Qantas flight QF31 from Sydney was on its final approach to Heathrow and as I peered through the right-hand-side window out over the Thames and the concrete expanse that flowed north, there was a new shape on the horizon. Clearly Wembley had developed a great deal in my absence. However, there was no arch visible, and within a few seconds I could make out the profile of the new national stadium. After several double-takes it hit me that I was looking at Arsenal's new stadium. The scale of the development and the progress that had been made during the past months left me breathless. Even with the Emirates marker, Highbury itself was still hard to see from the air – it had proved impossible for me to pick it out during numerous attempts down the years. Nothing in a physical sense could ever have driven it home to me that Arsenal were now about to arrive on the scene as a world power in the stadium stakes. Whilst Highbury would remain an icon and a marvellous moment to an era now gone, the Ashburton Grove development signals the start of something very real and incredibly significant.

It was no different later that same afternoon when I took my seat in the upper tier of the North Bank and gazed across at the new structure that had not just taken root in, but thrust itself into the sky. And there it remained a few days later as Everton were demolished by seven goals in arguably the best display of creative football ever seen at the stadium. That would have been a fitting last game at Highbury.

The Emirates Stadium dominates the Holloway skyline, swallowing up the surrounding sky and dwarfing the existing structures around it – almost overcrowding them as though about to expand and push them away. By the time the stadium is open for business, much of the surrounding hinterland will be on the way to a futuristic feel and look, as the development arm of the club sweeps up all around it.

The proposed redevelopment of Highbury will not take place until the club have fully relocated and are playing games in their new Ashburton Grove facility. This is a key factor in the business plan and its progression; something that must take place at the earliest opportunity so that the sale of the apartments and accumulation of hard cash can be realised. The importance is best illustrated by the changes made to the Ashburton Grove site. The club offices were due to be located at the Queensland Road end of the new stadium by the main entrance; however, this was behind schedule and would not have been available for relocation at the opening of the stadium. Leaving the club offices at Highbury was simply not an option and so an alternative plan was developed by incorporating a multistorey block at the north end of the site adjacent to Drayton Park (near Arsenal Tube station). Planning permission for this was fast-tracked through the council.

Many of the issues regarding the increase in dwellings at Highbury and the cut of affordable housing will make for interesting negotiation between Arsenal and Islington Council. It is unlikely that either party could have been fully aware of the full scope of what grew out of the original Ashburton Grove proposals and it is in the interests of the local council now to ensure everything happens.

The compulsory purchase orders for properties, such as the warehouse and work units along Queensland Road, have not been in any way vital for the stadium itself but have been an important aspect in allowing the financing of the stadium. The apartments constructed by the club are likely to generate profit far and above the Compulsory Purchase Order (CPO) price for which they were acquired. Whilst the morals of that might not sit too well with Islington Council, there is a realisation that the local council will experience a massive regeneration in an area that has long been an eyesore. With each new apartment block comes new income exceeding what was already there, so the club, the council and the local environment all benefit.

One issue that will not be resolved when doors to the new stadium open is that of infrastructure and communication. The redevelopment of local stations has stagnated as a result of governmental issues. This doesn't only affect matchdays at the stadium but also the ability to move the new population. Holloway Road Tube station will be that nearest the club's main entrance and yet will almost certainly be closed on matchdays. Its two small lifts are totally inadequate for the purpose and the heavy-duty Holloway Road itself is a potential nightmare and potential death trap for arriving pedestrians. Thus, Arsenal will move to a new stadium that itself looks likely to be finished on time; however, expect the area to be a building site for some time after as the infrastructure struggles to catch up.

The passing of Highbury as a football ground and the arrival of the Emirates Stadium heralds a very new and very different era for Arsenal Football Club and its supporters. It signifies a very new commercial era, way beyond the development of the South Stand and the introduction of the bond and all that.

I recall two occasions when the club has lost fans – how many I do not know, but I personally know people who have never returned both times. First, there was the introduction of the bond which, to many, went against the grain of the working man and, as the club became successful, made it more difficult to purchase a single ticket, let alone one for a sibling. Second, after ten years came the end of the subsidised season-ticket fees for those who purchased the bond, prices then catapulting fourfold to their true market value. Many saw this as a slap in the face and had strangely expected the prices to rise gradually. But the club had met their obligation in full. There was never any doubt in my mind the rise in price would come about.

In both cases the empty seats left by the loss of fans were easily filled, by the many thousands whose names are on a variety of lists either waiting to buy tickets or the right to buy them. The move to Emirates Stadium may well spark an end for another set of fans who simply do not wish to move into the next era of football supporter – it's a far cry from the days when Ted Drake had to go cap in hand to the club after an injury and the war. All cycles come to an end. It just remains to be seen whether Arsenal fans will meet the cost of their seats, in their full numbers on a regular basis. They certainly did when Arsenal spent several years playing UEFA Champions League games at the old Wembley Stadium – but then tickets were hugely reduced in price and had to be pre-booked for each Group stage. Thus, even later, non-essential games were sold out even if they were not fully attended.

Bond holders too have found that their large investment in the club is worth virtually nothing in the new scheme of things: initially, a choice of seat maybe, but none of the trimmings which had been secured for 150 years at Highbury.

In Spain and Italy the megaclubs with megastadiums, such as Madrid, Barcelona and Milan, often struggle to fill their facilities for run-of-the-mill games and this in countries where admission charges are substantially less than they are in England. It is an interesting potential dilemma that for the average fan the scarcity of tickets for games at Highbury has invariably been the reason for their demand. How that pans out in the future in the new facility, outside the corporate box, remains to be seen.

As they say, time will tell.

Timeline

DATE	EVENT
February 1913	League Management Committee agrees to Woolwich Arsenal's relocation from Plumpstead to N5; Norris secures a 21-year lease on the site at a cost of £20,000
March 1913	Archibald Leitch's assistant, Alfred Kearney, arrives to begin work on stadium planning
June 1913	With less than 60 days to go to the start of the new season, construction work finally starts on the new stadium
5 September 1913	The *Islington Gazette* starts campaign to name the ground Gillespie Road stadium
6 September 1913	First Highbury Game: some 20,000 supporters pack into an unfinished stadium to see Woolwich Arsenal win 2–1 against Leicester Fosse
7 September 1913	East Stand partially opens for the second fixture against Notts County, with around 4,000 spectators squeezing in to watch the game, which ends 3–0 to the home side

4 April 1914	First 'Arsenal' Game – Arsenal 1 Bristol City 1: Arsenal drop 'Woolwich' from their name
9 January 1915	First FA Cup game at Highbury: Arsenal 3 Merthyr Tydfil 0
24 April 1915	Arsenal finish fifth in the Second Division as the League is suspended for the First World War
1 June 1919	Arsenal 'voted' into the expanded First Division at Spurs' expense: possibly one of the biggest football scandals of all time
30 August 1919	First game in the First Division: Arsenal 0 Newcastle United 1
15 March 1920	First game of the Home International Championship at Highbury, ending England 1 Wales 2
12 March 1921	The first Football League representative game played at Arsenal Stadium
19 March 1923	England plays 'foreign' opposition for the first time at Highbury and record an emphatic 6–1 victory
June 1925	Herbert Chapman appointed manager of Arsenal; Sir Henry Norris purchases the Highbury site outright, paying around £64,000 for the ten-acre enclosure
22 January 1927	First football broadcast on BBC Radio: Arsenal draw 1–1 with Sheffield United
31 August 1927	Ticketing introduced at the Laundry End of the ground
7 February 1929	Sir Henry Norris, the mastermind behind Arsenal's move and growth in N5, is banned from football
16 March 1929	First FA Cup semi-final at Highbury: Portsmouth 1 Aston Villa 0
May 1930	The Arsenal board turn down Chapman's ambitious designs for Highbury

TIMELINE

6 September 1930	The landmark Highbury Clock is installed during the pre-season and used for the first time in a 3–1 win over Leeds United
28 January 1931	Record League win at Highbury: Arsenal 9 Grimsby Town 1
11 April 1931	Highbury stages the FA Amateur Cup final, in which Wycombe Wanderers beat Hayes 1–0 in front of 32,000
2 May 1931	First official Championship-trophy presentation: a crowd flocked to north London to see the official presentation to Herbert Chapman's side
May 1931	Claude Waterlow Ferrier appointed to develop the Highbury grounds
October 1931	Highbury Hill entrance created, work on West Stand started
9 December 1931	England 7 Spain 1: friendly international as England record their biggest win over Spain in front of a capacity crowd
9 January 1932	Biggest FA Cup win – Arsenal 11 Darwen 1: Cliff Bastin scored four of the goals. His match tally remains a Highbury record for an Arsenal player in the competition
5 November 1932	Gillespie Road Underground station renamed 'Arsenal'
8 December 1932	A Jacob Epstein-designed bust memorial to Herbert Chapman is unveiled in the main entrance hall in the presence of Mrs Chapman and her children
10 December 1932	Official opening of the East Stand performed by the Prince of Wales (later Edward VIII): Arsenal beat Chelsea 4–1 to complete celebrations
24 December 1932	Most goals in a League game by an individual player – Arsenal 9 Sheffield United 2: Jack Lambert scores five of the home goals which remains the most by a player in a single League game at Highbury

4 March 1933	Arsenal wear white sleeves for first time in a 1–0 loss to Liverpool
6 January 1934	Herbert Chapman dies. His death deeply affects everyone at the club
14 November 1934	The Battle of Highbury – England 3 Italy 2
May 1934	The famous Arsenal Clock is relocated to the south end of the ground, which will eventually become known as the Clock End. In two corners of the stadium scoreboards are installed alongside the edge of the terracing
1 September 1934	Shed over Laundry End used for first time: the designer, Claude Willow Ferrier, is killed in an accident before the shed's completion
9 March 1935	Biggest attendance at Highbury – 73,295: the crowd that packed into Highbury that afternoon accounted for more than a third of the total First Division attendance that afternoon
31 August 1935	Enumerator installed to control crowd size: 66,428 see Arsenal win 3–1 against Sunderland
May 1936	Work on new East Stand begins
24 October 1936	Official opening of the William Binnie-designed East Stand: at a cost of £130,000 the new stand is ready for use just six months after the demolition of the old East Stand began
2 December 1936	Arsenal hat-trick – England 6 Hungary 2: three Arsenal players represented in the England team this afternoon, one of whom, Ted Drake, scored a hat-trick
26 October 1938	England 3 Rest of Europe 0: Two Arsenal players took part in this high-profile encounter, as relations in Europe were degenerating quickly
6 May 1939	*The Arsenal Stadium Mystery* filmed: the final game of the 1938–39 season used to film the action scenes for the Thorold Dickinson movie

TIMELINE

3 May 1947	England 3 France 0: full-back Laurie Scott was the sole Arsenal representative in this first post-war England game at Highbury
19 November 1947	England 4 Sweden 2: Laurie Scott continues his run in the England side
2 December 1948	England 6 Switzerland 0: With no Arsenal player in the team, England gain revenge for the 1–0 defeat they suffered in Zurich
22 November 1950	England 2 Yugoslavia 2: England's first game at Highbury after the embarrassing 0–1 defeat by the USA in the World Cup in Brazil
3 October 1951	England 2 France 2: France became the only team to feature in two matches against England at Highbury
8 October 1951	First competitive fixture under floodlights: Hendon were beaten 1–0 in the London Challenge Cup. There were 13,548 in attendance to see Arsenal's reserve side win
17 October 1951	Official inauguration of floodlights: 62,000 pack into Highbury as Arsenal beat Rangers 3–2
11 March 1953	London FA 6 Berlin FA 1: an amazing 55,705 fans flocked to see this representative game under the Highbury floodlights, such was the pulling power of post-war football
20 February 1954	First Brazilian club side to play in England: Arsenal 7 Portuguesa de Desportos (São Paulo)
6 May 1955	The first of several England trial games held at the stadium with England playing Young England
17 December 1955	The 'phantom final whistle' goal – Arsenal 4 Blackpool 1
18 August 1956	New North Bank shed used for the first time: Arsenal drew 0–0 with Cardiff City
23 October 1957	First Inter Cities Fairs Cup game at Highbury: London beat Lausanne 2–0 to win the semi-final of this tie

HIGHBURY

1 February 1958	The greatest game ever? Arsenal 4 Manchester United 5
30 March 1960	First European Champions' Cup game: Rangers 3 Sparta Rotterdam 2
28 September 1961	England 4 Luxembourg 1: The last full England international at Highbury and a World Cup preliminary-round tie
15 October 1963	Eight-goal thriller – Arsenal 4 Tottenham Hotspur 4: The gate of 67,986 was Highbury's best for ten years and the second highest since 1934
23 October 1963	First European game involving Arsenal: Arsenal 2 Staevnet 3. The Danish select side secure a win just minutes from the final whistle
14 March 1964	Most goals by an opposition player: Bobby Tambling destroys Arsenal and gives League debutant Peter Simpson a torrid time at Highbury by scoring all four of Chelsea's goals
June 1964	Under-soil heating installed
5 May 1966	Lowest-ever attendance at Highbury for a top-tier League game. Just 4,554 turned up to see Arsenal lose their last home game of the season against Leeds United 0–3
21 May 1966	World Championship boxing – Henry Cooper v. Muhammad Ali
13 September 1966	First League Cup game at Highbury – Arsenal 1 Gillingham 1
28 April 1970	Arsenal win the European Fairs Cup 3–0 against Anderlecht: the Gunners end a frustrating spell of 17 years without a trophy, overcoming a 1–3 deficit to beat the Belgian side 4–3 on aggregate
June 1970	Under-soil heating system replaced with hot water pipe system

TIMELINE

22 August 1970	The greatest save – Arsenal 4 Manchester United 0: Trailing by a goal, United were presented with a golden opportunity to equalise. The Arsenal keeper somehow dived and snatched the ball away
9 April 1980	Cup-Winners' Cup semi-final – Arsenal 1 Juventus 1: Arsenal won the second leg in Turin to reach their second European final
28 October 1984	Diamond Vision screen erected at Clock End of the stadium
June 1986	Under-soil heating system upgraded again at a cost of £100,000
June 1989	East Stand repainted: the cream and green that had been a feature of the stand for so long was replaced with a more Arsenal-like magnolia and red
22 August 1989	New South Stand opened: at a cost of £6 million the corporate South Stand was complete and opened for the first game of the season
6 May 1991	Arsenal win the Championship – Arsenal 3 Manchester United 1: it is Arsenal's tenth title and puts the team into the European Cup – the first English entrant since the five-year ban imposed on clubs by UEFA following the Heysel disaster
2 May 1992	Last game in front of the North Bank – Arsenal 5 Southampton 1: an Ian Wright hat-trick was the highlight of Arsenal's thumping of Southampton before the North Bank was demolished
28 November 1992	Biggest crowd in front of the Mural: 29,739
July 1993	Sony Jumbotrons installed
14 August 1993	First game in front of the new North Stand: Arsenal 0 Coventry City 3
15 February 1994	North Bank stand officially opened by the Duke of Kent
12 April 1994	Cup-Winners' Cup semi-final: Arsenal 1 Paris St-Germain 0

6 April 1995	Cup-Winners' Cup semi-final: Arsenal 3 Sampdoria 2
22 September 1996	Arsène Wenger officially takes up the role of Arsenal manager
19 October 1996	Arsène Wenger's first game in charge at Highbury: two goals by Ian Wright ensure Wenger's first game get off to a winning start
16 July 1997	East Stand Listed nationally Grade II, West Stand listed locally
13 September 1997	Wright breaks Bastin's record: Ian Wright shoots himself into the Arsenal and Highbury record books with a hat-trick that takes him in front of Cliff Bastin as Arsenal's all-time top scorer at the time. The hat-trick gave him 180 goals
3 May 1998	Highbury's favourite goal – Arsenal 4 Everton 0: Tony Adams races onto Steve Bould's through ball to score a goal any centre-forward would have been proud of
15 May 2004	The Untouchables – Arsenal go unbeaten: having trailed at the interval, Arsenal came back, with goals from Henry and Vieira ensuring the dream was achieved: Arsenal 2 Leicester 1
14 February 2005	The all-foreign Gunners – Arsenal 5 Crystal Palace 1: Arsenal squad features six Frenchmen, three Spaniards, two Dutchmen, one Cameroonian, one German, one Brazilian and one player each from the Ivory Coast and Switzerland
12 May 2005	Biggest Premiership win – Arsenal 7 Everton 0: also Arsenal play in white-sleeved shirts at Highbury for the last time
14 August 2005	The return of redcurrant shirts – Arsenal 2 Newcastle United 0: to commemorate the final season at Highbury, the club decided to change from the traditional red and white shirts to plain redcurrant-coloured ones – the same shade the

club had played in when they moved to Islington in 1913

7 May 2006   The final game – Arsenal 4 Wigan Athletic 2: Thierry Henry scores the final hat-trick and final goal at Highbury as Arsenal end their tenure on a winning note.

Select Bibliography

BOOKS

Adams, Tony *Addicted*, Collins Willow, 1998

Inglis, Simon *Football Grounds of Britain*, Collins Willow, 1996

Smith, Bruce *The Virgin Arsenal Fact File*, Virgin, 2000

Harris, Jeff *Arsenal Who's Who*, Independent UK Sports Publications, 1995

Soar, Phil and Tyler, Martin *The Official Illustrated History of Arsenal*, Hamlyn, 2004

Spurling, Jon *Rebels for the Cause*, Mainstream Publishing, 2004

NEWSPAPERS

Islington Gazette

Islington Daily Gazette

Islington Daily Gazette & North London Tribune

Index

315